WRITING UNDER FIRE

STORIES OF THE VIETNAM WAR

WRITING UNDER FIRE

STORIES OF THE VIETNAM WAR

*Edited by Jerome Klinkowitz
and John Somer*

 A Delta Book

A DELTA BOOK

Published by
Dell Publishing Co., Inc.
1 Dag Hammarskjold Plaza
New York, New York 10017

John Somer wishes to thank the Faculty Research and Creativity
Committee of Emporia State University for a grant to begin
the study of the fiction associated with Vietnam.

Delta ® TM 755118, Dell Publishing Co., Inc.
Printed in the United States of America
First printing—August 1978

Library of Congress Cataloging in Publication Data
Main entry under title:

Writing under fire.

(A Delta book)
Bibliography: p. 271
1. Vietnamese Conflict, 1961–1975—Fiction.
2. Short stories, American.   I. Klinkowitz, Jerome.
II. Somer, John L.
PZ1.W94 [PS648.V5]   813'.01   78-17682
ISBN 0-440-59345-X

081989

ACKNOWLEDGMENTS

Grateful acknowledgment is made for permission to reprint the following copyrighted material.

"Dragon Lady" by Johanna Kaplan: Reprinted by permission of Russell & Volkening, Inc., as agents for the author. Copyright © 1970 by Johanna Kaplan.

"Troop Withdrawal—the Initial Step" by Thomas Parker: Copyright © 1969 by Thomas Parker. Reprinted by permission of Paul R. Reynolds, Inc., 18 East 41st Street, New York, N.Y. 10017.

"The Day We Named Our Child We Had Fish for Dinner" by Michael Rossman: Also known as "The Fourth Night of Cambodia." From *The Wedding Within the War* by Michael Rossman. Copyright © 1971 by Michael Rossman. Original publication in *New American Review*, 11 (1971). Used by permission of the author.

"On the Perimeter" by Robert Chatain: Reprinted by permission of International Creative Management. Copyright © 1971 by New American Review. First published in *New American Review*, 13.

"Gone Are the Men" by Thomas A. West, Jr.: Copyright © 1972 by Thomas A. West, Jr. Used by permission of the author. First published in *Transatlantic Review*, 29.

"The University of Death" by J. G. Ballard: Reprinted by permission of Grove Press, Inc. Copyright © 1969 by J. G. Ballard. Used by permission of C & J Wolfers Ltd.

"Portrait: My American Man, Fall, 1966" by Paul Friedman: Copyright © 1968 by Paul Friedman. Used by permission of the author. First published in *New Directions*, 20.

"God Cares, but Waits" by James B. Hall: Copyright © 1969 by James B.

Hall. Used by permission of the author. First published in *The Virginia Quarterly Review*, Volume 45, Number 2, Spring 1969.

"The Congressman Who Loved Flaubert" by Ward Just: Copyright © 1972 by Ward Just. Reprinted from THE CONGRESSMAN WHO LOVED FLAUBERT AND OTHER WASHINGTON STORIES by Ward Just by permission of Little, Brown and Company in association with the Atlantic Monthly Press. This story originally appeared in *The Atlantic Monthly*.

"He That Died of Wednesday" by W. C. Woods: Reprinted by permission of *Esquire* magazine, copyright © 1969 by Esquire, Inc.

"Evenings in Europe and Asia" by Don Porsché: Reprinted from *Prairie Schooner*, Summer 1972, by permission of the University of Nebraska Press. Copyright © 1972 by the University of Nebraska Press.

"Dossy O" by Clarence Major: Copyright © 1972 by Clarence Major. Reprinted from *Black Creation* 3/4 (New York: New York University Afro-American Institute, 1972), 4–5. Used by permission of the author.

"The Ambush" by Asa Baber: First published in *The Falcon* © 1972. Used by permission of the author.

"Vietnam-Superfiction" by Alain Arias-Misson: Grateful acknowledgment is made to the editors of *Chicago Review*, 23, 1971, in which this material originally appeared. Copyright © 1971 by Alain Arias-Misson. Used by permission of the author.

"A Birth in the Delta" by Tom Mayer: From THE WEARY FALCON by Tom Mayer. Copyright © 1967, 1971 by Tom Mayer. Reprinted by permission of Houghton Mifflin Company.

"The Biggest Thing Since Custer" by William Eastlake: From THE BAMBOO BED by William Eastlake. Copyright © 1969 by William Eastlake. Reprinted by permission of Simon & Schuster, a Division of Gulf & Western Corporation.

"A Simpler Creed" by Ronald J. Glasser: From 365 DAYS by Ronald Glasser. Copyright © 1971 by Ronald J. Glasser. Reprinted by permission of George Braziller, Inc.

"The Room" by Victor Kolpacoff: From THE PRISONERS OF QUAI DONG by Victor Kolpacoff. Reprinted by permission of the author. Copyright © 1967 by Victor Kolpacoff.

"Illumination Rounds" by Michael Herr: Copyright © 1969 by Michael Herr. Reprinted from DISPATCHES by Michael Herr by permission of Alfred A. Knopf, Inc.

"The Negotiators" by Harvey Jacobs: Copyright © 1969 by Harvey Jacobs. Used by permission of the author. First published in *Esquire* magazine.

For Eugene McCarthy

"I declare the war is over . . ."

—Phil Ochs
Central Park, New York
Spring 1965

" . . . peace is at hand."

—Henry Kissinger
Washington, D. C.
Fall 1972

CONTENTS

WRITING UNDER FIRE

STORIES OF THE VIETNAM WAR

INTRODUCTION

Jerome Klinkowitz and John Somer

Telling stories is one of the things we do to make tolerable the affairs of life, to rescue them from banality, and charge them with significance. It is no wonder, then, that the Vietnam conflict spawned such an array of stories and authors. During the war, over fifty stories were published in periodicals ranging from the *Ball State University Forum* to *Esquire*. Who knows how many more were rejected for publication, abandoned by authors, or left stillborn in the fantasies of dreamers.

Vietnam veterans, unlike their counterparts from World War II, seem to feel a need to talk about their "tour of duty." And, if we can judge by the stories that have made their way into print —those written by combat soldiers, reporters, artists, and writers who have been to Vietnam and those who have not—Vietnam epitomizes for them the frightening side of contemporary life. We must ask as well: what does it mean for all of those whose stories remain unpublished, or unwritten?

In Vietnam, wayward Americans—utopian products of the Great Society and Haight-Ashbury—met head-on with the reality of a long-term, peasant-agrarian, revolutionary struggle. The fact that Americans in olive drab were playing the part of the British Redcoats of nearly two hundred years earlier gave ironic testament to much that was wrong with the times. But for the trooper standing up to his waist in the muck of a paddy, there were even greater wrongs. In Vietnam, the individual was subsumed by a technology of warfare that served only itself. All that was real was a senseless repetition of events. Because language had been devalued by the governments and the media, attempts to explain the experience usually failed (or were intended to fail) and created hallucinatory gaps between the senses and imagination, be-

tween experience and understanding. While drugs provided
temporary bridges across these chasms, the questions remained.
The novels and short stories about Vietnam reveal a common,
desperate search for meaning—a search for any shred of authenticity in this experience—that may be traced back decades before
"our" Vietnam War.

The first Western novelist to write about Vietnam was André
Malraux, who as early as 1930 saw that the Indochina experience
could be a metaphor for "man's anguished alienation from an
absurd society within a meaningless universe." Malraux's *The
Royal Way* was the beginning of a line of books that followed
the Western involvement in Vietnam from colonial exploitation
to ideologically based warfare. By 1966 Norman Mailer could
state, "If World War II was like *Catch-22*, this war will be like
Naked Lunch." Malraux's anguished alienation had become a full-
blown nightmare, suggesting that this shard of the Asian continent was indeed bound up with the subconscious of Europe and
America, and that to deal with it in art would take on the
dimensions of a dark encounter with the more unpleasant aspects
of our lives.

Two dozen novels about the war were published during America's active involvement in it. In 1965, Robin Moore first introduced the war to a literary audience with *The Green Berets*,
which concluded: "What the outcome in Vietnam will be is anybody's guess, but whatever happens, Special Forces men will
continue to fight Communism and make friends for America in
the underdeveloped nations that are the targets of Communist
expansion." The war did not turn out that way, and neither did
our country's appreciation of it. Coming to a final understanding, and expressing it in art, has become an ongoing effort as
arduous as any trial described in the existential novels of Kafka,
Sartre, or Malraux. From a European perspective it would have
been nothing new. But in Vietnam, America lost its innocence,
and by that process grew immeasurably in its art.

The processes of art inevitably tell us more about ourselves
than the matter at hand. In this sense there is no novel or story
"about" Vietnam. But the Indochina experience is especially self-
revealing, and with Malraux's *The Royal Way* the measure of
self begins. In the jungles of what we now call Thailand, Cambodia, and Vietnam, Malraux explores the roots of what two
subsequent generations of novelists must face: "that fabulous
aura of scandal, fantasy, and fiction which always hovers about
the white man who has played a part in the affairs of indepen-

dent Asiatic states." The jungle itself is a strange and exotic contrast to the civilizations of the West, a place where Malraux's protagonist finds that he was "growing aware of the essential oneness of the forest and had given up trying to distinguish living beings from their setting, life that moves from life that oozes." Even in 1930 Vietnam is a place where "some unknown power assimilated the trees with fungoid growths upon them, and quickened the restless movements of all the rudimentary creatures darting to and fro upon a soil like marsh-scum amid the steaming vegetation of a planet in the making." In such a place one asks, "Here what act of man had any meaning, what human will but spent its staying power?"

The overt action in *The Royal Way* is colonial adventure. The soldier of fortune, Perken, would plunder the land of its treasure and organize a military force to become its political ruler as well. But as in every subsequent Vietnam fiction, there is a deeper current turning back upon the characters. As Perken explains his motives to his skeptical assistant, Claude:

> "And then—only try to grasp all that this country really is. Why, I'm only just beginning to understand their erotic rites, the process of assimilation by which a man comes to identify himself, even in his sensations, with the woman he possesses—till he imagines *he is she*, yet without ceasing to be himself! There's nothing in the world to match it—sensual pleasure strained to the point when it becomes intolerable, the breaking-point of pain! No, for me these women aren't merely bodies; they're . . . instruments. And I want . . ." Claude guessed his unseen gesture, the gesture of a hand crushing out life. ". . . as I once wanted to conquer men."
>
> What he's really after, Claude mused, is self-annihilation. I wonder is he more aware of it than he admits. Anyhow he'll achieve it easily enough.

Perken's immediate quest fails. He cannot take his plunder out of Vietnam, and his private army is decisively beaten. But his greatest defeat is just as Claude supposed:

> Frenzied with self-centered passion, her body was withdrawing itself from him irrevocably. Never, never would he apprehend, never share, this woman's sensations; never could the frenzy which thrilled her body be for him anything but a proof of the unbridgeable gulf between them. Without love there can be no possession. Carried away by forces he could

not control, unable even to make her realize his presence by tearing himself away from her, he too closed his eyes, thrown back upon himself as on a noxious drug, drunk with a wild desire violently to crush out of existence this stranger's face that urged him on to death.

It would be thirty-five years before American fiction came to grips so closely with these dark matters of the self. Westerners in this novel took their first steps into an experience destined to constrain and diminish their imperial selves, but the challenge was irresistible.

Some historians date the beginning of American involvement in Vietnam from 1954, with Vice-President Nixon's advocacy of intervention at Dien Bien Phu against Eisenhower's wish to remain neutral. Graham Greene's Vietnam novel of 1955, *The Quiet American*, witnesses the awesomely quiet birth of American interest in this country recently deserted by the French. The narrator is a British journalist, seasoned by events in his personal life as well as by his nation's experience, before whom the quiet American A.I.D. official, Pyle, is the epitome of collective innocence: "He was absorbed already in the dilemmas of democracy and the responsibilities of the West; he was determined—I learned that very soon—to do good, not to any individual person, but to a country, a continent, a world. Well, he was in his element now, with the whole universe to improve." This innocence, of course, is Pyle's downfall. As the journalist tells him, " 'I wish sometimes you had a few bad motives; you might understand a little more about human beings. And that applies to your country too, Pyle.' " Innocence, we learn, "is like a dumb leper who has lost his bell, wandering the world, meaning no harm." The young, well-intentioned man "with a crew cut and a black dog at his heels" is as out of date as an Errol Flynn movie where the hero "rescued a girl and killed his enemy and led a charmed life. It was what they call a film for boys, but the sight of Oedipus emerging with his bleeding eyeballs from the palace at Thebes would surely give a better training for life today." Vietnam was already gaining a reputation as "an experience," and Americans were from the first cast as hapless (if dangerous) innocents.

Greene's novel portrays the personal and national havoc created by Pyle's "involvement," the consequences of which are a vivid preview of what was to happen from 1962 to Christmas week of 1972. During these same years *The Quiet American* went through seventeen printings in the United States; but few Americans came forward to write a Vietnam novel with such a mea-

sured and controlled view. The first attempt was Robin Moore's
highly dramatized journalistic account, *The Green Berets*. Its
tone was set by the dust-jacket advertisement, boasting that
Moore "was paid the 'supreme compliment' of being sent along
as the second Special Forces 'sergeant' on all-Vietnamese or
Montagnard patrols. On one such patrol Moore so distinguished
himself that the Montagnard commander offered him the rare
privilege of cutting off the ear of a dead VC!"

In the years since 1965 Robin Moore has remained an apolo-
gist for the war in Vietnam. David Halberstam is not. A journalist in Vietnam the same time as Moore, Halberstam incurred
Administration disapproval for his Saigon dispatches, which
Graham Greene characterized as not taking at all "the conventional line about the American presence in Vietnam." In 1967
Halberstam wrote *One Very Hot Day*, a novel which follows an
American sergeant through a day's patrol—the same role Moore
took for his own book, but with very different results. Halberstam's Sergeant Beaupre is the first American literary character to
face Malraux's jungle, the first to sense that "the heat was the
enemy of all white men, but it was more an enemy of his, he had
less resistance and resilience." It is 1963; he is only a military
"advisor"; and there is a strict limit to his tour of duty, so the
magnitude of Malraux's primeval landscape need be nothing
more than "his imagination turning Vietnam into 365 days of
this." But the artificial limits on time and on his military role are
distressing. "He wished the troops would go faster, would move it
out, and he wished he were a real officer, someone who could give
commands and then see them obeyed, who could send a patrol
here and another there, could make the troops go fast, go slow,
be brave, be strong; wished to be hated, to be feared, even to be
loved, but to be an officer and in charge." His experience is
perplexing, since Vietnam is a different kind of war for him. A
veteran of World War II and Korea, the sergeant can instruct his
young lieutenant (a scene which is to reappear in several Vietnam fictions) in just how strange things are compared to the war
against Hitler:

"We didn't know how simple it was, and how good we had it.
Sure we walked, but in a straight line. Boom, Normandy
beaches, and then you set off for Paris and Berlin. Just like
that. No retracing, no goddam circles, just straight ahead. All
you needed was a compass and good sense. But here you walk
in a goddam circle, and then you go home, and then you go
out the next day and wade through a circle, and then you go

home and the next day you go out and reverse the circle you did the day before, erasing it. Every day the circles get bigger and emptier. Walk them one day, erase them the next. In France you always knew where you were, how far you had walked, and how far you had to go. But this goddam place, Christ, if I knew how far I had walked, it would break my heart. From Normandy to Berlin and back, probably."

Halberstam's novel also begins the search for structure common to most subsequent Vietnam novels: how to organize this war which defies all previous military and political patterns. The novelist starts with basics, a single day's patrol, but on it his veteran sergeant loses all sense of purpose and achievement. Even in the simplest of conventional terms, the experience of Vietnam makes little sense.

Whether experienced by journalists on Guggenheims or by literate infantrymen on patrol, Vietnam proved to be a war unlike any other. Tom Mayer, a representative of the first group, writes about such difficulties in his collection of stories, *The Weary Falcon* (1971), which includes the situation of "the US Marine landing at Chu Lai where the troops came storming out of the amtracks and up the beach like John Wayne in 'The Sands of Iwo Jima' only to find twenty photographers on the top of the first dune taking pictures of it all." In similar terms William Pelfrey's *The Big V* (1972) fails as a realistic combat novel, since the war, measured first against its familiar image on television, never has the chance to escape the tired pop-art clichés assigned to every act. "I fired one round on semiautomatic. His body jerked erect, almost like a gangster blown back by a sawed-off shotgun, only screaming, hoarse, with his mouth gaping; more like an Indian, his arms flying up and dropping the rifle." Pelfrey's narrator can find no vocabulary for the war beyond that of its television images because his vision extends no further than the video-adventures of his youth. That Vietnam was fought on such a level is less frightening than the thought that it was so comprehended, by soldiers and citizens alike.

Outstripping the politics and military theories of earlier wars and older generations, the truth of Vietnam became a test of the artist's imagination. Hence three of the best books about the war were written by authors who were never there as participants, and who remove the action of their books to points of broader perspective. In *The Prisoners of Quai Dong* (1967) Victor Kolpacoff suggests the sense of Vietnam by writing about a military jail, where the order of life has all the tedium, uncertainty, and

senselessness of the war going on outside—particularly when the
narrator is asked to participate in the interrogation/torture of a
Viet Cong suspect. William Eastlake's *The Bamboo Bed* (1969)
finds an even more appropriate perspective on this surreal war—
above the jungle combat, above even the monsoon engulfing
that action, in a rescue helicopter used for in-flight trysts by
a modern Captain Tarzan and Nurse Jane. The ship is more
noted for the people it has not rescued, including an infantry
company directed by its captain into a ritualistic re-creation of
Custer's Last Stand, with the Viet Cong as obliging Indians. Asa
Baber sets his *The Land of a Million Elephants* (1970) in a place
of make-believe not unlike Vietnam in its geography, and quite
like Vietnam in its role in our international fantasies. Baber's
strategists submit that America has been deadened by civil unrest
and political assassination: "I submit that if you had a National
Blood Pressure Monitor at the moment people heard the news
you would have found virtually no response. No orgasm."

Baber's depiction of the lack of imaginative possibilities in
Vietnam may be closest to the truth of what the war really
meant. But within the limits of actual events, it remained the
role of fictionists to find a structure. Ronald J. Glasser's *365 Days*
(1971) admitted the problem: "There is no novel in Nam, there
is not enough for a plot, nor is there really any character devel-
opment. If you survive 365 days without getting killed or
wounded you simply go home and take up again where you left
off." Yet within this artificially imposed structure of a duty
tour Glasser sketches many aspects of the war: the suicidal role of
helicopter pilots, the medics' psychotic altruism, and the case of a
veteran commander who against the military silliness of Vietnam
applies World War II tactics with great success until he is
fragged by his most decidedly Vietnam-era troops. Airmen's
routines—bombing Vietnam on office-hour schedules from comfortable bases in Thailand while intimately involved in affairs
back home in Washington, D.C., or Schenectady Falls, New
York—are used by George Davis as the structure for *Coming
Home* (1971). In counterpoint, Davis places the problems of a
Black officer, unique even in the Vietnam-era Air Force, for
whom "this war is like Harvard. Nothing in it seems real. Everything is abstract. Everything is an argument or a question."

In terms of structure, the most successful novel to portray the
military situation in Vietnam is Josiah Bunting's *The Lion-
heads* (1972). A major and former commander in Vietnam teaching history at West Point, Bunting finds the essence of the Vietnam insanity simply by viewing it through the traditional form

of Army chain-of-command. His novel begins at the top, where a major general knows that

> commanding a Division in the combat theatre can be the capstone of an excellent career of service, leading to one further assignment . . . or, if he truly distinguishes himself, the assignment will lead to another promotion—the big step to three stars (only 15 percent of two-star generals are promoted to the three-star rank). . . . He wants to be Chief of Staff—of the Army.

With the visit of a branch secretary imminent, the general mounts a campaign, implications of which are carried down-staff with the orders. At brigade, he charges one of his colonels in the manner of a sales director: " 'Your body-count is a standing joke. Tell you what, Robertson, you have one week to produce.' " Among the three brigades there is a scramble for the division's helicopter assets; inevitably one brigade is shorted and sustains a frightening number of deaths, but overall the casualties are "moderate" enough for the general to claim a significant victory. As the battle has progressed from planning to execution, Bunting has followed the action down to company, platoon, and squad, until he reaches what the Army calls the "real sharp individual" —the soldier in the field, in this case PFC Compella, the single person in the book devoid of all but purely human ambitions. In the first chapter, at division, he has been temporarily assigned as an aide, displaying maps for the coming battle. "PFC Compella notes that the officers take no notice of him, but follow only the movements of the tip of his pointer as it plots the new locations on the briefing map." His presence is as unreal as the deaths orchestrated by these same commanders. At the novel's conclusion, when he himself is the fine point of the war's action, the officers again take no note, for he is killed on a day for rejoicing, when casualties are light. His experience in Vietnam is absolute, but unmeasurable.

But the Vietnam experience was bewildering even to the military. To Army veterans the war made little sense. Confused sergeants, whose twenty years of service span the end of World War II, Korea, and the beginnings of Vietnam, are familiar characters in fictions emerging from the war—and in few cases do they find a solution, or even an understanding of what is going on. The larger dimensions of America's involvement remain the province of the professional novelist. Two young novelists wrote their first books about the war, James Park Sloan with *War Games*

(1971) and William Crawford Woods with *The Killing Zone* (1970). Both have since broadened their writing careers, but these first novels are the two best to come out of the Vietnam war.

For *War Games* Sloan faces the familiar problem of finding a structuring device. This is why his protagonist has joined the Army—he has two theories to test, one of which he hopes to use for a novel:

THEORY ONE

The timid hero goes to Vietnam like a sissy dipping his toe in the pool. Suddenly he realizes that he can be a cold-water swimmer. This happens because Vietnam provides him with a character-molding experience. It is both purposeful and earthshaking. There is a flash of insight. He realizes that he is now fully mature. He has become a soldier and a man.

This is only a hypothesis. Then there is Theory Two.

THEORY TWO

A tough-minded young man, who unsuspectingly has above-average sensitivity, goes to Vietnam. For the first time in his life he encounters genuine brutality and tragedy—perhaps his first tragic love affair. The experience shocks him into his own humanity. There is a flash of insight. He comes home in total revulsion at war and probably writes a book.

The story of his book becomes the story of his attempts to write "the definitive novel of Vietnam," and its structure becomes one natural and unique to the young college drop-out ripping off the Army in Vietnam. Discovering that if the service does dental work on any tooth it is responsible for the care of that tooth, and the two adjacent, for the rest of the soldier's life, Sloan's protagonist begins a program of systematically complaining about every third tooth. The organization of his dental chart becomes the structure of his novel.

The chart is the most real thing in the book. Like other writers before him, Sloan finds that there are many unreal things in this new war: airliners that race the sun across the Pacific, serving breakfast every hour; APO mail that sends the same letter back and forth across the world twenty-seven times; a peace-time army staffed by uniformed civil servants who must suddenly fight for their careers; and dozens of other incongruities that suggest that Vietnam and its war are a world apart from anything America

has previously known. Officially, the Army contrives its own un-
reality to match. It is a nonlinear war, with no objectives to seize
nor end-date in sight:

> Each departure is festive in its own way. Since there has
> been no mass homecoming, it seems that each individual's
> leaving must represent a victory in miniature. Since the
> rotations after one-year tours are staggered, victory is a con-
> tinuous process. It is thus more sustained than the sword
> tendering, paper signing, and ticker-tape marching of previ-
> ous wars. On the other hand, it is followed by an equally con-
> tinuous reappraisal. Newcomers are always groaning that
> "that bastard has left me in a bind."

The service treats it as a game, a matter of duration and simple modal exercise:

> I have standardized the statistics as well. Ours. Theirs. We
> lead by a steady three-to-one. Which is good, but not good
> enough. Any worse and there would be alarm. Any better
> and the statistics would be checked. No one really reads the
> reports. I never bother with the facts. When a town comes
> up on my roster, I put the monthly battle there. That's the
> way it is with this war.

Sloan's protagonist learns that if he is to have a real war, he
must make it up himself. "The hero must not merely thrash the
villains, but create them. Set them up for the kill like the mata-
dor his bull. Lay hold to a portion of the banal, flog it to life,
and from it fashion an adversary worthy of his steel. I shall
remember to cite Hamlet: devise the play, then act in it!" Others
had to make a separate peace, Sloan observes; "I had to find a
separate war." As he makes progress through his war, which has
become his novel, he wonders, "Have I begun inventing things?
A man who goes to war should return with tales to tell. God
knows, I would like to take part in tellable stories. Is my life
merging with my imagination?" He fears that he is "tramping,
step by step, in the direction of the implausible. Was it possible
that my life was becoming like that of a literary device?" On
patrol with a group of ARVN rangers, his dream catches up with
him: sickened by his allies' torture of villagers and disgusting
acts with animals, he sets his rifle on automatic fire and destroys
them all. For this he expects court-martial and execution, but at

least he has performed a significant act in this otherwise insignificant war.

The writer and his "separate war" are saved by his new boss, Colonel Rachow, who has authored the Army manual *Creative Leadership and Collective Tunnel Vision*, and who in other times "would have been magnificent . . . as a paper lawyer in the twelfth century. Or perhaps as the head of a noble family encroaching on its vassals." Rachow sympathizes with the protagonist's behavior because he can articulate many of the young soldier's feelings about the unreal war against Vietnam:

> War, said Rachow, has ceased to be tied down by facts. It has become metaphysical; one might say a platonic form. He asked me to picture an amphibious landing across Lake Michigan. Then imagine, he said, such things as landings by Martians; invaders from liquid planets formed of molten lava, surprised and threatened by our explorations. This is the future of military planning. War is no longer waged merely to achieve ends; it is waged as proof of its own possibility.

Moreover, technologically "war had come to a state of entropy! It was more and more complex, but in the process its energy was spent. If he had known sooner, he might have quit the army and written a book—on the war which had made his profession obsolete." And so Sloan's protagonist ends his tour with the creation of his small novel about a small war, *War Games*.

In *The Killing Zone* William Crawford Woods employs even more artifice to come to terms with this most artificial of wars. A confused sergeant stands at the center of the action, which Woods places not in Vietnam but rather in a New Jersey training camp where the strategies of Vietnam are first rehearsed. Sergeant Melton has rejected a career which would have led him to Josiah Bunting's managerial officer caste of Vietnam. Instead he finds himself first sergeant of a company with no executive officer, its C.O. having been stricken with a heart attack on the golf course; and so he is in a position of command when a new lieutenant arrives to test a demonstration plan of computerized warfare—a plan being implemented in the Vietnam War for which the inductees are training. The war and its methods, of course, are like none other; and the lieutenant helping to plan it is equally new:

Twenty-four years old. BS and MS in electrical engineering
from the University of California. Master's thesis on some
military application of information retrieval. ROTC commission deferred until after graduate school. Part-time pro-
grammer for Armed Resources Corporation—one of those
ambiguous concerns that hide in the rolling countryside of
Maryland and Virginia within fifteen minutes by chopper of
the Pentagon.

Lieutenant Track's experiment is "to find out how closely and
how well a computer can perform with a small line unit in a
rapidly changing combat situation." The unit chosen is led by
Sergeant Cox, Track's age but in spirit more akin to Melton's
Army, who despite the strange nature of the war and the even
more incongruous circumstances in which one trains for it ("the
training area . . . was a parking lot; they were learning to kill
like cavemen in a place where the pizza truck would stop that
night") resists computerized warfare in favor of the personal vir-
tues of soldiery.

Track's computer plans an action, issues plastic-headed war-
game ammunition, and follows the training exercise with all the
deliberation of a division commander, receiving information from
the field and determining the best strategies to continue. But an
error is made: the operator has not routinely cleared the computer's storage, and as a result two boxes of live ammunition
have been issued. There is no way the computer can discover or
correct its action. That remains the prerogative of the common
foot soldier, in this case Sergeant Cox, who has but one way to
save his men from total slaughter:

He had been hit four times by the gunner who was still firing
when he reached him. Mr. Track's computer had provided
an unbeatable realism which had gone into his belly, and one
bit of realism had ruined his left arm, taken it out altogether.
So it was with the rifle in one hand that he came over the
barrel, calmly, indifferently, almost sweetly, and with practiced smoothness and precision slid the bayonet into the
boy's chest, up to the hilt, not seeing the frightened and
finally knowing glance down at the explosion of blood as
cloth and skin and muscle and then bone gave way to the
rushing pouring steel. Cox's finger jerked on the trigger and
a short stream of plastic bullets squirted into the open
wound, splashing hot into the welling lake of blood. The

sergeant and the private fell together behind the finally silent gun.

Because he has attacked the technology itself, Sergeant Cox can affirm both himself and the real matter of death, each of which the military technicians of the Vietnam War try to efface. *The Killing Zone* stands as the best novel to define, amid the surreal confusion of a war planned by computers and practiced in parking lots, what field remains for honor. The villains are those who disavow such honor, whether they be technocrat lieutenants who fight weekday wars with weekends in New York, or a military establishment which has lost sight of the purpose of soldiering. Again, the sergeants, both young and old, suffer. But in Woods' novel their acts have meaning and their minds comprehend the meaning of what's going on. The lieutenant can drive away in his red Corvette, radio blaring; the first sergeant remains, to write letters of bereavement but also to understand:

> Melton paused, because the melody from Track's radio was surfacing in his mind, and he wanted to name it. It mingled with others, then came clearer. Rock-and-roll, or what they now called just rock, the new music—he hated most of it— but he had heard before, and liked, this quiet tune: there it was: "Ruby Tuesday," by the Rolling Stones. A really beautiful song.

* * *

The immediacy and chaos of the Vietnam experience is illustrated more readily in the short story, where the scope of action may be more limited and intense than in the novel. The stories contained in this collection provide a wide spectrum of responses to both the experiential and moral dislocations visited upon Americans by Vietnam.

Tom Mayer's book of stories, *The Weary Falcon*, is the best introduction to the soldier's lot, bringing Vietnam intellectually and emotionally to the reader in a rich catalog of experience. We learn the names of helicopters, rockets, and gadgets of seeming omnipotence. We make small talk and swap cigarettes, dope, and girls. We stand on tarmac islands in the middle of dense jungles, climb into choppers and swoop into battle against an invisible enemy. We slosh through rice paddies, swear like real GIs, and cower like frightened children, wondering whether heroism or death will reach us first. Mayer's stories, all written well, form a panorama of the war, exposing a corrupt military bureaucracy and the brutalizing nature of war.

The brutal initiation—inevitable for all who become involved in the war—is a central theme of much of Vietnam fiction, in which innocence is often an evil. Don Porsché captures this ambience dramatically in "Evenings in Europe and Asia." During the first evening, set in Europe, the young narrator feels uneasy talking with a German youth because his sheltered suburban childhood in America seems such ridiculous preparation for life. The German views enlistment in the military, even in peacetime, as a serious moral issue. Although the narrator is self-conscious about his background, the remoteness of Vietnam insulates him from its moral implications. At this point he, like so many American literary figures before him, affirms his fundamental innocence. There is a dark quality to this blindered optimism as we see such characters time and again undergo traumatic awakenings in the reality of a kill-or-be-killed situation. Innocence becomes a cage rather than a shield—a state so threateningly inconsistent with reality that escape from it is fundamental to survival. Porsché's initiate comes to terms with his innocence during the second evening related in the story, in Vietnam. He finds his freedom in violence, as he coordinates the reports of scouts with artillery batteries from a radio shack. He can say, "I didn't kill anybody," but he is at the same time obsessed with the distance created by geography and technology that separates him from the consequences of his acts. His need for sensual contact and direct meaning in what he is causing is finally released in an orgasmic slaughter of the exotic oriental insects in his quarters. His only regret amid the frenzy of destruction is that he is "too squeamish" to kill them with his bare hands. Porsché's character thus overcomes his abstract innocence and plunges headlong into the real, albeit deathly, world.

More seasoned, morally solidified characters also suffer their initiations into the ambiguities of Vietnam. Paul Friedman's "Portrait: My American Man, Fall, 1966" dramatizes this problem. The narrative voice that weaves throughout the story, addressing first one mysterious audience and then another, questions the chaotic state of his times and wishes he knew what it all meant. But simple good will and even honesty cannot remedy the political and existential complexities created by Vietnam. In "The Congressman Who Loved Flaubert" Ward Just's delineation of political power, of moral confusion, of the conflict between personal and public commitment exposes the clumsy

machinery that we call government. This is the story of a politician whose noble intentions become mired in pragmatism and
political expediency as he is forced to slither through the bureaucratic swamp of Washington. In Harvey Jacobs' "The Negotiators" this moral atrophy reaches the international sphere. The
negotiators, who could politically ease military tensions, fail, but
create a separate peace—a friendship based on the rich, carnal
pleasures of the international nightlife.

The atrophy of the self in the realm of abstraction leads to
both riotous situations and to moral aberrations. Thomas Parker's "Troop Withdrawal—The Initial Step" is a rollicking study
of personal hatred. Throughout his career the protagonist has
been plagued by a garrulous fool. For his revenge he uses his
bureaucratic post to place his antagonist's name on the plastic
bag of an unknown soldier, thereby murdering his enemy on
paper. An official form altered here and there and the enemy is
cut adrift on a sea of technical abstraction. The most vicious
studies of human atrophy, however, deal with the interrogation
of prisoners. Victor Kolpacoff's "The Room" (later incorporated
in his novel *The Prisoners of Quai Dong*) is a subtle analysis, not
merely of torture and endurance, but of the heroic preservation
of dignity under stress. The protagonist, himself imprisoned for
refusing to kill the enemy he had come to see as human, must
help interrogate a Viet Cong because he speaks the prisoner's
language. But what might be a moral quagmire evaporates when
he finds he can still make a decision. He transcends the abstract
realm by seeing himself, the other prisoner, and their mutual
captors as individuals. The narrator's triumph here underscores
the problem generated by an abstract, absurd, irrational war:
when men fail to respond concretely to the fact of death,
they consequently fail to discover a purpose and direction for
life.

This difficulty of acknowledging death is the theme of two
stories not included here. Robert Bonazzi's "Light Casualties" is
a story of brothers, one a foot soldier, the other a medic, both of
whom write lies home to their mother to comfort her. The lies
seem to work even for them, especially the medic, until he oper-
ates on the mangled body of his own brother, and the nature of
his business becomes real. Stephen Erhart's "As the Hippiest
Doctor Almost Grooved" studies the use of chemicals to alleviate
the daily pressure of this impinging reality. While white physi-
cians cloud their minds with alcohol to escape the routine press
of carnage, Black orderlies stoned on grass live with mangled

limbs and distended flesh as though they were rare and exotic flowers.

The most vivid dramatization of the confrontation with death is the final story of Tom Mayer's *The Weary Falcon,* "Birth in the Delta," a stark, realistic study of guerrilla war. After "taking a village" (in fact a mere collection of huts), the soldiers find a corpse in the act of birthing. The bizarre event transforms the attackers into saviors, as they frantically deliver the child. When they realize that it is stillborn, they also understand that death is the issue of death.

In the stories that deal with death as an irrefutable reality, it can become a motive for action. William Eastlake, the author of *The Bamboo Bed,* tackles this problem most successfully in his self-contained chapter, "The Biggest Thing Since Custer." The story deals with a detachment analyzing the remains of a battle to determine how it was fought and lost. The evidence suggests that the carnage resulted not because the massacred squad was outmaneuvered by a superior force, but because its commanding officer indulged himself in heroic fantasies that proved disastrous for his men. A young reporter, along for the ride, notices one body stirring and grasping for life. This struggle pierces the abstract analysis of casualties and etches in blood the only concrete enemy in the Vietnam experience—death. The vague hatred the men feel for the Viet Cong, the war, the draft, the officers, and even presidents is marshalled against the one enemy common to all men in Vietnam, the one enemy that can be fought on an individual level. For a brief moment the men come together, applying every medical aid they know to the dying soldier. Death wins, but the brief community that surrounded it offers the only nourishment in Vietnam. Eastlake ends the story with the living digging in under the corpses for protection from a sudden bombardment. The theme again is clear: war is the issue of abstraction—what were players on the surface of the battlefield now become cover from incoming fire.

As different from each other as many of these stories are, they all suggest that the central human dilemma of the Vietnam conflict was the moral vacuum created when death was abstracted by geography and technology. Because our sophisticated weaponry enabled killing at a distance—even indiscriminately—the essential facts of life were dissolved into an abstraction so pervasive that only the concrete horrors of death could stand against it, and then only for the moment.

Given such a context, the imaginative life of the individual must confront the problem directly or collapse. In "Vietnam-

Superfiction," Alain Arias-Misson analyzes the problem of abstraction as it is experienced in language. The story is a series of news releases and pictures of ambassadors, generals, soldiers, and Viet Cong. In counterpoint to each of these releases is the author's response to the reported event. The story lies in the tension between the "media" and the author. Arias-Misson probes behind the picture, through the article, to the humanity imagined to be there. His tone is restrained, disinterested, but above all sharp. The juxtaposition of styles in the news stories and the author's interpretations emphasizes the moral dimensions of language. Concrete language evolves into a way of life and becomes a significant human response to the abstractness of life generated by technology.

J. G. Ballard dramatizes the value of concrete language in "The University of Death" (incorporated into his novel *Crash*). It is a series of cameos, all vividly sensual but irrationally arranged. In their totality, these observations of war, sex, famous men, and the characters of the story blend into a sensible cacophony. The story probes the facts and implications of Vietnam, working indirectly through its absurdities toward an "interval of neutral calm" that resolves the story. There is no human narrator, but the arrangement of details suggests a controlling force behind the story deliberately maintaining a technical absence. The story, then, responds to abstracting forces by creating the possibility of identity rising from vivid, concrete language.

Clarence Major confirms this possibility in "Dossy O." The speaker (or thinker) of the story generates and maintains a consistent identity in an environment that denies his presence. Major endows his character with a private Black dialect that serves as a protective realm where the self can exist intact and unthreatened. Because this linguistic identity is rooted in real experience, it supplies the concreteness needed to live in the moral vacuum of Vietnam.

Concrete language can rescue more than morality or psychology, however; it can also revivify the imagination. Robert Chatain's "On the Perimeter" illustrates this point. His story is a series of vignettes of army life, emphasizing the empty, boring days that affect an active imagination. The realistic fabric of sensory details, descriptions of ants, rats, mundane conversations, and references to events back home (such as Nixon's nomination) establish the reliability of the narrator. We are not disturbed, then, by a long maniacal military exchange, nor startled by the vivid reality of the jungle sounds and forms. A vague reference to a third world war seems innocent speculation, at first. Then rumors of international chaos, bombs dropped, and major cities destroyed by nuclear holocaust rush upon us with the same controlled vividness of the earlier realism. Slowly we become aware that the narrator's fantasies have become concretized in language. The boredom and insanity of the perimeter are so great that the narrator has expanded them for his own amusement, and thus ends by filling the void with himself. The imaginative exercise is therapeutic for him, and quite successful: he collapses into "helpless laughter" while his comrades can only cry in their frustration. Chatain's use of concrete language makes storytelling possible; it creates at least one way to respond to the experience of Vietnam.

While all of the stories in this collection deal specifically with Vietnam, they speak also to other literary and social concerns. The fact that amateur and professional writers of all ages and abilities wrote on every aspect of the war in a wide range of styles and modes demonstrates that writing, that telling stories, is an essential reflex to the human dilemma. More specifically, these stories argue that literature is man's private weapon against lies and hypocrisy, that a precise and concrete use of language is a moral act. The Vietnam conflict made less of an immediate impression on domestic America than any other war in its history; there was no mobilization of the homefront, and America was, simultaneously, going through one of the most culturally fertile periods in recent times. In his book *Standard Operating Procedure: Notes of a Draft-Age American* (1971), James Simon Kunen ponders what he will be able to tell his future grandchildren:

> They won't understand why the war did not become the center of our lives, why stopping it did not pre-empt all other concerns, why opposition did not progress far beyond *dissent*. They won't understand how it was possible that, while the war was going on, a new football league grew and merged with the old, hemlines rose and fell amid great controversy, and the nation rediscovered romance.

The task of making such explanations ultimately falls upon literary artists. The peculiar nature of Vietnam, both at home and abroad, has made that task all the more difficult. But long after the politics, economics, military theories, and sociologies of the war have been outdated, the fictions of those artists will remain as evidence of how the war affected our imagination. And for all its struggles, their writing is perhaps our most reliable record of just what Vietnam was. For the argument of this literature is not only that poetry is the supreme fiction, but that life itself is the ultimate superfiction.

CHRONOLOGY OF VIETNAM CONFLICT

207 B.C.   China first enters Vietnam.

1010 A.D.   Vietnam wins independence.

1802   Gia Long unifies Vietnam from the China border to the Gulf of Siam.

1873   Francis Barnier, a French adventurer, attacks Hanoi and declares the Red River open to international trade, beginning French dominance.

1890   Ho Chi Minh born.

1901   Ngo Dinh Diem born.

1940   France falls in Second World War, and Japan takes its place in Vietnam.

1941   Ho Chi Minh founds Vietnam Independence League.

Aug. 19, 1946   Ho Chi Minh establishes Democratic Republic of Vietnam in Hanoi.

Dec., 1946   French army returns to Hanoi.

1950   United States subsidizes French in Vietnam. President Truman sends a thirty-five-man military aid group. Diem visits the United States and meets John F. Kennedy.

1954   United States supplies eighty percent of France's war expenditures in Vietnam. John Foster Dulles tells France that the United States will not commit troops. France surrenders.

April, 1954   The Geneva Conference declares a demilitarized zone at the 17th parallel.

1955   Diem, in defiance of the Geneva accords, organizes the "Republic of Vietnam" as an independent nation. United States Military Aid and Assistance Group arm seven divisions of Vietnamese with American weapons.

1957   Diem visits the United States and is received as a hero.

1960	John F. Kennedy is elected president.
1961	American buildup begins. Kennedy commits 3,200 soldiers. James Thomas Davis from Tennessee is the first official American casualty.
June 16, 1963	Thich Quany Due burns himself in downtown Saigon, rallying Vietnamese Buddhists.
1963	Diem and Kennedy assassinated.
Aug. 4, 1964	Gulf of Tonkin incident. President Lyndon Johnson orders bombing of North Vietnam.
Feb., 1964	Johnson administration begins the covert bombing of Laos.
Fall, 1964	Johnson runs as "peace" candidate.
March, 1965	American regular troops land at Da Nang.
Jan. 31, 1968	Tet Offensive.
March, 1968	Johnson announces that he will not run for re-election.
Spring, 1968	Columbia University riots.
June 23, 1968	Vietnam becomes the longest war in United States' history.
Jan., 1969	United States troops reach peak of 542,000.
May 20, 1969	Peace talks begin in Paris.
Sept. 3, 1969	Ho Chi Minh dies.
July 8, 1969	President Nixon announces first troop withdrawal.
Apr. 30, 1970	Nixon announces invasion of Cambodia.
Spring, 1970	Kent State and Jackson State killings.
Dec. 19, 1972	Headlines: "U.S. Stages Heaviest Attack of War on Hanoi, Haiphong. . . . Official News Blackout Imposed by Order of President Nixon."
Jan. 31, 1973	Peace agreement signed at a twenty-three-foot, green-beige, circular table in Paris.
	John Rucker, a twenty-one-year-old Texan, is the last American officially killed in Vietnam.

DRAGON LADY

Johanna Kaplan

SAIGON (AP)—Police indicated today a woman arrested in connection with the shooting of a Nationalist Chinese officer may be the Dragon Lady who has been gunning down people from the back of a motorcycle.

The National police director, Brig. Gen. Nguyen Ngoc Loan, said Miss Phung Ngoc Anh, a 24-year-old Vietnamese of Chinese descent, was arrested carrying a .45 caliber pistol which ballistics tests show was used to kill five persons, including two Americans. Loan said the woman admitted three of the shootings.

The Dragon Lady has been variously described as having long hair and short hair and wearing a red scarf and a blue scarf. Loan said a search of Miss Anh's apartment turned up a red and a blue scarf and two wigs.

"Draw your own conclusions," Loan said.

The Dragon Lady shot most of her victims from the back seat of a motorcycle driven by a male accomplice. She operated in Cholon, Saigon's Chinese quarter.

Loan said the woman had admitted she was a Viet Cong who learned to shoot a .45 at a secret base in Cu Chi. "She shoots with both hands," Loan said.

"Miss Phung Ngoc Anh, a 24-Year-Old Vietnamese of Chinese Descent"

There are places where it does not rain every day at a certain time, but the girl tripping over the mosquito netting in the heat does not know them. Not that she really hears the rain—it rains every day and she's used to it. She pays no attention to the whirring fan from the gambling club across the street, and can

even disregard the clatter of dishes and pans from the cookshop
through the alley. What she cannot stand is the goat: every time
he moves, the bell around his neck rings, and hopping back and
forth on his tether in the back, there is enough sound of bells to
make it seem like a pagoda. Many people could gain calm from
this idea, but she doesn't—all it does is make her trip, and ring
up through her mind certain things she has to live with.

> *I built my hut among the throng of men*
> *But there is no din of carriages or horses.*
> *You ask me how this can be.*
> *When the heart is remote, earth stands aloof.*

It's her grandfather's favorite poem, this one, by T'ao Yuan-
Ming, and on long walks he often recites it for her, in a way, as a
lesson. But as it is, her heart is not remote enough. Not yet.
When will it be? And who is she?

First of all, her name is not Phung Ngoc Anh. Not yet. From
such a Chinese family, how could it be? She is named Sut On
(Snow Quiet), and from the Ling family, so Ling Sut On, and for
most of the years before she was twenty-four, lived in Cholon, in
the rooms above her uncle's go-down. He is her First Uncle, her
mother's oldest brother, and though all he's supposed to have
downstairs in the warehouse is rice, what else he might have his
stained fingers into is a secret between them and his abacus,
which, no matter what else is going on in the world, never seems
to stop moving. Really there's not as much there as Wu and his
round-bottomed wife always like to pretend, but still, even Sut
On's grandfather, First Uncle's own father—who cannot com-
plain of being thrown out or not supported (it's not as if Wu
were actually unfilial)—even Sut On's grandfather says to no one
in particular when Wu is around and looks as if, for a minute, he
might have stopped moving beads in his head, " 'If a state is
following the Way, it is a disgrace to be in poverty and low estate
within it. If not, it is a disgrace to be rich and honored.' " And
sometimes, when Wu's gambling cronies come upstairs, Sut On's
grandfather smiles, looks straight ahead of him, and, pretending
that he's talking to himself, says, " 'Ill-gotten wealth and honors
are to me as wandering clouds.' " With that kind of smile on his
face, he looks as if he might *be* a wandering cloud, and half the
enjoyment for him is throwing them all off and leaving that
impression. Wu gets the point, though. He puts down his teacup,
makes a quick bow, and heads down the stairs, his friends clack-
ing after him like mah-jongg tiles. His attitude is well known:

One—you're not in Canton anymore, Old Man. Two—I don't care *who* you were there. Three—what good did all your study and Confucius quoting do you when famine came? And four—if it weren't for me, every single one of you in this house would be out in the street and starving. Not that Wu would ever dare say this to his father himself: he leaves it for his perfect, quiet wife to shriek it out to Sut On's mother. In Wu's presence, you could think that First Aunt, Ping, had no tongue at all—stolen by the fox-fairies maybe. She is silent and sweet-faced as she bends down in her *cheongsam* to give him things, and always cooing with her children, but as soon as Wu is out of the room, and especially when he takes his old secondhand Renault and goes out buying rice in the Delta, Ping begins shrieking, and for all her concern with perfection, suddenly doesn't even care how much she offends her husband's father. "It's my house," is one of her favorite beginnings. "Everything here is mine, and when we move, even if we let you stay here, you would be left with nothing." And another one: "When we move, even if we let you visit us, you wouldn't know what to do."

"And the goat?" says Sut On's mother, very familiar with this conversation. "Will he know what to do when you take him?"

It's not much of an argument, though, because everything in the house does belong to Wu, goat included, but he is a miser and would never move. Besides, who would watch the go-down? Not his sickly brother Lim, who also lives upstairs with his whiny wife and children and cannot even watch what he says or to whom he says it, so busy is he darting around in his leather cap and dreaming up schemes for anyplace else—Hanoi, Macao, Bangkok. Nor would Wu trust Sut On's father—a man who could not even properly take his wife to his own home. This is what makes it so hard on Sut On's mother, who is in any case practically a barren woman: two sons stillborn and another one so puny he did not last a month. Of course, there is Sut On, but she is only a girl, and naturally there are people (one of them Sut On's father) who blame it on Vietnam: what kind of country has *women* for heroes, keeps up statues of women who drove off invaders mounted on elephants? But Sut On's mother never gives up, goes to fortune-tellers constantly, and every morning before she sets out rice cakes and tea (while French ladies are having coffee and long hot rolls), she lights her joss stick and prays to Kwan Yin. With no sons, Sut On's father could take another wife if he wanted, but this is impossible to imagine. Once, in the time of the Japanese, he ran a public letter-writing stall, but for as long as she can remember, her dim, red-eared father has always

worked for her uncle and usually smoked enough opium pipes to
not even know who she is. If anyone spilled tea on him, he
wouldn't feel it. So no one pays attention to him, least of all her
mother, who never suspected how lowly she had married, and
there is no respect for him in this house. Every so often, though,
his face changes, and suddenly as if he were one of the Forty-
seven Beasts, he is forced out of his thinness and quiet, and above
all the usual racket, even over explosions or bombs, he begins to
scream and stamp his feet, cursing in peasant Cantonese that Sut
On cannot even understand. Which one of the Forty-seven Beasts
is what she tries to figure out when this happens. For instance:
there once was a man who spent all his days and nights in wick-
edness and unbelief. His family pleaded with him, his friends
argued and cajoled, his neighbors warned him, but it was all
useless, for in his arrogance he would not change his ways. Suddenly, in the middle of his life, he was overtaken by a strange
and mysterious illness: for ten years he would neither speak,
receive visitors, nor move from his bed. His son, who was dutiful,
hovered by his father's doorstep, and finally one day heard the
old man call for a bundle of hay. As quickly as the hay was
brought, so quickly was the door now shut again, for to the poor
obedient son's horror, he saw that his father had been turned
into an ox.

Or another one: in a village, a farmer known for his idleness
and covetousness one night stole into the yard of his friend and
neighbor, and, in the false glow of darkness, came away with his
neighbor's most prized duck. Swaggering in the moonlight, he
cooked the duck that very night, ate it, and later in the midst of
his sleep, felt his skin begin to itch. In the morning, his body was
covered with a thick growth of duck's feathers, so painful that he
cried out. "Quack," came the farmer's voice in his agony: he had
been turned into a duck.

If Sut On were a French girl, she would not have to listen to
such scenes of stamping and cursing; they would not happen, and
if through some accident they ever did, she could go off and turn
on the water faucets, tremendous silver spigots known to shine
through French villas, and in the rush of French water, drown
out all the noise.

How does Sut On know so much about what happens in
French houses? In a roundabout way, the answer is her grandfather, and in an even more roundabout way, it's certain big-
time Cholon merchants, much richer than Wu, so much richer, in
fact, that when they appear at the house unexpected, it sends Wu

running up and down screaming orders and bumping tea-things. By mistake, he even bowed at a no-good friend of sickly Lim's, whom he had forbidden to ever come back. This is the perfect situation for Ping, who is always waiting for the time her smiling smug ways would get a deserving reception. But it's not Wu these whispering, dark-suited merchants have come to see. Instead, it's Sut On's grandfather—whose reputation they have not forgotten, whose words and even name, because he was once their teacher, can still recall them to fear.

" 'Man's life-span depends on his uprightness,' " says Sut On's grandfather immediately. Naturally, they are up to something. Why waste time? " 'He who goes on living without it escapes disaster only by good fortune.' "

"My grandfather was a *lettré*," Sut On would say later on in her school years, simply to make an impression, because otherwise she was ashamed of her household. But in much later years and in a very different place, this old misused sentence came back to her head with a certain surprise.

The merchants leave without even saying good-bye to Wu. This is the reason for their visit: they have managed to secure an extra place for a Chinese child in the French school, and they wish to honor their old teacher by offering it to him, for one of his grandchildren. Sut On's grandfather is very pleased—not so much by the offer, but because they remembered to quote for him from Feng Kui-fen: " 'There are many brilliant people in China. There must be some who can learn from the barbarians and surpass them.' "

Wu is furious, he stalks around and cannot even go back to his abacus. What does he care about French schools? The richest men in Cholon have been in his house, drunk his tea, have come and gone as if he were nonexistent. If they truly want to honor his father, then help make the old man's life more prosperous and comfortable by entering into business arrangements with the son. But Ping sees it differently: "Think of Chen. When he goes to the French school, he'll be able to help *his* father"; and because Wu is still fuming, children on the floor are crying, and Chen, a loping sneaky boy, is nowhere around. Ping shrieks out in an unwifely voice, "Chen! Find Chen! It's his grandfather who wants him."

"Do they think I have no ability?" says Wu. "Do they think my contacts in the Delta would be of no use to *them*?"

"If you don't find Chen immediately," Ping screams at all the other children, "you are disobeying your grandfather!"

Lim's listless friend, who has taken off his shirt, yawns very loudly, the goat rings his bell in the back, and Sut On's grand-father, who does not at this moment look like a wandering cloud at all, says, "It's time for my walk with Sut On."

There is nothing at all unusual about Sut On's grandfather taking her out for a walk. It's been a habit of his for years, and rarely is the walk itself very different. For years he has held her hand and walked slowly through the different streets in Cholon, only speeding up a bit or ducking into an alley when he sees the face of someone he does not respect and would rather avoid. Occasionally they go along the docks and this is the only part Sut On does not like: the coolies, wearing no shirts and sweating, load things on their backs and mutter to themselves peasant Cantonese curses, just as her father does in the times he is angry. Her grandfather does not allow her to look away, but because he knows she does not like it, he buys her a slice of pineapple or a fruit drink to suck on. Usually, though, they walk slowly through the streets and the stalls and he tells her about his life in his village in Canton, which even her parents have never seen, tells her stories from ancient China, and sometimes when he thinks of it, recites pieces of poems. What she likes best is the story of Chuang Tzu, who was a philosopher, a real person, but was never sure of it. One night he dreamed he was a butterfly, and when he woke up he couldn't decide whether he was Chuang Tzu who had dreamed he was a butterfly, or whether instead he was really a butterfly who kept on dreaming he was Chuang Tzu. "Is it I, Chuang Tzu?" her grandfather says, changing his voice when he comes to this part of the story, and thinking about it now, Sut On is about to ask her grandfather to tell it to her again, but he is holding her hand more tightly, and walking along so quickly that they are no longer even in Cholon, but in Saigon itself where Vietnamese live, and there are no more signs in Chinese.

"Look very carefully, Sut On," her grandfather says, and being in a strange place, how can she do otherwise? She hardly knows any Vietnamese, having lived in Cholon all her life, and always gone to a Chinese school. Once, in one of his strange, unpredict-able fits of anger, her father knocked down a Vietnamese police-man, leaving him sprawled out right on the street. Probably he had said something against the Chinese or looked at her father in a way that made him think so, but since it had happened in Cholon, even though there were many people watching, natu-rally it had all come to nothing, except for her mother for whom it was just an extra reminder of how she lived in shame.

Sut On looks around her and knows what she will never be: a lithe Annamese girl, pretty in an *ao dai*. Her bones are too broad, her legs are too heavy, and even if she ever put on an *ao dai* and got accustomed to the material, just above it her face would be a dead giveaway—she will always look Chinese. That's not what her grandfather has in mind, though.

"They have nothing," he says, and will not even look at all the Vietnamese who crowd through the street. "No Empire, no culture, no language, no energy. They couldn't even keep their alphabet, which in any case was really ours. What do they have that isn't borrowed?" and walking along in his long Mandarin coat and his beard, Sut On's grandfather does not dodge around trishaws or pedicabs, but passes right by them as if they were shadows and not there at all.

And soon they aren't: they have walked so far, Sut On and her grandfather, that by this time there are no more trishaws or bicycles, only Frenchmen in cars. Their eyes blink too much against the sunlight, their feet seem stuck as they push them, in big shoes, along the street.

"I've never told you this story before, Sut On," her grandfather says. But she's in no mood for a story. No other street is so wide and so shiny, no other street has no markets or stalls. Instead, people walk in and out of glass-covered stores wearing the same kind of clothing that stares out from the glass. With their very pink faces, they climb to the top of high-windowed buildings, and when they get tired of being so high, they come down to the street, tip back in strange chairs, and unfolding their newspapers, they sip cups of coffee and don't suck their gums. Not one of them knows enough to hold a cup with two hands, and despite this, they live in big white houses hidden by gardens, where maybe occasionally they take off their wide shoes. Even their little children have pink faces and red and yellow hair, and when they take rides on airplanes do not come home to goats.

What story can have come to her grandfather's mind? Heng O, the Moon Lady? The Sisters in the Sun? How the Eight Old Ones Crossed the Sea? What on this street could make him think of any of them?

"A hunter went into the woods and in them found a young deer, a fawn so lovely that he could not kill her. Instead, he brought her back with him to his home, and let her play there within his yard. At first, he worried that his dogs would attack the shy creature, so different from themselves. But it was not so. For months on end the fawn played and frolicked with the dogs in his yard, and grew up with them so well that the hunter saw no reason to return her to the forest. One day, however, when the gate to his yard was open, the deer ventured forth and seeing some dogs in the distance, she scampered up to play with them. But these were strange dogs who had never seen a deer before. They tore her up from limb to limb and that is the end of her story. For so long a time she had lived with dogs, she no longer knew she was not one of them."

"I've never even seen a fawn," Sut On says, though she's never made this objection to stories about fox-fairies. But they're no longer on the Rue Catinat now, so she skips on the streets that are increasingly familiar, and her grandfather buys her a slice of pineapple.

"A deer is a fleet animal," he says very carefully: it is Sut On who will go to the French school.

"Draw Your Own Conclusions"

In French books, the paper is very glossy. Touching it, in her European schoolgirl's smock, Sut On is no longer a girl who comes home each day to a room above a go-down in Cholon, or even a strangely pink-faced girl whose mother in thin, high-heeled shoes plays tennis at the Cercle Sportif and thinks nothing of walking in and out of shops on the Rue Catinat. Instead, she is someone named Françoise or perhaps Solange, whose face she cannot quite imagine, but whose feet take her along broad, tree-lined boulevards, broader than any in Saigon, and down into underground trains where people around her sit down politely with armfuls of long thin breads. Sometimes this Françoise or Solange takes her small dog, Coco, for a walk into gardens called the Tuileries. She is totally unfamiliar with goats, though sometimes in August she and her family—moustached, firm-voiced father, smiling mother, and perhaps a small brother named Jean-Claude—take trips in a car which they own, past farms to the countryside. Here there are animals, maybe even a goat, but Françoise or Solange occupies herself with the fruit orchards. She sings a song to herself in a perfect French accent about a shepherdess, all the while she is picking cherries and dropping them one, two, three into a basket. She is very careful to avoid picking any mushrooms, and when it is time for a meal, eats veal in a sauce of wine and butter, and potatoes that have been cut up thin and fried. Never in her life has she tasted bean curd, and if she saw a lichee nut, she wouldn't know what to do with it.

"She'll grow up to be a taxi-girl," Ping shrieks whenever she sees Sut On in her smock, carrying home her schoolbooks and writing out her lessons. It's the one thing Ping ever learned from Chinese literature: educated girls may bring great pleasure to men, even Emperors, but never, never are they marriageable. Sut On's mother pays no attention to this, goes on pouring out her many cups of tea as usual, and worries only that her daughter, almost grown now, has become much too concerned with ordinary noises and everyday smells. Because of this, Ping has begun to call her Madame Oo-la-la, and still rails to Wu about his father, "How can he have shown such preference? He must have been as blind and deaf then as he is now."

He's not truly deaf yet, Sut On's grandfather, but he is blind enough so that it's very difficult for him to read. Instead of taking walks together, Sut On reads out to him from old issues of a Chinese newspaper whose office has been bombed. Luckily he cannot tell that these are articles which he's heard before, and is pleased enough with Sut On's blurry presence and the rising and falling of her voice as she reads. After his death, when his picture —taken so far back in his youth that Sut On does not even recognize him—is hanging on the ancestral altar, her mother says, "He was a very fair man, your grandfather. He had no illusions about his children." What, in Sut On's opinion, was there to have illusions about?

These are things about her, though, which he has never known. First, her greatest mistake at the French school: a picture in drawing class. The drawing was in honor of Christmas, a feast day celebrating peacefulness and serene joy. Sut On drew a great-winged bird flying slowly from high mountains to a quiet pond. All around her, other children drew a fat, bearded man, Père Noël, or a pink, yellow-haired baby surrounded by donkeys. The French girls laughed aloud, the Vietnamese girls looked at each other and giggled, the drawing teacher tore up her paper. Sut On looked up at the drawing teacher: blond and doughy, his face looked like a countryside in a European child's picture book— the sheep on hills in French nursery rhymes. So, once again Sut On drew a picture for the joyful holiday—a pink, yellow-haired baby, and put him right next to a goat.

"Do you *live* in Cholon?" the French girls would ask her sometimes. "My parents like to go there to eat Chinese food. Do you walk all the way?"

Sut On walks all the way, she has never tired of it. No longer a small child on the arm of her grandfather, there are streets in Saigon she has gotten to know as well as Cholon. These days, though, there are almost no French girls left in her classes, and the Vietnamese girls who once giggled at her drawing hop into their brothers' sportscars, wearing sunglasses and giggling still. This time they're off to Vung Tau, to the seashore. Perhaps soon they'll go to Paris or even America. In the meantime, they buy new scarves, look through *Paris-Match*, and watch the American secretaries whose hairdos, incredibly, rise up like so many new buildings: floors and floors of immovable, perfect curls.

Sut On will not go to Paris, nor to the university at Hue as she had wished. In the room above her uncle's go-down, cousin's children lie awake on the floor, Lim sucks his gums with his cap on, the goat rings his bell in the yard. If she takes this teacup from her mother's hands, it will not rest between her fingers, but fling itself in all directions: like a dragon or one of the Forty-seven Beasts, there is nothing that it will not smash.

"A Secret Base in Cu Chi"

Narrator: "The village of Quoc Tri, once a place of cheer and hearty, joyous activity, found itself suddenly plunged, through no fault of its own, into one of lassitude and woe. No longer did the sultry winds whistle through the green and gold stalks a happy, continuous melody as busy as the chirping of crickets. It was not floods which were drowning the crops and sturdy spirits of the villagers, but great sheets of fire and flame, falling from the skies, which ruthlessly consumed, sparing nothing; neither fields, nor homes, nor sons. The villagers who remained could not contain their puzzlement. What had they done to so anger their ancestors? The women wept and wailed over the loss of those most dear, and the men, sunk in anger and sorrow, did not know what there was to be done nor what indeed was the cause of this terrible misfortune. As they sat, still tormented by grief and astonishment, soldiers appeared amidst the ruins. From their speech and appearance, the villagers could ascertain that these soldiers were Southerners like themselves and rushed out to greet them with hope innocent in their hearts. Alas! Neither hope nor innocence lasted beyond that instant. The soldiers, as rude and ruthless as the flames themselves, gave no heed to the cries of their countrymen. Cruelty flickered on their features and they swooped through the desolated village, ravishing the young daughters, torturing its Elders and temporary Chief. But still they had not contented themselves, for they began to vie with each other in wringing the necks of the few miserable, squawking chickens scratching mournfully about in the scorched yards. These they carried off to heavy, rumbling trucks nearby, trucks whose massive sides were labeled U.S.A. And finally the villagers understood! These soldiers were the puppet troops of the usurper government, and the sheets of flame, the cause of their misfortune, did not fall from the sky, but were thrown upon them by giant planes flown from the land of Hollywood."

What has happened to Françoise or Solange? And where, for that matter, is Sut On? Called Anh now, she is wearing black trousers still strange to her and standing to the side, watching, as a small theatrical troupe performs a pageant for the villagers. It is NLF holiday, so members from her base which is close to the village have come with the troupe to celebrate. It's not the first time she's been in a village like this one: years before, when Wu drove out to buy rice, Sut On and Chen occasionally went along. Chen would lope along with his father, but Sut On almost never got out of the car. Sitting in it, stuck to her seat by the heat and the sun, she would look out the windows, closed against mosquitoes, and staring at the red-tiled roofs behind small palm trees, at the little orchards of mangoes and jackfruits, and above all, at a certain slow quietness so different from Cholon, she would wish that she was one of the small girls she could see running barefoot past the monkeys, sucking on a piece of cane or perhaps a coconut. She looks no more like them now than she did then: it's girls like these she's met at Cu Chi, girls to whose bodies black trousers are not strange, girls who have run barefoot for miles and miles through wild panther country and think nothing of it. Bits of rice and *nuoc-mam* are what they're used to, and jungle sounds at night do not make them jump. Their Vietnamese is so quick she can barely understand it. Naturally she is still not trusted.

The troupe is finishing up, waiting for the musicians. They sing with a guitar:

> *An American plane is like a tiger*
> *Ferocious from afar*
> *But helpless against determination!*

Sut On is still watching a small-boned girl from the troupe, a dancer, who played out with slow, huddled movements the grief of a widow. The sadness, which just minutes before crept and bent through all of her, is gone now, transformed. She stands up straight, and, in a plain cotton blouse her mother might have

worn in the Viet Minh, is singing with all of them, "helpless
against determination!"

"Other women bring forth children, you bring forth rifles,"
said the official who arrested Ho's sister in the days of the Viet
Minh. Her father was a *lettré*. "My grandfather was a *lettré*,"
says Sut On that night, when they are back at Cu Chi, far beneath foliage. In the darkness especially, the feeling of holiday
persists: there are coconuts and an orange or two from the village, and some of the younger boys are strumming on guitars.
But Sut On is impatient with it. In a headiness, an elation she
cannot explain to herself, she pushes a guitar out of someone's
hands, and in her high Chinese voice—she hears her accent but
doesn't care—begins to sing:

> *Dors mon amour*
> *Fais do-do mon trésor*
> *On crie chez la voisine*
> *Chez nous une câline*
> *Tu se traînes dans la fange*
> *Tu vas dans la soie*
> *Dans la robe d'un ange recalée pour toi.*

The song is from *Mother Courage*, a record Sut On once found
hidden behind books in the French school.

> *Dors mon amour*
> *Fais do-do mon trésor*
> *L'un repose en Pologne*
> *Et l'autre je ne sais où.*

"Why are you singing a French song?" says the cadre. He is a
wiry man, quick, nimble, and for that reason called Squirrel.
No one's name is their own.

Why is she singing a French song? For a second, in her headiness, Sut On thinks she will tell Squirrel about *Mother Courage*,
about the Thirty Years War, but is afraid that just like with
machine-gun fire, when her head drums so quickly that the
rounds seem too slow, her thoughts are going so quickly her voice
would make no sense.

"It's a lullaby," she says and, looking at him directly, knows
perfectly well that was not the way she sang it.

The cadre begins tapping rapidly on a bamboo length he has
sharpened. In his staccato Northern voice, he says, "You should
not stay in the jungle any longer."

"A Red Scarf and a Blue Scarf and Two Wigs"

There is no street in Cholon, no house, no door, no stand, no stall that Sut On could not find in her sleep. It is in fact this feeling of sleep that stays with her now as she walks through the market in a short wig and a Western dress, seeing no one and smiling dimly, politely at hawkers who, noticing a stranger, shout out elevated prices in broken Vietnamese. She could tear off her wig, pull out her voice, and scream and haggle with them in Chinese, but luckily the sleepiness stops her. In some ways, nothing even seems familiar, so she walks on, with her sunglasses, to a certain teashop where she picks up instructions. In front of it, there is a row of old women who are selling radios and cameras in cartons marked PX. One of them suddenly looks up at her and in a hoarse, tired voice calls out in Chinese—it is *not* her mother. Inside, the message is more or less what she has been expecting: "The mountains around you do not have higher peaks than the one on which you already stand! There is no going back."

In the bare Cholon apartment rented to Miss Phung Ngoc Anh, Sut On lights a joss stick, and in its old, missed smell folds and unfolds the scarves, staring at the red and blue squares in the dark room. Over and over again, she turns them inside out and around and smooths down the edges; it's as if they were someone else's, she has never been so neat.

"Should I wear the red or blue?" she says, and feels like giggling, so much does she want to pretend that this is her dilemma.

Asleep on the straw mat which belongs to the apartment, she dreams that her grandfather is walking through the long narrow halls of her uncle's go-down. He is coming to greet her but does not call out her name or even beckon to her. He just keeps on walking slowly with a slice of pineapple held out in his hands.

"There is no going back." To what would Phung Ngoc Anh go back? There is a girl with a flowing red scarf who speeds through the streets on the back of a motorcycle. If her heart is remote, she'd be the last one to know it. Fleet as a fawn, she shoots with both hands.

EVENINGS IN EUROPE AND ASIA

Don Porsché

The youth hostel at Avignon is on an island in the Rhône River. During my first visit there, in May or early June of 1963, I had a long talk one evening in the embankment by the edge of the water with a young man, a German, of about my own age. We were both in our early twenties, born at the beginning of the Second World War. He had hitch-hiked from Hamburg and was going, I believe, to Marseille.

As often happens in such conversations, there was a quick establishment of trust, and we were soon talking about personal topics. He asked me about my early childhood; I said my first memories were of a porch full of toys at a friend's house around the corner, and tarred alleys and running under the hose in the summer.

"You were in the States, I suppose, all during the war?"

I said yes, I was born and grew up there.

"And the war didn't make much impression on you, as a small child?"

"No. I'm not sure I even knew there was a war going on. I don't remember anything about it except V-J day; there was a parade. And ration stamps, but I guess my memories of ration stamps are from afterwards. There was an embarrassing moment in kindergarten or the first grade when it developed that I didn't really know the difference between ration stamps and money."

He smiled.

I asked if he had been in Germany during the entire war.

"Yes. My earliest memories are of the air raids: sirens in the night, running down stairs, explosions in the distance. Waiting, everybody frightened. Sometimes nearby explosions and crumbling walls. My father was killed on the Russian front and my cousin, one of my older cousins, died in an air raid a few blocks from where I was. It was terrible. I dreamed about it for years afterwards. Sometimes I still do."

My first impulse—and it was a foolish one, I admit—was to envy him for his early memories. I thought vaguely that it might be better to begin one's life with something decisive, something that cut into the depths of existence, rather than the trivial embarrassments I remembered from my suburban childhood in the United States. I had the idea that I was living only on the surface of my life and that my shallowness was partly the result of a banal childhood. My German friend appeared neither shallow nor trivial.

We went on to talk about Germany in the years immediately after the Second World War, and I tried to imagine the feeling of waking up after the end and finding oneself still alive. We also talked about the German Youth Movement: its beginnings in the early part of this century, and what's left of it now. When we got back to our own travels I said I had spent the winter in Spain and was now on my way up the Rhône, by bicycle, going to Germany. By the third week of June I had to be in Frankfurt, to take a pre-induction physical at a U.S. Army hospital. If I passed, as I surely would, I expected my induction notice by the end of the summer.

"Are you going to let yourself be drafted?"

I said yes, I didn't like the idea but there wasn't much I could do about it.

"You could refuse."

"And go to jail? I suppose I could, but that would be even worse than being in the army. And it wouldn't really accomplish anything."

"At least you wouldn't kill anyone."

I scoffed. "I won't kill anyone in the army, either. I'll be given a desk job, I'll put in my two years of mindless busywork, and that will be that. The only thing that remotely resembles a war right now is in Vietnam, and all we've got there are a few 'military advisors.' They're all volunteers, career men. Marines and such." I had read articles saying they weren't sending any American draftees over there because the Vietnamese were doing all the fighting. Like most people in 1963, I had only a vague idea where Vietnam was and what was going on there.

The sun had set behind us, and its glow was fading from the massive stone palace of the medieval popes, across the river to the east. Now the pale aluminum light from a half moon was reflected in the swiftly moving water between us and the *pont d'Avignon,* the remains of the bridge that was danced upon in the French folk song.

"I know so many people," he said, "who have drifted into the army—various armies—thinking the same thing. 'There's no war. I'll have a desk job. I'll just serve my time.' And then they find themselves in the middle of something they want no part of. When my father was drafted there was no war, and everyone said there wouldn't be one, *der Führer* wouldn't allow it. I never knew my father, but I'm told he had no intention of fighting. He just got entangled in the military, and then it was too late."

I nodded, but said nothing.

"Suppose you *do* find yourself in a war," he said. "Suppose someone was aiming a gun at you. Would you kill him?"

My answer was that I really didn't know.

After a pause he said: "Actually I shouldn't have asked you that. It's the sort of question they ask at hearings for conscientious objectors, to determine if you're 'really' a pacifist: 'What if someone attacked your grandmother on the street?' Any way you answer is wrong."

I asked if he was a conscientious objector himself.

"Inside, yes. But if you mean do I have the official status of a C.O., no I don't, not yet. I've applied, and had some hearings and appeals, but nothing's settled yet. Of course I haven't served and don't intend to. If all else fails I'll stay out of Germany, or go to jail. I haven't really decided if a direct refusal is essential, or if it's enough simply to avoid service by whatever means. Maybe I'll just move to West Berlin. We have that advantage, in the Federal Republic, that if we move to Berlin we can no longer be inducted. But of course you Americans have no such island."

I said I had considered just staying in Europe. "In many ways I prefer Europe to the States, anyway . . . But still, it *is* my native country, and if I could never go back there it might be quite a hardship."

He asked if I had considered conscientious objection, and I said I hadn't, as it was very difficult in the States except for members of certain religious groups. But I wasn't religious, and couldn't really claim to have any great moral principles. "No," I went on, "the one possibility is being deferred as a student, and I've done that to the point where I just can't go on doing it any more. I've graduated from college in the States, I've studied in Switzerland and Paris, and last fall I enrolled at Barcelona but I couldn't go through with it. I rode around Spain on my bicycle all winter instead. The trouble is that by now I *know* what I want to learn and I know how to go about learning it. The more

I study in universities, the more they seem to get in the way. I'd have given up on universities a year or two ago, except that I wanted to stay out of the army. But now I'm so sick of doing pointless things to avoid it that I think I'll just let myself get drafted, serve my two years, and have done with it."

"Of course, that's just the way they want you to feel."

"I suppose. Or it may be that they don't care how you feel, just so they get you one way or another."

The moon had risen higher in the sky. It was nearly closing time for the youth hostel, and groups of people were drifting inside.

"I know how you feel," said my German friend, "but if I were you, I wouldn't do it. Somehow, I'd refuse."

Later, when I was in Vietnam, I often thought of our conversation by the river in Avignon. I wished I had written down his name and address, so I could write him a letter.

One thing I was right about: I didn't kill anybody. At least I didn't kill anybody directly, personally, with my own hands or my carbine. Like everyone else, though, I was involved in complex processes that resulted in people being killed—many more people than I could possibly have killed just by shooting them.

Sometimes when I was working nights in the radio shack at Ngheo Nan there was a light observation plane overhead, and the pilot would call me on the radio and say: "This is Hawk one-seven. I see some lights, they look like campfires, by a bend in a small river south of your location. I believe they're within your artillery radius. The coordinates are . . ." and he would give me six numbers indicating the location on the map. Occasionally I thought of changing the numbers in some way before passing them on, but I never did it. Mainly I was afraid of getting caught, I suppose, but another reason was that I didn't know the area well enough, and I was afraid I might bring down artillery fire on some innocent people, other than those the pilot had in mind. At any rate I plugged a jack into the hole marked "ARVN OCC" on the field switchboard, turned a crank to ring a phone on the other side of the compound, and read the six numbers to an American lieutenant on the other end. "ARVN OCC" meant "Army of the Republic of Vietnam, Operations Control Center." Why the people at OCC couldn't have had their own radio and talked to the pilot directly I don't know, but they didn't. The American lieutenant who took my call had to give the numbers to a Vietnamese lieutenant who in turn had to phone them out to the Vietnamese artillery crew. Usually everyone at the artillery position was asleep, and the Vietnamese lieutenant had to go out and wake them up.

After a while the pilot called again: "Are those people ever going to fire?" I said I'd ask, and then I called the American lieutenant over at OCC, who said: "Beats me, I gave them the coordinates and that's all I know. Hold on a second." Then I would hear the American lieutenant calling to the Vietnamese lieutenant: "Hey, Thieu Uy, why aren't they firing?" Pause. "They're sleeping? Then why don't you go wake them up?" Pause. "Well? Why don't you?" Pause. "Do you want me to go with you?"

Most of the Vietnamese lieutenants were city boys from well-to-do families in Saigon. They appeared to be afraid of the dark or afraid of the enlisted men in their own units, or both. Sometimes the Vietnamese lieutenant would leave the room (ostensibly to wake up the artillery men), remain outside for a few minutes, then return and slip behind his desk without saying anything. "Well?"——"They no wake up? How come they no wake up? Did you yell at them? Did you shake them? You tell them you're the Thieu Uy, they damn well better wake up." Some of the American lieutenants were infuriated, some only amused, depending on their temperament.

Even I got impatient sometimes, because all this talking back and forth on the radio and telephone was keeping me from my reading. I kept telling myself I should encourage inefficiency; at least no one was getting killed while the Vietnamese were sleeping and fooling around. But I was worried (as the U.S. command doubtless wished me to be) that this habitual inattention might be the death of us all, in case we ourselves were ever attacked.

Some nights, in spite of everything, the artillery eventually fired.

"Hawk one-seven, this is Tunafish Control," I said over the radio. "One round on the way."

"Roger. About time. I'm getting low on fuel. Stand by to adjust fire." I clicked my microphone button twice, which meant all right.

Our call sign had been "Tunafish Control" for so long that no one found it the slightest bit odd. Eventually it was changed to "Able Mable" and still later to "Antique Bed Five-Zero."

Soon I heard the pilot's voice again: "Up two hundred, right three fifty." "Roger." I relayed the instructions to the American lieutenant, who told the Vietnamese lieutenant, who phoned the artillery crew. A moment later there was another loud bang.

"Hawk one-seven this is Tunafish Control, another round on the way." "Roger." He gave a further adjustment, I relayed it, another round went off. Invariably I felt an odd satisfaction now that everything was finally clicking, now that the system was finally working the way it was supposed to. Somewhere I once read that rhythmic interdependent motions performed by a group of people, such as workers in a factory, can be satisfying regardless of what is being accomplished. In my case, this was certainly true. I didn't like what was being accomplished, but I couldn't help enjoying the rhythm of doing it. "Tunafish Control, this is Hawk one-seven, they're putting out some of those campfires. Tell them up fifty and fire for effect." I relayed the message and soon heard a series of explosions: boom-boom, boom-boom, boom-boom. . . . There were two artillery pieces that fired one right after the other, then reloaded and fired again. It always reminded me of a Gregory Corso poem: *Boom-bam ye rivers, Boom-bam ye jungles.* . . . Boom-bam ye Vietnamese peasants who happen to be in the way.

Some nights the colonel, who lived in an adjoining building, came over in his pajamas to see what was going on. He was small, grey-headed, and slightly pigeon-toed, but even in his pajamas he somehow managed to look authoritative, at least to me. "What was that artillery a while ago? Just H-and-I?" That stood for Harassment and Interdiction; it meant firing a few rounds at random into the jungle. "No, sir. Hawk one-seven was up, and he spotted some campfires to the south." "Any trouble with the artillery?" "No more than usual." The colonel nodded, glanced at the radio log on my clipboard, and then said: "Very good. Tomorrow I'll try to talk my counterpart into sending a battalion or two in there, to see if we hit anything. Maybe we can at least get a body count."

His counterpart was Colonel Quan, the South Vietnamese zone commander, an enthusiastic tennis player. Our colonel's job, as Colonel Quan's advisor, was to advise him over and over again to *do* something: strengthen the defenses, conduct an operation, send out patrols, anything besides play tennis. When I was running the switchboard I often listened to their conversations: ". . . oh, yes, Colonel Williams, we do that right away, maybe middle next week." "I really think, Colonel Quan, that since your last operation was, ah, such a success, you really should, er, strike again while they're still off balance." "Oh, yes, but men tired. All the time operations. . . ."

My own attitude toward Colonel Quan was problematical. Emotionally I found myself identifying with Colonel Williams's anger and frustration—identifying with aggressive American know-how against dark-skinned native sloth—even though I knew perfectly well, intellectually, that playing tennis was more rational than leading hundreds of men around the countryside trying to shoot people. I also knew that these "operations" did nothing to increase our own security; on the contrary, at that particular stage of the war the local Viet Cong seemed generally content to leave us alone, provided we did the same to them. But my emotional response often refused to agree with my intellectual understanding.

I worked the evening or night shifts whenever I could. Between calls I read books, looked up words in my foreign-language dictionaries, drank tea that I made from an immersion heater plugged into the wall, wrote letters, and did calisthenics under the breeze of the ceiling fan.

In the rainy season there were swarms of insects, especially in the first few steaming hours after a heavy downpour. They came in an astounding variety, big and small, flying and crawling, biting and nonbiting. Somehow, in my previous experience, large numbers of insects had only come at me in homogeneous hoards, one species at a time, for instance mosquitoes in Maine so thick you couldn't take a breath without inhaling a few of them, or tiny hard-biting black flies in Canada, or plagues of grasshoppers in Colorado, where one summer a local radio station offered a free "Purple People Eater" record to anyone who brought in a quart jar of grasshoppers to the studios. Fortunately in Vietnam the biting insects were in a minority, outnumbered by the moths and stink-beetles and especially by the clumsy golf-ball-sized monsters I privately called "Caribous" because they were slow and awkward like the fat two-engine Caribou airplanes that brought us our mail and beer and Coca-Cola every day from Saigon. These "Caribou" insects lumbered around the room, crawled all over the switchboard and the radios, flew around your face, smacked into your head and arms, fell into the tea-water and drowned, landed on the light bulb and singed themselves to death, blundered onto your open book and crawled across the line you were trying to read. Once when I was on a three-day pass in Saigon I looked through several book stores on the Boulevard Le-Loi trying to find a guide to Southeast Asian insects, but I never found one and so I never learned the official name for these monstrous flying bugs. Sometimes I closed the doors of the radio shack to keep them out, but that made the room too hot, and they got in anyway through the holes that had been drilled in the walls for antenna cables and telephone wires. It helped somewhat to turn off all the lights except the little fluorescent lamp on the table in front of me; then at least the light wasn't visible from so far away, and that seemed to keep the numbers down. But of course those insects that were already in the room all congregated around me and my lamp. Inevitably I got annoyed and started swatting at them with a rolled-up newspaper, and before long the cement floor was littered with dead insects.

There was a spray can on the shelf, but I never used it. I insisted on swatting each insect individually with a newspaper, both because I didn't like the smell of insecticide and because of something I called "refusal to kill with technology." One night I was explaining this to someone when Colonel Williams came in, and to my surprise he smiled in his grim way and said: "Well, I'm glad someone has some comprehension of what's involved over here." He never elaborated, and I'm not sure his comprehension was the same as mine, but at least he gave me credit for some sort of understanding, and I reluctantly did the same for him.

To be consistent I should have put the newspaper aside and killed each insect with my bare hands, but I was too squeamish for that. To be absolutely consistent I shouldn't have been there at all.

A BIRTH IN THE DELTA

Tom Mayer

The company was spread out behind a series of dikes, taking a lunch break. The sun thrust down, glared with steady eye-aching intensity off the muddy paddy water. Some of the men had taken off their shirts, others wore undershirts, which were dark with sweat. Now, resting, they had all taken off their helmets. They were all also caked with mud to their thighs. The mud was drying in the sun, beginning to crack.

The company had been in the field in the Delta for a week, plowing across an interminable series of paddies, always working through the muck and never along the hard packed dikes, because the dikes were where you ran into ambushes and mines and booby traps. Before this operation they had had a one day stand-down, complete with warm orange sodas and new uniforms, after having been in the field for ten days. Before that they had had a one day stand-down . . . etc.

The headquarters element was grouped in the center, around the company commander, Captain Harkness. Harkness looked to be perhaps eighteen, with the tanned athletic aspect of a lifeguard or an assistant tennis pro, his face smoothly brown and his hair thick and blond, close cropped. His appearance was somewhat deceptive, for actually he was twenty-six, a veteran commander, now in the eighth month of his second tour. A paratrooper, an instructor at ranger school, a survivor of two dozen bitter firefights in the Central Highlands two years ago. He was studying the map—it often seemed to him he had spent the major part of his adult life studying maps—and half listening to the desultory luncheon conversation going on around him.

"I'll trade you ham and eggs for them Salems," said Corporal Blacksides.

"Fuck that," said Top Sergeant Himmlemann.

"You can have my coffee too."

"Shit. I got plenty of coffee."

"They give me the fucking shaft. I'm too fucking short." That was PFC Leyba, the radio man, who was scheduled to leave in three days. "They shouldn't have sent me to the field again. Fucking Roth didn't go on no operations, and I'm shorter than he was."

"Roth was a fucking fuck-up, Leyba," said Spec 4 Burns, the medic. "We need you."

"Fuck you."

"Ask the old man. You're indispensable, Leyba. They ain't never gonna let you go home."

"Watch your fucking lip. I'll fucking bust it for you."

"I'll give you my peaches."

"I don't know."

"Peaches, you asshole. You don't even like Salems."

"I got to think about it."

"Fucking eighty more days," said Rifleman Upshaw. He drew a line through the number 81 on his helmet. Many of the troops' helmets were virtually covered with numbers.

"You can't cross it off yet," said Private Prissholm, who was on his first operation. "We're not through the day."

"I can cross it off if I fucking want."

"Of course you can," Prissholm said. "But it doesn't mean anything."

"Shit."

"A can of peaches for a pack of fucking cigarettes, you dip. You don't even like the fucking brand."

"Maybe I don't like peaches neither."

"Don't shit me, Top."

"I never shit nobody."

The captain glanced at his watch, went over the map another time, making sure he had not missed some obvious ambush site. "All right, Top," he said. "Tell 'em to put it on."

"Where do we go now?" Prissholm asked.

"Across some more fucking paddies, you idiot," Upshaw said. "Where do you think we're going? On fucking R and R?"

"Put it on," Top was bellowing.

"Maybe we'll get us a fucking vil," Leyba said. "I like to burn them hootches."

"Rape, loot, pillage, burn," Burns said.

"Lay off that shit," Top said. "There ain't no fucking TV cameras around."

Men were standing up, slowly, drawing each move out, feeling the sweat begin to run again as they donned shirts, slid packs and webbing over shoulders, fastened buckles, slung ammunition containers and belts of machine gun bullets, placed the hated weights of the helmets. Harkness gave instructions to the platoon lieutenants over the radio. The point element, which was several dikes ahead, moved out. The company unfolded forward like an opening accordion. Harkness checked to either side that the flank security was out. They had not had a contact for two days, and he was not particularly expecting one, but he knew you got hit when you expected it least, and worked constantly to keep himself and his troops alert. Two or three kilometers ahead of them a treeline shimmered in the heat, a dancing band of cool across the glare. It could almost have been a mirage, but he knew from the map it was real enough.

It was headquarters' turn to move. One by one the men went over the dike, hesitated, and stepped down into the muck on the other side. The Delta was the most work of any place in the country, Harkness thought. In the mountains at least you were on firm ground. There were always twice as many heat exhaustion cases here. Several times he thought he had come to the end of his own rope. But you learned how to move in the muck, how to hop from one rice plant to the next and never, almost never, slide off into the gumbo, which might be knee or even thigh deep.

They slogged through the paddy and over the dike and into the next one and the sun kept pouring down. Some of the men wore sunglasses, but most did not bother. Glasses fogged up and you sweated so much they were impossible to keep clean. Every so often a man fell down, slipped off a rice plant and lost his balance and sprawled forward or sideways into the water and mud, then scrambled up swearing. They crossed one deep canal. They held rifles and ammunition overhead, but a machine-gunner, a Negro named Dillard, slipped going up the far side, slid back into the water on his chest, dragging weapon and ammunition through the ooze. Two men helped pull him out and they stopped while he cleaned the gun, wiped off the belts.

After an hour they stopped for a five minute break.

"I'm almost out of water," Prissholm complained. Most of the men were drinking deeply, carried four or five canteens on D-rings and webbing.

"Don't look at me, dickhead," Upshaw said.

"I wasn't asking for any. I just wonder when we'll get a re-supply."

"Shit," Upshaw said.

"Maybe tomorrow," Burns said. "Maybe tonight. Maybe never."

"I could pill this paddy water."

"Sure," the medic said. "Put enough pills in piss and you could drink it."

"Don't shit this dickhead, doc," Himmlemann said. "He might try it."

"Top," Harkness said. "Make sure they're taking their salt."

"Right."

"I got plenty of salt pills," Burns said. "Iodine too. If anybody needs them."

"Good, doc," Harkness said.

"Blacksides, have you got some extra water?"

"How much you got left?"

"About half a canteen."

"You got plenty. Tell me when you're out."

"Thanks a million."

"Anytime, dickhead."

"This fucking operation eats shit," Leyba said. "It sucks."

"Nobody'll argue with you about that," Burns said.

"It's a goddamn ratfuck. I'm too short to get zapped on a ratfuck."

"You aren't going to get zapped."

"Fucking A I ain't. But you can't never tell."

"Don't sweat getting zapped, Leyba. I'll fix you up."

"Shit, doc. You don't know how to get a Band-Aid on straight."

"Well, motherfuck, just hope you don't have to try me."

"Now don't get pissed off."

"O.K.," Harkness said. "Let's move out. Get 'em moving, Top."

Harkness called ahead to the point and out to the flanks on the radio, told his people to stay alert, to watch the treeline. They were less than a kilometer away now. The map showed several hootches, which did not necessarily mean that there were people, or even hootches any more. However, Harkness was aware of how naked his people were coming across the paddies, how they might look through a pair of binoculars or a telescopic sight. He called Battalion, made sure they wanted him to push on. They did.

"It's typical," he said to Sergeant Himmlemann. "They haven't got a fucking blocking force so anybody in there can DD if they feel like it."

Himmlemann, his bull neck luminous with sunburn, the color of windblown coals, was too busy hopping from rice clump to rice clump to answer.

Leyba, slogging behind the captain, bent under the weight of the radio, loathed Harkness, focused his hate at a point between the captain's shoulder blades. He hated Harkness for bringing him out again, was sure he could have gotten him a dispensation. In fact, he had hated the captain for eight months, ever since Harkness had come to the company and made him a radio operator in the first place. The radio cut down into his shoulders and tendons, caused a burning sensation and numbness, almost as if the straps were eating their way through his flesh and sinew. He had humped the captain's radio and never gotten used to it: it was his ball and chain, an extra thirty pounds of knobs and transistors and batteries that nagged him like a lead growth. He had nightmares where he was drowning in a canal, floundering face down in brackish water, the weight on his back pressing him inexorably toward the muddy bottom. He thought of shooting Harkness if they got into a contact, a recurrent and favorite daydream. He had read about things like that happening, good soldiers shooting unjust officers in the field, in men's magazines. As far as he knew it had never happened in their brigade or their division. But there was always a first time. But they might catch him, and then he wouldn't deros, wouldn't ride the freedom bird, they would put him in LBJ, the Long Binh Jail. If he wasn't so close to leaving he wouldn't even mind that. Sometimes he thought anything would be better than the radio, than humping the boonies week after week with that dead weight on his back. He would shoot Harkness without a qualm if it weren't such bad percentages with only three days left.

Private Prissholm was simply miserable. He had gotten over being frightened—the first few days out he had been carried by sheer nervous energy, had imagined every odd shape and terrain feature concealed his doom, had not slept ten minutes—but now he was only tired, indescribably weary through his thighs and calves, and thirsty. How was he supposed to have known most of the water here was so saline as to be undrinkable, even when liberally laced with purification tablets? And even if he had known about that, how was he to have guessed that resupply would be so erratic? He assumed that somehow things like water and food got taken care of. This was, after all, the American Army, and the one thing everyone admitted Americans were superior at was logistics. That was supposed to be our genius. Six million cans of hair spray for the Saigon PX and air bases with ten thousand-foot runways of solid reinforced concrete every twenty miles up and down the country, but no water for one infantryman in the Delta.

He imagined a confrontation with the battalion lieutenant colonel, a mean-eyed Swede who affected a fatherly attitude, called everyone from his most senior major on down lad, in which he, Private Prissholm, told the colonel that it was a fucked-up Army that expected its troops to fight without water, and the colonel, amazingly, agreed with him, assured him it wouldn't happen again. Momentarily Prissholm was pleased with the vision, his victory, and then he thought that he was deluding himself. He was losing touch with reality. He was Michael Edwin Prissholm, college graduate, political science major, former vice-president of the sophomore class, and all of this, the colonel, the water, the muck, the heat, cretinous Sergeant Himmlemann, Leyba the obvious psychotic, Harkness who was running for eagle scout, everything since basic training, since induction, all of it was unreal, had nothing to do with the real world and real people. The only way to survive mentally was to turn off his mind.

Burns, the medic, was content. He was light, very lithe, and he was not weighted down with ammunition as were the other men, so he hopped easily, mechanically, from plant to plant. He had learned long ago how to turn off his mind, divert its focus, on marches like this, to concentrate his physical attention on the next step, never farther ahead than two steps, while he let the thinking part of his brain slip off on little trips. Burns was always well equipped with marijuana, and had even devised a way of taking it in public. He smoked Kools, the most noxiously mentholated of cigarettes, and he had discovered that by carefully repacking the tubes with a mixture of tobacco and grass the pot odor was lost in the menthol. He was so expert at this that it was completely impossible to tell one of his repacks from an original until you smoked it. He had smoked frequently in front of the captain, and had even considered offering him one just to see what would happen.

Now Burns was imagining being rich. He was a licensed chiropractor, a profession he had chosen for its large remunerative potential. He had just completed school when the Army drafted him. At first he had been indignant—at being drafted at all, then at not being treated like a doctor. They had no right to make him a mere medic while doctors were automatically officers and never left the air-conditioned hospitals. But then he had gotten over here, and all he cared about now was living through his tour so that he could go home to San Jose and start his practice. His Army record might even help bring in patients. Burns was a good California boy, born and raised there, and he happily imagined a weekend house in Santa Cruz where he could surf all year around. He would need a wet suit, for the water there was very cold, the Japan current brushed the coast at that point, but the surf was excellent. The house in Santa Cruz and a sports car—today he was torn between a Jag XK-E and a Corvette, with one of the new Porsches running slightly behind—to get him there from San Jose. Maybe a helicopter. He had never thought of a personal chopper before. He would learn to fly, buy one of those Loaches like the colonel had. They couldn't be all that expensive. He pictured the house on the cliff overlooking the beach and the long waves breaking and his Loach skimming in over the hills and landing in front of the house.

Harkness was getting worried. They were closing on the treeline and he was reflexively worried. He had been shot at from too many treelines. He pushed the point out a little farther. In a few minutes he would begin to recon by fire, let his lead platoon shoot. If you shot first, even if you were wild, they would sometimes open up themselves when you were still out of effective range, give their position away. Usually, of course, they weren't there at all. And this time there might be civilians. Down here in the Delta there was always a chance of that. There were not supposed to be, Intelligence said they had all been moved out, but few things worked out the way they were supposed to.

It was precisely then that the point man in the lead squad, which was only 150 meters from the treeline, climbed across a grassy dike and tripped off a booby trap, a grenade with a wire attached to the pin. The fuse had been removed, and the grenade detonated instantaneously, blowing off the point man's right foot and sending fragments into his inner thighs and groin. The man behind got a few pieces in the chest.

There was a moment of general confusion, men stopping and crouching, trying to place the explosion, fix its type and source. Then a few of the new ones scurried headlong for cover, for the protective backsides of the dikes, and the platoon sergeants shouted at them to stay calm, to watch for trip wires. Harkness called to the point squad leader, asked what had happened.

"Fucking booby trap. Two WIA."

"Who?"

"Fraily. And that new guy. Walinski. He got a foot blown to shit and got it in the nuts."

"He was on point?"

"That's affirm."

It was usual practice to put the new men on point. It slightly minimized the risk for the veterans. The new men either died or were wounded or learned quickly enough to live until there was someone newer than themselves.

Harkness called for a Medevac, then called Battalion, told the colonel what had happened. They discussed the best way to proceed. They had to assume there were unfriendlies in the treeline. They could try to flank it, then drive in, or call in arty and air.

"There might be some civilians," Harkness pointed out.

"I know."

"S-2 says they got them out."

"I know that's what S-2 says. The province chief told him." The colonel paused. "It's up to you, lad. You're the man on the spot."

"Let's get arty and the gunships then. Maybe we can get an air strike."

It was better them than us, Harkness thought. Though there might not be any of them there at all. But if there were and the place wasn't prepped he'd take more casualties getting in, and probably have nothing to show for his blood. The advantages of position, of camouflage and fortification and field of fire, were all with the enemy. He knew of at least two company commanders who had been relieved after such incidents. It was fine to be thoughtful of the civilian population, but not at the expense of the kill ratio.

He called up to the lead platoon, had it withdraw a hundred meters. Within five minutes white phosphorous marker rounds began to drop in the trees and paddies in front. One was short, hit right on his platoon's old position. He adjusted the fire, called in the high explosive.

They brought the wounded back to the captain's position. Burns had gone forward immediately after the explosion, tied off Walinski's leg. Fraily was a Band-Aid case, a question of picking out a few splinters. Burns gave Walinski two morphine shots, which did not seem to have much effect. He kept trying to clutch the mangled wreckage of his genitals. Every so often the stump of his right calf jerked, as if a doctor were testing his reflexes.

Prissholm watched Walinski in fascination. Walinski was the first seriously wounded man he had seen. Prissholm felt giddy, lightheaded. He was breathing rapidly, through his mouth. Walinski had come only a week before he had. He, Prissholm, had been incredibly lucky to be assigned to HQ rather than a regular squad. He would have to keep in Harkness's favor no matter what.

Leyba, as did the others, with the exception of Burns, ignored

the wounded. They were out of it, it did no good to look at
them. Leyba sat on a dike top, the radio on his back, connected
to the captain by the flexible umbilical cord of the microphone,
and hunched over, looked as if he were trying to touch his forehead to the ground between his feet, made himself as small a
target as possible. There had been no incomings yet, but there
might be any second, or short artillery rounds, or the fucking
gunships. Cobra pilots didn't know their dicks from their ass-
holes. Harkness stood beside him easily, map in one hand, the
mike in the other, occasionally shading his eyes with the map,
giving corrections and instructions to the artillery and then the
gunships as casually as if he were conversing in a living room.
Harkness was forever exposing himself—he probably thought he
had to set a fucking example or something—and Leyba, because
he was the radio man, usually got exposed with him. Leyba
imagined a short round hitting out in the paddy in front of
them, dinging Harkness but sparing him.

While the gunbirds were working, the Medevac came in and
loaded the wounded. Walinski was crying and Fraily was grinning.

The gunships expended, flew off, and the artillery started
again. Salvos of 105 and 155 alternated. Whole trees were blown
up by the 155's, cartwheeled through the air.

"Sock it to 'em," Upshaw said.

"Look at that shit," Blacksides said. "That's beautiful. Beautiful."

"You know Charlie's shit is weak now," Upshaw said.

Prissholm was watching the treeline with the others, but was
unable to keep from wincing at each series of explosions. Several
fires were started.

"It's burning. Beautiful."

"Burn, baby, burn."

"Fucking arty is O.K."

"Except when they're short. Sometimes those dickheads can't
hit a bull in the asshole boresighted."

"They're beautiful today."

When the shoot was over Harkness moved them forward cautiously, placed his machine guns behind the dikes for covering
fire, probed with the riflemen of the lead platoon. There was no
fire from the trees or huts, no more booby traps. Two of the huts
were burning. As HQ approached there was a wild burst of fire
and everyone but Harkness, even Himmlemann, threw himself
into the mud. Several individual shots. It all seemed to be com-

ing from near one of the burning huts but no one could tell where it was directed.

"Ammo cache," the captain said. He was standing there looking down at them, not haughtily, almost sympathetically. "Get 'em going, Top. It's only some ammo in the roof cooking off."

"Right."

They moved on in. The lead platoon was set up in a fan around the edges of the clearing where the huts were. Occasional rounds kept popping off in one of the flaming hootches and the burning bamboo made loud cracks, like a small caliber pistol. The lead platoon lieutenant showed them several bunkers, and part of a body. There were several clips for an AK-47 in one of the bunkers. The whole place smelled of explosive, a lingering acrid odor.

Prissholm and Upshaw went to check out a hut at the far corner of the clearing.

"Should we throw a grenade in?" Prissholm asked.

"You fucking idiot," Upshaw said.

"There might be somebody in there."

"You think a goddamn grenade wouldn't blow through these walls and get you too? That's thatch, you asshole, not brick."

Upshaw stood beside the doorway for a few moments, his eyes closed, adjusting them for the dim light inside. Then he pushed through the opening. Along the back wall were bags of rice, gunny sacks filled to the bursting, and several big earthen jars. The hut had been hit many times by shell and rocket fragments, and there were gashes in the thatching that admitted oblongs and sickles of light. Along one wall was a low Vietnamese-style bed, a platform of planks covered with reed mats. Lying on it was a figure. Upshaw turned his rifle on it, index finger taking up the slack in the trigger, thumb automatically checking that the fire selector was off safety, in the full auto position, rock 'n roll. Then he saw the figure was a woman, pregnant and dead, a great rip torn in her throat. The blood was still bright. Flies were buzzing in it.

"Go tell the old man we got a greased dink in here."

A few minutes later the captain, Burns and Leyba arrived. As the captain approached the woman seemed to move, twist slightly.

"I thought you said she was zapped?"

"Let me see," Burns said.

"She's pregnant."

"No shit."

Burns was holding her wrist, feeling for pulse.

"She's gone," the medic said.

"She moved," Harkness said. "I saw her."

"Reflex. I think she may have been in labor."

The woman twitched again, rolled slightly. The flies buzzed away from the wound at her throat.

"My God," Harkness said.

Leyba looked quickly at the captain. It was the first time he could remember seeing a crack in his composure, and he had seen him in and after four or five real fire-fights, seen him any number of times when anyone normal would have been shitting in his pants. Harkness's composure was one of the things Leyba hated about him most.

"Yeah," Burns said. "She's in labor." He pulled away the blanket that covered her legs. "It's coming out."

The medic stood up, wiped his arm across his forehead.

"Christ. I don't know how to handle something like this."

"It's not alive, is it? The baby?"

"I don't know."

"My God."

"Can you call Battalion, sir?"

"What do I say? That I've got a dead woman having a baby?"

"I guess so. Something like that."

"Leyba, let's go outside."

The body moved again.

"I need some forceps. I can't do a fucking thing without big forceps. I ought to have some boiled water too."

"I'll call Battalion."

The captain and Leyba left.

"It can't be alive," Prissholm said.

"It might be. I've never even read anything about a case like this."

"You could write it up, doc," Upshaw said.

Lebya came back in.

"They'll send out a fucking chopper if you want, but the colonel said he hasn't got any forceps. Upshaw, Top wants you."

"I need forceps," Burns said. "I don't think she ought to be moved."

"The old man didn't say anything about getting you any. Only a chopper."

"Because they haven't got any."

"What do you want me to tell the old man?"

"Tell him let me work on her awhile."

Leyba returned, put his radio set down by the door.

"O.K. Only he says don't take too long. We gotta make the next fucking objective."

"Find me some water," Burns said.

The top of the baby's head was showing. Burns was pushing on the women's abdomen. Her contractions were not forceful enough to do any good, he thought.

Leyba discovered that the earthen jars held fresh water, filled his helmet. He stood over the medic watching. It reminded him of once at home, at his family's farm in northern New Mexico. They had had a cow that couldn't calve. His father had not wanted to call the vet, had not wanted to have to pay. The cow had grown weaker and weaker. Finally, when it was obviously going to die if something was not done, his father had tied the cow to the corral gate post, put a rope around the neck of the half-born calf. He attached the rope to his saddle and slapped the horse. The calf had been jerked out, its neck broken, but the cow had recovered. He thought of suggesting something like that to Burns, but of course the mother was already dead, and there weren't any horses around.

"It's stuck," Burns said. "I'm going to have to cut."

He stood up again. Sweat was popping out of his forehead. He ought to have boiled water to sterilize his knife at the least, but he didn't think there was time. He drew the knife, a Navy K-bar, an excellent knife that he had traded away from a corpsman for a half pound of good Lao grass. He did not like bayonets, which were what they were issued, because they would not hold an edge. He liked good tools, had promised himself the finest instruments when he got out. He seared the blade with the flame from his zippo.

"That won't sterilize it," Prissholm said. "Lighter fuel is full of grease."

"Shut up, dickhead," Leyba said.

Burns wiped his forehead, knelt, and began to cut. "Throw some water on," he told Leyba.

"Easy. That's enough."

"It ain't bleeding much."

"She's dead. No circulation."

Harkness came in, watched for a moment, and left. Leyba was grinning.

"More water."

Burns worked quickly, but carefully. Once he stopped, wiped the sweat away again. Several times he asked Leyba for water.

His first incision was not big enough, the abdominal muscles clamped shut, he could not get hold of the baby.

A crowd gathered outside the hut. Harkness came back, stood just inside the door, prevented the men from pressing in.

"Water."

"That's getting it," Leyba said. "Cut some more sideways."

"Enough water."

The medic pried the slit open, reached in.

"He's taking it out," Leyba said for the benefit of the crowd.

Burns pulled the baby free, tied off the cord with a boot lace, slashed it with the bloody K-bar, and held the form up by the heels in best Ben Casey fashion. He began to slap it.

"It's dead," Leyba said.

"Throw some water on," someone suggested from the door. "Dunk it."

"That's enough," Harkness said.

Burns kept slapping, could not think what else to do, harder now, urgently, as if he could force life into it, but he produced no response. Finally he put it down beside the mother, pulled the blanket over them both. He was still sweating unnaturally, the beads popping out quickly and big on his forehead. He wiped his face on his shirt front, but it was too wet already to absorb much. He felt drained, almost as if he had dysentery. It was the way he always felt after he had lost someone.

"That's it," he said. He started for the door. "That's the ball game."

They formed up, moved through the trees and into the paddies on the other side. There was another treeline barely visible on the horizon.

As they hopped along through the muck Harkness was worried. They had lost a lot of time, would have to press hard to reach the safest position to spend the night. Automatically he checked that the point and flank security was out, that the men were spacing themselves far enough apart.

The war down here was pure shit, he reflected. He had seen more blood spilled in the high country along the border two years ago, but there hadn't been problems with civilians, and up there he'd never seen anything like this today. It had been a cleaner and more honorable war, a soldier's war, with fights between regular units of real armies, without much booby trapping, without the muck and the people. Down here there were limitless complications. It occurred to him that when the enemy came back to the hootches, and they surely would come back, they might take pictures of the woman and child, use them as anti-American propaganda. GI dogs murder pregnant woman, rip infant from womb. If they did that and our own psy war people ever hooked the stuff to his company, he'd have a helluva time explaining what had really happened.

Also, he should have done something about the rice. There had been a ton, maybe more, in that hut. He hadn't even called it in. He had been so involved with the other thing. Next to getting confirmed kills, or weapons, capturing rice was about the best thing that could happen to a commander. He could at least have had the men urinate on the sacks; that was what they did if there was not time or means to haul a cache in. That was a stupid thing to have missed.

Harkness had not had to come back to Vietnam, and he now thought, as he had often the past few months, coming back had been a mistake. After instructing at ranger school he had been an aide to a general at the Pentagon, and the general had been assigned to the mission in Brazil, had wanted to take him along. But he had volunteered to come back here instead. His friends had all come back, and he had felt that somehow it was wrong for him not to. The general, he knew, had been disappointed, thought him a fool. He had thought that when he told the old man he'd understand, would pat him on the back, realize that a job in an advisory mission was not like commanding troops in the field, that an infantry officer should always try to be with the men, had an obligation to them and to himself, to his profession, but the general had only shrugged, told him he was sorry. It was not wise to lose the favor of a general, even an obscure brigadier, and Harkness had tried to explain that he'd learn more on a second tour than he had on the first. He might, the general had said, and gave that cold shrug again. Well, learn he had, especially this today, although what you could not say exactly, or what use it would be.

Leyba was feeling better than he had all day, better than at any time since the last stand-down. He figured they'd had their action for a while, he could scratch this day, which left only two more to be lived through. He was even pretty sure he was going to make them. He could not say why, but for the first time in months he really believed he'd get out of it.

Which did not make him feel any more gently toward Harkness. Maybe he felt so good because Harkness was obviously shaken. Next to seeing the bastard dinged, seeing him blow his cool was the best thing he could imagine. He had already mentioned it to Blacksides and Upshaw. In fact, the only things wrong were that he was still here, and the radio was still cutting down into his shoulders.

Prissholm was horribly, terribly thirsty. The back of his throat was the consistency of stale cotton candy. He had drunk his last half canteen and would have to wait for the next break to get some water from someone. He should have filled his canteens from the earthen jars, but he had been too absorbed. Now he thought that he must not think about what had happened, it was another unreal event, another threat to his imperiled sanity, and he must not dwell on it. If he did not think about it, it would not touch him, and he'd be all right. It was like his fraternity initiation, when they had gang-banged the whore hired for the purpose, everyone very drunk, people sitting and standing in the bedroom watching. He had been very drunk and had climbed on himself finally, when there had been no graceful way left to refuse, surprised at his own potency, that he could even be potent in such a situation—degrading and ludicrous—and even during the act telling himself it did not matter unless he let it matter.

And Burns, the good medic, rolled himself a huge joint, a real bomber, a B–52. He needed it, the real thing, with no menthol or tobacco or filter to cut its effect. He had tried to slip back into his daydream, reconjure the Loach and the house on the cliff and the surf, but he was too tired to make his mind go the way he wanted it to, to force out the woman and the cutting and the slapping, the defeat, so he reached into the side of his bag where he kept morphine and his cache of grass and papers, and stopped on an especially firm clump of rice, standing in plain sight of Harkness and Top Sergeant Himmlemann and anyone else who wanted to look, not really giving a damn, and rolled his bomber, and lit up. No one even cast a curious glance.

THE BIGGEST THING SINCE CUSTER

William Eastlake

The chopper came in low over the remains of Clancy's outfit. Everyone below seemed very dead. They were as quiet as lambs. Sometimes you could see what looked like smoke coming up from a fire, but it was only ground fog. Everyone with Clancy was dead. All of Alpha Company. It was the biggest thing since Custer.

Mike, the correspondent, had to watch himself. The correspondent tended to take the side of the Indians. You got to remember that this is not the Little Big Horn. This is Vietnam. Vietnam. Vietnam. They all died in Vietnam. A long way from home. What were the Americans doing here? The same thing they were doing in Indian Country. In Sioux Territory. They were protecting Americans. They were protecting Americans from the Red Hordes. God help Clancy. You could tell here from above how Clancy blundered. Clancy blundered by being in Vietnam. That's a speech.

The chopper circled now low over the dead battle. Clancy had blundered by not holding the ridge. Clancy had blundered by being forced into a valley, a declivity in the hills. It was the classic American blunder in Vietnam of giving the Indians the cover. The enemy was fighting from the protection of the jungle. The first thing the Americans did in America was clear a forest and plant the cities.

Concentrate on the battle below. Do not always take the side of the Indians. You could see here clearly from above how Clancy blew it. In the part of the highlands of Vietnam near the Cambodian-Laos bunch-up, there is no true open country. Everything is in patches. You could see where Clancy's point squad had made contact with the enemy. You could see, you could tell by all the shit of war, where Clancy had made, where Clancy had tried to make, his first stand on the ridge and then allowed his perimeter to be bent by the hostiles attacking down the ridge. Then Clancy's final regrouping in the draw where all the bodies were.

Clancy should have held that ridge at all costs. If you must fight in the open, fight high. Then the only way the enemy can kill you is with arching fire. Mortar fire. You can dig in against mortar fire. When they force you in the valley, you are duck soup. They can hit you with everything from above. From the way the bodies lie Clancy had mounted three counterattacks to get the ridge back he had too early conceded. The attacks were not in concert. He did not hit them all at once. There should have been more American bodies on the ridge. Clancy should have paid any price to get back the ridge. The ridge was the only opportunity. The valley was death. Ah, but the valley is comfortable. The hill is tough, and the men are all give out and dragging ass, tired and leaking blood. See where they stumbled up and were shot down. See where they failed. See where they tried again and again and again. Where they were shot down. See the paths of bright they made with their blood. See Clancy pointing them on with his sword. War is kind. See Clancy pointing them on with his sword. The son of a bitch had one, like in an old movie. See Clancy pointing them on up the ridge. Once more into the breach. Once more, men, for God and Country and Alpha Company. I blew the ridge. Get it back. Get it back. Get it back for Clancy. Go Smith, go Donovitch, go Lewis, get that——back! I need it. Now Shaplen, now Marshall, now Irvine, get me the——back. I will lead this charge. Every man behind me. Where has every young man gone? Why is that native killing me? Why, Shaplen? Why, Marshall? Why, Irvine? All dead. The valley is beautiful, warm, and in this season of Vietnam, soft in the monsoon wet. Contemplative, withdrawn, silent, and now bepatched, bequilted with all of the dead. Alive with scarlet color. Gay with the dead.

The helicopter that carried the correspondent made one more big circle to see if it would pick up ground fire, then came in and hit down in the middle of Clancy's dead with a smooth chonk noise.

The grave registration people got out first. They ejected in the manner of all soldiers from an alighting chopper, jumping out before it quite touched the ground, then running as fast as they could go to escape the giant wind. When they got to the perimeter of Alpha's dead, they stopped abruptly as though they had come to a cliff, and then they came back slowly, picking their way among Alpha's dead, embarrassed and wondering what to do about all this. The lieutenant got out and told the body people not to touch any of the bodies until the army photographers had shot all the positions in which they had fallen. This was important, he said, so Intelligence could tell how the battle was lost. Or won, he said. We are not here to draw conclusions right now. The lieutenant was very young and had red hair. The grave registration people just stood now quiet among the dead, holding their bags in which they would place the dead folded over their arms, like waiters.

The army photographers alighted now holding their cameras at high port like weapons, and began to shoot away at the dead it seemed at random, but they began at the concentric of the perimeter and worked outward in ever widening waves of shooting so that there was a method to their shots. The young lieutenant kept telling them not to touch. The photographers kept having trouble with the angle of repose in which many of the Alpha bodies lay. They had not fallen so that the army photographers could shoot them properly. It was important that they be shot so Intelligence could tell the direction they were pointing when they were hit, how many bodies had jammed guns, how many bodies ran out of ammo. What was the configuration of each body in relation to the configuration of the neighbor body, and then to the configuration of the immediate group of bodies in which the body rests? What relation does said group of bodies have to neighbor groups? To all groups? Bodies should be shot in such a way so that patterns of final action of dead are clear and manifest to establish Alpha's response, if possible, to loss of ridge. Does bodies' configuration show aggressive or regressive response to ridge objective? Where body position of men and commissioned officers? Does body position of noncommissioned officers manifest immediate body group leadership? Neighbor body group's leadership? Photographer should manifest if possible commissioned officer's response to command situation. Does command officer placement of body manifest command presence? Lack of same? Does placement of commissioned officer's body manifest battle plan? Lack of same? Find Clancy. Photographers should shoot all mutilations. Does Captain Clancy's body show normal kill? Planned mutilations? Do commissioned officers' bodies show more mutilation than ear men? When battle situation became negative did ear men attempt to throw away ears? Hide ears? Display ears?

"Don't touch," the lieutenant said.

The correspondent was examining the bodies. He had never seen it so bad.

"Don't touch," the lieutenant said.

"What's this about ears?" the correspondent said.

"Ears?" the lieutenant said.

"Yes."

"You must mean years," the lieutenant said. "We have some five-year men, some ten-year men."

"I see them," the correspondent said.

"I wouldn't write about it if I were you," the lieutenant said.

"You'd pull my credentials?"

"Yes."

"I'll have a look-see," the correspondent said.

"Don't touch," the lieutenant said.

The correspondent leaned over a soft-face boy whose M-16 had jammed. The boy body had never shaved. He was that young. The boy had something stuck in his mouth.

"Jesus," the correspondent said.

The young lieutenant knelt down alongside the correspondent now.

"You see how bad the enemy can be."

"Yes," the correspondent said. "Why has it got a condom on it?"

"Because Alpha was traveling through jungle swamp. There's an organism that gets in the penis opening and travels up to the liver. The condom protects the penis."

The correspondent made a move to remove it.

"Don't touch," the lieutenant said.

"Why don't you bag him?"

"Intelligence wants pictures."

"Bag all of them," the correspondent said, "and let's get out of here."

"It won't be long," the lieutenant said.

"If I report this you'll lift my credentials?"

"I don't know what the brass will do," the lieutenant said. "I do know the people at home can't take it."

"They might stop your war," the correspondent said.

"They don't understand guerrilla war," the lieutenant said.

"You're tough," the correspondent said.

"Listen," the lieutenant said, and touched the correspondent.

"Don't touch," the correspondent said.

"Listen," the lieutenant said, "it makes me sick. I hope it always makes me sick."

The correspondent stood up. There was an odor in the jungle now from the bodies that the correspondent had not noticed when the chopper rotor was turning. Now the chopper was dead. It was very quiet in the jungle.

"How did Clancy get into this?"

"He asked for it," the lieutenant said.

"I heard different."

"You heard wrong," the lieutenant said.

"I heard he was ordered out here."

"He ordered himself out. Clancy's an old ear collector. Alpha Company always had that reputation. Clancy's an old ear collector."

When the lieutenant became angry, his white skin that could not tolerate the sun became red like his hair. His red hair was clipped short under his green helmet, and when the young lieutenant became angry, his white skin matched the hair.

"Clancy wanted to provoke the VC, Victor Charlie. Clancy wanted to collect more ears."

"I don't believe that."

The lieutenant kicked something with his boot.

"Why not scalps?" the correspondent said.

"Because they're too difficult to take. Did you ever try to take a scalp?"

"No."

"It's difficult," the lieutenant said.

"What makes you think Alpha Company asked for this?"

"Because Clancy could have made it up the hill," the lieutenant said pointing. "But he stayed down here on the narrow ridge hoping Charlie would hit him. You see," the lieutenant said carefully. "Look. It's only a hundred more meters up the ridge to the top of the hill. That makes a perfect defense up there, you can see that. And Clancy knew Charlie could see that too, and he wouldn't hit. That's why Clancy stayed down here. Clancy wanted Charlie to try to take him."

"A full battalion?"

"Clancy didn't know Charlie had a full battalion."

"How do you know that?"

"We had contact with Appelfinger, his RTO man, before radio went dead. Clancy guessed the Unfriendlies as maybe an over-strength company."

"Unfriendlies?"

"NVA. North Vietnamese Army. Clancy knew that. They are quite good." The lieutenant almost mused now, looking over the dead, reflective and sad.

"We got a man alive here, Lieutenant," someone called.

The jungle had been most quiet, and everyone had been moving through the bodies with caution, almost soundlessly, so that the announcement was abrupt, peremptory, and rude, almost uncalled for.

"Don't touch," the lieutenant said. The lieutenant raised his arm for a medic and moved toward the call, sinuously winding through the bodies with a snakelike silent grace. The man who had called, the man who made the discovery, was a body man, one of the grave registration people. He had been standing gently with his bag over one arm waiting patiently for the others to finish when he noticed a movement where there should have been none.

"Don't touch," the lieutenant said, standing over the alive. "See what you can do," he said to the medic.

Each of the American dead had received a bullet through the head, carefully administered to each soldier by the enemy after they had overrun the position, to make absolutely certain that each was dead. The soldier who was alive had received his bullet too, but it had been deflected by the helmet, and you could see when the medic removed the helmet from the head of the young Mexican soldier that it had only torn through the very black, very thick hair and lodged in the head bone. The soldier was dying of natural causes of battle. You could see this when the medic removed the boy Mexican's shirt, which he did skillfully now with a knife. The boy Mexican had been sprayed with hostile machinegun fire, eight bullets entering the olive-colored body just above the pelvis. The boy Mexican with the olive body in the American olive-colored jungle uniform was cut in half. But he lived for now, taking in sudden gusts of air terrifically as though each were his last.

"Nothing can be done," the medic said without saying anything. The medic's hands were just frozen over the body, not moving to succor, just antic and motionless like a stalled marionette's.

"Water?" the lieutenant asked.

The medic shook his head no.

"If he's going, it could make it easier," the lieutenant said. "He seems to be looking at us for water."

The medic shook his head OK. Nothing would make any difference.

When one of the photographers tried to give the boy Mexican water from his canteen, the water would not run in the mouth; it just poured down the Mexican's chin and down his chest till it reached his belly and mixed with the blood that was there.

"I think the son of a bitch is dead," one of the army photographers who was not pouring the water said.

"No," one of the body men said. "Let me try it."

"That's enough," the medic said, letting the body down. "I think he's dead now."

"How could the son of a bitch last so long when he was cut in half?"

"We have funny things like this all the time," the medic said. "Another funny thing is I've seen guys dead without a mark on them."

"Concussion? But there's always a little blood from the ears or something, isn't there?"

"No, I've seen them dead without any reason at all," the medic said, wiping clean the face of the Mexican boy with the water the Mexican could not drink. "If you look good at the guys around here I bet you'll find at least one that doesn't have a mark on him that's dead. It's funny. Some guys will die without any reason at all, and some guys will live without any reason at all." The medic looked perplexed. Then the medic allowed the boy's head to rest on his smashed helmet. "You'll find some guys with just that one bullet in the head given by the Unfriendlies after they overran Alpha."

"Some guys will play dead," the army photographer said, "hoping to pass for dead among the dead."

"They don't get away with it though too much," the medic said. But the medic was not listening to himself. He was still perplexed that the Mexican boy could have lived so long when he was cut in half. "It's funny, that's all," the medic said.

"You want them to die?"

"I don't want them to suffer," the medic said.

"There's another live one over here," someone called.

"Don't touch," the lieutenant said.

No one moved. There was a hiatus in the movement in the jungle, as though, the correspondent thought, no one here wanted to be deceived again, no one wanted to be taken in by another illusion. The problem was that Alpha was all dead. You could tell that with a glance. Anyone could see that they were ready to be photographed and placed in bags. It wasn't planned for anyone to come back to life. It made all the dead seem too much like people. The dead should stay dead.

"Maybe this one's real," someone said.

That started a drift toward the caller.

"Don't touch," the lieutenant said.

The correspondent got there early. It was a Negro. It did not seem as though the boy were hit. He was lying in a bed of bamboo. He looked comfortable. The Negro boy had a beginning half-smile on his face, but the smile was frozen. The eyes too were immobile. The Negro boy's eyes looked up, past the correspondent and on up to the hole at the top of the jungle canopy. There were two elongated fronds that crossed way up there at the apex of the canopy. Maybe that's what he was looking at. Maybe he was staring at nothing. The Negro boy said something, but nothing came out. His lips moved, and words seemed to be forming, but nothing came out. Maybe he was saying, the correspondent thought, that he had come a long way since he was dragged up with the rats in the ghetto. He had never been close to white people before, except relief workers. Now he had joined the club. In death do us join.

The young Negro stopped breathing. The white medic was on top of the Negro like a lover. In one sudden deft movement the white medic was down on the bed of bamboo with his white arms around the black boy, his white lips to the black lips, breathing in white life to black death. The Negro lover did not respond. It was too late. The white boy was late. The eyes were all shut. Then abruptly the young Negro's chest began to heave. The eyes opened. But not to life, the correspondent thought, but to outrage, a kind of wild surmise and amaze at all this. As though he had gone to death, to some kind of mute acceptance of no life and now come back to this, the lover's embrace, the lover lips of the white medic.

The white medic ceased now, withdrew his lips from the young Negro's and tried to catch the erratic breathing of the Negro in his hand to give it a life rhythm. He was astraddle the boy now, up from the bamboo bed, and administering a regular beat with his hands to the young Negro's chest.

"Ah," the Negro said.

"Ah," the white boy said.

"Ah ah ah," they both said.

Now the medic allowed the boy beneath to breathe on his own.

"Ah," the lieutenant said.

"Ah-h-h-h . . ." everyone said.

Now the jungle made sounds. The awful silence had given way to the noises that usually accompany an American motion picture. The cry of gaudy birds seemed fake. The complaints of small animals, distant, were remote like some sound track that had blurred, some other mix for a different cinema, so that you not only expected that the next reel would announce the mistake, that this war would have to start all over again, but that the whole damn thing would be thrown out with whoever was

responsible for this disaster here at Dak To, this unacceptable
nightmare, this horror, this unmentionable destruction of Clancy
and all his men. But more, the correspondent thought, this is the
finis, the end of man in this clearing, this opening in the jungle,
the end of humankind itself and the planet earth on which it
abides. And shit, the correspondent thought—and Ah— He
found himself saying it too now, celebrating the rebirth, the
resurrection of the black man and the rebirth and resurrection
after the crucifixion of humankind itself. And shit, he reflected,
they, Alpha Company, are the ear hunters, and maybe not shit
because all of Alpha were standing in for us, surrogate, and all of
us are collectors of ears.

"Will he make it?" the young lieutenant said.

The medic looked perplexed. It was his favorite and especial
expression. Then he went down in the bamboo bed in lover
attitude to listen to the heart.

"No," he said from the black heart. "No."

"No?"

"Because," the medic said from the black heart. "No. Because
they were supposed to be all dead here, and we needed body
room in the chopper, and there was no room for my shit."

"Blood plasma?"

"We didn't bring any," the medic said.

"Can he talk?"

"Yes." The medic passed a white hand in front of the black
face. The black eyes did not follow it.

"Ask him what happened to Clancy's body. Clancy is missing."

The medic made a gentle movement with his hands along the
throat of the Negro and whispered to him with lover closeness,
"What happened to the captain?"

"He dead."

"Where is the body?"

"The RTO man," the Negro pronounced slowly.

"Appelfinger carried him off," the medic said to the lieutenant.

"Can you give the boy some morphine?" the lieutenant said to
the medic.

"I don't like his heart."

"Risky?"

"Yes."

"Can he talk more?"

"I don't think it would be good," the medic said.

"All right, keep him quiet," the lieutenant said.

"They was so nice," the Negro said.

"Keep him quiet," the lieutenant said.

"They gave us each one shot," the Negro said. "They was so nice."

"Keep him quiet."

"They was so nice—"

"I said keep him quiet," the lieutenant said. And the lieutenant thought, war is so nice. Looking over all the dead, he thought ROTC was never like this, and he thought in this war everything is permitted so that there is nothing to be forgiven. And he thought about the ears that Clancy took, and he thought a man can read and read and read and think and think and still be a villain, and he thought there are no villains, there are only wars. And he said, "If the photographers are finished, put the men in the bags."

And then there was that goddamn jungle silence again, this awful and stern admonition and threat of the retribution of Asia to white trespassers. But that is metaphysical, the lieutenant thought, and it is only the VC you have to fear. More, it is only yourself you have to fear. It is only Clancy you have to fear. Clancy is dead.

"When you find pieces of body," the lieutenant said, "try to match them and put the matched pieces into one separate bag. Remember a man has only two arms and two legs and one head each. I don't want to find two heads in one bag."

And the lieutenant thought, Clancy is dead but the crimes that Clancy did live after him. Custer too. Custer liked to destroy the villages and shoot up the natives too. Listen to this, the lieutenant told Captain Clancy silently. I did not spend all my time in the ROTC. I spent some of the time in the library. What you did in the villages is not new. Collecting ears is not new. Listen, Clancy, to Lieutenant James D. Connors after the massacre of the Indians at Sand Creek, "The next day I did not see a body of a man, woman or Indian child that was not scalped by us, and in many instances the bodies were mutilated in the most horrible manner. Men's, women's and children's private parts cut out. I saw one of our men who had cut out a woman's private parts and had them for exhibition on a stick. Some of our men had cut out the private parts of females and wore them in their hats." I don't think you can top that, Clancy. I don't think war has come very far since then. I don't think your ears can top that, Clancy.

"What's happening, Lieutenant?" the correspondent said.

"Happening?" the lieutenant said. "I was thinking."

"This man is dead," the medic said, pointing to the Negro.

"Bag him," the lieutenant said.

"What were you thinking?" the correspondent said.

"That this makes me sick. Awful sick."

"Have you ever seen it this bad?"

"No, I have never seen it this bad," the lieutenant said, spacing his words as though the correspondent were taking each separate word down. "No, I have never seen it this bad in my whole short life. I have never seen it this bad. No, I have never seen it this bad. Is that what you want me to say?"

"Take it easy," the correspondent said.

"OK," the lieutenant said. "I'm sorry." And then the lieutenant heard something. It was the sound of a mortar shell dropping into a mortar tube in the jungle. It was the sound the lieutenant had heard too many times before, then the poof, as the enemy mortar came out of the tube, then the whine as it traveled to their company. The symphony. The music of Vietnam. Incoming! The lieutenant hollered as loud as he could make it. "Incoming!"

Incoming? Where? Who? Why? The shell hit their helicopter, and it all exploded in a towering orange hot pillar of fire in the jungle.

"Pull the bodies around you, men, and try to dig in. Use the bodies as a perimeter!" the lieutenant hollered. Then the lieutenant said quietly to the correspondent, "I'm sorry I got you into this."

"You didn't," the correspondent said.

"I'll try to get Search and Rescue on the radio."

"You do that," the correspondent said.

A SIMPLER CREED

Ronald J. Glasser

Watson had been a troublemaker since he was six. He was a bitter, imaginative, hate-filled kid who had been drafted and somehow had survived basic training without ending up in prison. He was assigned to the medics at an evac hospital and then to the field. When he went on line, the hospital personnel gave him a week to be busted and sent back to the States in irons.

When I met him he had been up front with his unit for almost five months. He was soft-spoken, but marvelously animated and alert. The old abusiveness was gone; even the adolescent arrogance I'd been told had for so long been the central pillar of his personality had disappeared. He was perfectly at ease and open. Those who had known him before were pleasantly surprised, if still a bit leery.

Watson didn't mind talking. "Why not go all out, man? They need me, and I know what I'm doing out there. Hundreds of cases—fuckin' hundreds. The big-shot dermatologists, they come down once a week. They look at all that rotting skin and shake their heads and leave. Know what we did? We got a Mixmaster, threw in a couple of quarts of calamine lotion, a few kilograms of Mycolog for the fungus, and figured some tetracycline and penicillin couldn't hurt, just in case there was any bacteria around. Called it jungle mix and bottled it and handed it out. Fuckin' dermatologists couldn't believe it. Wanted to know where we'd read about it, what medical journal. Sure, I take chances. That's my job—to save lives. The VC—well, I ain't got nothing against 'em. Guess they're doing their job, too."

On a routine sweep through Tam Key, a squad of the American Division was ambushed. Watson was hit twice, both rounds shattering his leg. He kept helping the wounded, dragging himself from soldier to soldier until he was hit in the neck by a third round and paralyzed.

All the medics talk the same and they all act the same, whether they come from the ghetto or the suburbs. No one planned it this way. It was the kids themselves, caught between their skeptical seventeenth or eighteenth years, and the war, the politicians, and the regular Army officers. Growing up in a hypocritical adult world and placed in the middle of a war that even the dullest of them find difficult to believe in, much less die for, very young and vulnerable, they are suddenly tapped not for their selfishness or greed but for their grace and wisdom, not for their brutality but for their love and concern.

The Army psychiatrists describe it as a matter of roles. The adolescent who becomes a medic begins after a very short time to think of himself as a doctor, not any doctor in particular, but the generalized family doctor, the idealized physician he's always heard about.

The excellent training the medics receive makes the whole thing possible, and the fact that the units return the corpsman's concern and competence with their own wholehearted respect and affection makes the whole thing happen.

Medics in the 101st carried M & M candies in their medical kits long before the psychiatrists found it necessary to explain away their actions. They offered them as placebos for their wounded who were too broken for morphine, slipping the sweet between their lips as they whispered to them over the noise of the fighting that it was for the pain. In a world of suffering and death, Vietnam is like a Walt Disney true-life adventure, where the young are suddenly left alone to take care of the young.

A tour of Nam is twelve months; it is like a law of nature. The medics, though, stay on line only seven months. It is not due to the goodwill of the Army, but to their discovery that seven months is about all these kids can take. After that they start getting freaky, cutting down on their own water and food so they can carry more medical supplies; stealing plasma bottles and walking around on patrol with five or six pounds of glass in their rucksacks; writing parents and friends for medical catalogues so they can buy their own endotracheal tubes; or quite simply refusing to go home when their time is over.

And so it goes, and the VC know it. They will drop the point, trying not to kill him but to wound him, to get him screaming so they can get the medic too. He'll come. They know he will.

THE ROOM

Victor Kolpacoff

There were the six of us and the prisoner in a room that was thirty feet long and half as wide, and the table took up a quarter of the space. It was made out of heavy sheet metal and had strong vises at either end, as if it had once been a workbench. Above it was a low ceiling of corrugated tin, sagging in the middle where the rusted sheets had been bolted together. All the heat in the room seemed to come from that ceiling. It leaked in under the sagging plates like lava. The walls, too, were made of tin sheets. The ruts of the corrugated surface did not look comfortable, but I had a prisoner's instinct to keep my back against something, and I marked the hot corners of the room as a retreat. On the wall opposite the door there was a tool rack that stood as high as a man's head. It was divided into thick plywood boxes, black with grease, and each box was marked with a number that had been burned into the wood. The tools had been thrown in on top of each other by the last occupants of the room, but I could see the gleaming black handles of wrenches and metal hammers. Deeper back, where the electric light did not reach, there were dark coils of rope and wire cable. The floor was dirt, hard-packed from use, and as dry as the parade ground. Only the cots were new. For the moment they gave the room an odor of new wood and canvas that almost covered the musty smell of tin and human sweat.

Then there were the faces: Cowley's heavy, ugly face, squinting up at the light; and McGruder, as ugly as Cowley, but with no humor around his eyes or mouth, watching the prisoner; and Buckley's handsome pink face, clean-shaven, with his pale blue eyes moving from place to place; and finally Nguyen, whose impassive, patient eyes were fixed on Buckley. Only the prisoner seemed to want to see nothing. He kept his face lowered out of the light and fixed his eyes on a long streak of rust that ran down a leg from the top of the table, as if the metal were slowly bleeding.

When I saw that, I wanted to get out, but I had been carefully taught that escape from Quai Dong was impossible. I tried not to think about it. The soldier, Russell, was still holding his carbine at the ready. He looked frightened and dangerous, as if he might squeeze the trigger and shoot through the ceiling.

Not that he wanted to hurt anyone. For the time being, I didn't think that any of them wanted that. They only seemed frightened or unaccountably angry.

Buckley and Nguyen began to argue quietly between themselves about how to begin with the boy. Buckley was in a hurry, but Nguyen was telling him that "such things" took time. Finally Buckley turned his back to the light and looked at us. "You all know why you're here," he said, "and what we have to do."

"Let's get it started," McGruder said.

"No, we're going to do it properly," Buckley replied sternly, and McGruder moved away with a shrug and watched the crack of sunlight under the door.

"Now listen to me," Buckley said, raising his voice, though we had heard him perfectly well before, "we're a rest camp and a military stockade. We don't have the right people to do this kind of job, but we're going to do the best we can and get it over with. Now," he added, stepping forward and dropping his voice, "I've got a Vietnamese interpreter who says this thing will take a long time. Do any of you think you can do better than that?"

"Let me have him, Lieutenant," McGruder said, and he turned toward the boy hopefully—but Buckley was looking only at me and seemed not to hear.

"Kreuger?" he asked.

"I don't know what you want," I said.

Cowley dug his fingers into the back of my arm. "Keep out of it!" he whispered.

I wanted to tell Buckley that I did not know why I was there at all, but Cowley was right; it was safer to be quiet and I said nothing. Among the six of us in the room nothing seemed clear. I did not know if Cowley and I were counted with the interrogators or as convicts. We still wore our prison uniforms. Our position was awkward, and if something went wrong it could be dangerous, for we would be witnesses to whatever took place. Buckley knew it as well as I did, but he tried to hide it from us.

"You're here as an officer," he said.

"What about Cowley?" I asked.

Buckley shifted his feet and did not answer for a moment, then he frowned up at the light. "We've had trouble from a local guerrilla outfit for a month. We need your help. Forget the stockade."

"I thought the district was pacified."

"It is officially pacified," he said, tightening his lips, "and we want it to stay that way."

"What does the boy have to do with it?" I asked, despite the pressure of Cowley's fingers on my arm. Finally I felt his hand slide down, and he let me go.

McGruder turned around slowly and looked at me. "We took him off the Weichu Road," he said. "He was trying to get through our patrols."

I watched McGruder for a moment. He looked at me full of hate, as if he thought that I was somehow a threat to him or to what he wanted to do. I wanted only to stay clear, but there was no way to tell him that.

"What will happen to the boy?" I asked Buckley.

"Leave that to us," he replied quickly. "You do your job and you'll come out all right."

I agreed with him, since there was nothing else for me to do, and I retreated to one of the cots along the walls and sat down where I would be able to watch what happened from the farthest possible distance. Cowley followed me. All that puzzled me was what my "job" was supposed to be. It was not until I looked up across the room at Buckley that I realized that I had turned my back to an officer and walked away. I had taken a seat, in spite of my prison khaki, and had not been immediately jabbed with a swagger stick and ordered to get back on my feet. That had never happened to me before at Quai Dong. Only then did I realize how much of our punishment in the stockade had been made up of simple humiliation. Already, somehow, I had acquired this simple privilege. I was grateful to Buckley. I couldn't help it, and that made me distrust him.

Still, it seemed that we had been granted a reprieve for as long as the interrogation lasted. At the moment that was all that mattered. I thought of the other prisoners still working on the beach, trudging from the hollow to the shore with their sacks full of sand. The corrugated shed would be a diversion, at the very worst. All that remained was to make the most of it, and to keep out of the way of whatever was about to happen.

Cowley, however, put another face on our good luck. He leaned close to me and asked me if I knew why they had brought me to the hut instead of taking someone from the regular camp.

"I know some Vietnamese," I said, watching the prisoner's head.

"They've got a translator," he whispered. "What the hell do they need you for?"

I shrugged. "We'll find out soon enough."

"Use your head," he said. "Guys in the rest camp go back to the States after a year out here. They can talk and make trouble. We're easy to keep quiet because we aren't going anywhere."

He added that he had seen interrogations before; and then he grinned ruefully, as if to make the best of a bad thing.

I began to ask him what he meant, though I understood it well enough, when Lieutenant Buckley suddenly turned impatiently away from Nguyen, with whom he had again been arguing about the prisoner, and rapped the table angrily with his knuckles to silence us.

"This is no joke," he said, raising his voice again, but now to an official tone, as if he were about to address a staff meeting. "We need definite information about these guerrillas, and we need it fast. We've finally got a prisoner of war that can tell us everything we need to know, and our Vietnamese ally says that he'll need at least a day to make him talk."

McGruder said, in a very matter-of-fact way, that the guerrillas might attack again somewhere during the night.

"You don't need to tell me that," Buckley replied.

He was so earnest that he couldn't stand still. Yet it was what he said, not the way he moved, that made me uneasy, for certainly McGruder and Nguyen knew perfectly well what they had come to do. Therefore Buckley was speaking only to me, which was either dangerous or foolish, depending on what he meant by it.

"They've hit us everywhere," he said. "Fuel dumps, quartermaster convoys, rest camps. Last week they mined the road to Doc Thieu. At dawn we lost a jeep and three men."

He added that all the attacks had come at night. It seemed to be a personal affront to him. "In six weeks they've cost us fifty casualties, and as far as we know we haven't killed one of them yet—or if we have, they carry their dead with them. This is a little peasant outfit. Saigon says there isn't a hard-core Viet Cong in the district. All the help they're getting from the outside is equipment, and they're careful with that. They don't take on combat units. Only isolated patrols or a single vehicle. They like to win," he added, "and so far they've had it all their way."

He looked angrily at the boy—the prisoner—and said that he

was one of the guerrillas. He called them Victor Charlies as was the custom at staff briefings. I glanced up at the broken tin roof, thinking more about the heat than what Buckley was saying. He turned around and looked down at me as if to gauge the effect of his words. Of course none of it meant anything to me, and I didn't try to hide it. Buckley frowned with disapproval and nodded to McGruder.

"Show the lieutenant what the prisoner was carrying," he said. He used the title that was no longer mine, as if to place me still further in his debt. I began to hate Buckley a little.

McGruder swung a string of grenades off his shoulder and held them up to the light. "They were rolled inside the little bastard's blanket," he said, and, for the first time, he seemed satisfied that things were going the way they should.

I recognized the grenades, as they doubtless knew that I would. They were Chinese, in a North Vietnamese Army sling. I felt a dim memory of anger, of ambushes and night patrols, but I did not let McGruder see it.

"It's clear that he was running supplies for the guerrillas," Buckley continued, as though he were satisfied with his evidence. "The patrol that took him off the road found drugs on him as well as grenades. Now all we have to do is make him tell us where he was meeting his contact, and our job is finished." He cast one last official look around the room. For a second he even looked at Russell, but Russell only gripped his carbine tighter and stared back at him.

"Saigon says that this zone is a military backwater," Buckley said quietly, watching the boy's lowered head. "A rest and recreation camp and a stockade. The entire district stinks of it. According to the brass, we have nothing to do out here but sit on our ass and play cards. We're a joke in Saigon bars. I've heard it. Well now," he said, "we've got a little operation of our own, a tough little guerrilla outfit that just asks to be cut up—and we're going to do the job without any outside help, no interpreters from division, no Special Forces people butting in where they don't belong. This kid is our first break," he concluded, looking at each of us in turn. "He can lead us to their base and supplies, and by God we're going to make him do just that."

Cowley and I sat perfectly still. We had nothing to say. It seemed simple enough, to hear Buckley tell it, though it was their job and not ours. I wondered why they had sent for us at all, since they already had an interpreter who knew more Vietnamese than I did. There seemed nothing for me to do, and even less for Cowley, who was good for nothing but fighting.

However, Buckley told McGruder to untie the prisoner without offering us any further explanation, and the boy was brought under the light. The interrogation got under way.

Nguyen began the questioning slowly. Buckley was almost immediately moving back and forth from one wall to the next as if he could not control himself now that his ignorance of the language had forced him to surrender the proceedings to Nguyen. He seemed to consider the business an urgent affair that had to be finished in the shortest possible time. Within the hour, if Nguyen could do it; before sundown, at the latest. Buckley chain-smoked, but the cigarettes didn't help him and he kept pacing around the room. Now and then he glanced down at me, as if I had somehow let him down; but he said nothing.

We waited. There were no provisions for the night in the room—only the heavy table, the bare light bulb, and the three cots without blankets. Not even drinking water had been brought in. The walls were bare except for the tool crib, but the tools were no part of the interrogation, as far as I could see. We seemed to be locked in alone with the prisoner.

Nguyen asked him where he had gotten the grenades. When I listened to the Vietnamese, which only Nguyen and the prisoner and I could understand, I felt even more alone than I had before. Buckley, McGruder, and even Cowley could not follow me as far as my understanding of the language forced me to go. I didn't like it, for it made me feel a party to anything that Nguyen said, but there was no escaping the sound of his voice in that small room.

I looked up to see what the boy's answer would be—and it was then, for the second time, that I felt uneasy certainty that something unreasonable was going to happen. It was happening. I could not connect the frail-looking boy with Buckley's account of guerrilla raids and dead Americans. I knew better, but I could not do it. And yet Buckley, and McGruder, and even the quiet Nguyen looked at the prisoner as if he were unquestionably the enemy, and were all waiting only to hear his confession, not to hear the truth, whatever it was.

When I looked up at the boy's face, caught under the cruel light, I saw only the stiff black hair, the delicate forehead, the high cheekbones, the small brown eyes that hardly moved behind their tightly drawn lids, the full, impassive mouth, and the narrow chin where the blood had dried and turned black—and stamped on it all was a look of immovable fear, as though he were staring at death, without hope. I knew that face. It bore sisters and daughters who were beautiful—for the face was inherently feminine—and who now filled the brothels in Saigon. And I had seen it, and a hundred of its brothers, in the quick glimpses of highland skirmishes; and once, the last time, I had not been able to see the enemy. Only the face itself. Disembodied. Waiting. I was kneeling in tall grass at the mouth of a valley near Darlac when it happened to me. Barren hills rose on three sides of us. Our captain had been killed in the morning, and I was left in command of two hundred men. Four other companies of infantry were dug in on the ridges on top of the hills, ready to open fire on the remnants of a Viet Cong outfit that we had trapped on the floor of the valley. My job was simple. When the company commander on the hilltops had his machine guns and mortars in position—the anvil—I was to give the order for my men to move in. We were the hammer: machine guns, grenades, flame throwers, automatic rifles, and finally bayonets. There would be no survivors, unless we took one or two prisoners out of the valley for questioning. The Montagnard tribesmen who would move through the valley after we had gone would see to that. I watched the Vietnamese trying to dig in, sweeping my field glasses from one knot of them to another; and then, perhaps because the sun was hot on my back, or because I was tired, I began to see, not the enemy, but faces. Only faces. Here and there I would glimpse them for a fleeting second, unreal through my glasses, enlarged, yet tense, expectant, certain of death. Suddenly two mortar shells exploded among them, taking the range. My radioman signaled me. I took the receiver and heard the order to attack when the barrage lifted. My company was braced, waiting. I waited too, kneeling in the sunlight, listening to the whirring of insects in the tall grass, gazing at the small figures of the men we were about to kill—and then I pulled my company back. The men were veterans and they obeyed my order. We opened up one end of the valley like a hinged door and withdrew up the side of the hill to our left. The Vietnamese were quick and they fled through the gap before the outfits on the hills understood what had happened. There were one or two mortar hits. A few men were killed. But that was all.

At my court-martial I was accused of refusing to obey an order under fire, and of "aiding and abetting the enemies of the United States." I was given legal counsel, an Army lawyer from the Military Justice Division. He pleaded that I had suffered a nervous breakdown; "combat fatigue," he called it, and cited my past record to show that I had been a good soldier and, as he put it, a patriot. He was a hardworking man and I bore him no ill-will. The court found me guilty of willfully failing to obey an order under fire, which was only right, and was about to sentence me when a colonel dropped in—I don't remember his name— and discovered that I knew two thousand words of Vietnamese. He asked me if that was true, and I said that it was. Then he decided that I was Army property, and too valuable to be disposed of entirely; and thus it was that they only broke me to the ranks and sentenced me to hard labor in the camp at Quai Dong, where my two thousand words would be available if anyone wanted to use them.

Once or twice during the first weeks of my imprisonment I was called to the mayor's quarters to interpret. A village headman complained that his chickens had been stolen; the mother of a dead child wanted compensation for its funeral. Then they seemed to forget about me, and my days went on undisturbed. No doubt someone mislaid my file; or, which seemed more reasonable to me, they had decided that I was unreliable, and could not be trusted.

Now I was expected, once again, to look at a boy's face and see the face of my enemy. It was very remote from my life after so long a time at Quai Dong, where there were no enemies and no friends, but only endless days of waiting. Still, Buckley and the others showed no doubt. Obviously, I was expected to follow their lead and to make my stand with them. We were to show solidarity in the face of the enemy. Yet it seemed a difficult question, and it was one, moreover, on which the Army could no longer force me to give an answer.

The other questions that Nguyen asked the boy, the simple ones that centered around concrete facts like hand grenades and medicines, were always the same; the boy's answers, too, were identical each time. It puzzled me at first, then it became tiring to hear. But Nguyen seemed undisturbed by it, as if he had expected it. The prisoner's replies were made in a voice so low that it was barely audible. That, too, was irritating to hear, for, though I did not want to listen to any part of it, I could not keep from straining to catch his words. Only later did I realize that it was difficult for him to speak through his broken lips.

"Where did you get the grenades?" Nguyen asked. He spoke with a razor's edge to his voice, though his voice remained quiet. Unlike Buckley, he did not have to shout.

"From the dead soldier," the boy replied humbly.

"Was he American?"

"North Vietnamese."

"Where was he?"

"On the road to Weichu."

"There are no dead soldiers there."

"He was in a ditch."

"Why did you take the grenades?"

"To protect myself."

"Where did you get the medicine?"

"From the dead soldier."

"Soldiers of the Democratic Republic of North Vietnam do not carry penicillin and morphine!"

"This one did, sir."

"Where were you taking your supplies?"

"I was going to Saigon, to my sister."

"The Weichu Road does not go to Saigon."

"There was fighting on the other side of the hills. I was afraid to go that way."

"You will tell me now," Nguyen said, "where you were told to meet your comrades."

"I am alone, sir. I was only going to my sister. Our parents are dead."

Nguyen studied the boy's lowered head for a moment, then he turned to Buckley. "You see," he said, "he is obstinate."

McGruder approached with a businesslike expression on his face, but Buckley waved him back before he could reach the table. He told Nguyen to begin again. "Keep after him," he said.

Nguyen put the same list of questions to the boy. Buckley began to pace back and forth between the close walls of the room. I watched him, for I was already tired of watching Nguyen. It seemed reasonable enough, I thought, for him to want to find out where the guerrillas were meeting to launch their raids. He was impatient and angry, but he looked honest. I supposed that if he broke the prisoner's resistance he would be able to save some lives and do his career some credit. There was little enough chance for that at Quai Dong.

But when I looked back from Buckley to the boy, who had been dragged off the Weichu Road and locked in a windowless room with four Americans and a Vietnamese that he could not trust, it all seemed more questionable, somehow, than when I looked at Buckley alone.

"There's no way of knowing whether he's a guerrilla or not," I observed quietly.

"What do you mean by that?" Buckley snapped, looking at me for the first time as if I were a convict.

Cowley nudged me hard, and I said nothing more.

But McGruder was aroused. He looked at me vengefully, as if
he had been waiting for me to make a mistake, and said that you
could never tell one Vietnamese from another until he shot you.
"But we caught this little son of a bitch red-handed, and we ain't
gonna let him off!"

I admitted that he was right, but still he wasn't satisfied, and
told Buckley that Nguyen was wasting time. "Throw the China-
man out of here, Lieutenant," he begged. "Let's do it our way."

I saw the boy's arm stiffen when McGruder raised his voice;
and I knew then how his mouth had been covered with blood.

McGruder saw his involuntary motion too, and a look of pleasure came into his eyes. "I can make him squeal like a monkey,"
he said, and took up a threatening position behind the boy, not
quite touching him but so close that he must have felt his breath.
McGruder's head nearly touched the hot bulb, but he was too
interested in the boy to feel anything. For a moment I hated him.
I was fascinated and sickened by the thought of driving my fist
into his unshaven jaw. But I stopped myself, for I did not want
to get involved, and I leaned cautiously back and listened to the
droning sound of Nguyen's voice, which went on undisturbed in
spite of McGruder.

By three o'clock the interrogation had made no visible progress.
I passed the time watching a cockroach moving in the shadows
along the floor. It was pushing its snout against the wall behind
Cowley's foot, trying to find its way out. The floor was dirt, but
the metal walls had been driven in too deep for it to have a
chance. Still the bug felt up and down, inching along. But it was
going in the opposite direction from the door, where it must have
come in. There seemed no reason to step on it. If it was patient
and went all the way around, behind the heels of the other men
in the room, it might find its way out; if not, it was its own
fault.

From time to time I listened to the questioning. It remained
unchanged, and the prisoner's answers remained identical. Finally I saw that Nguyen was forcing the boy to repeat his meaningless replies by quietly menacing him if he varied them in the
slightest way from the answers that he had first given. The word-
for-word repetition puzzled me. It was wearing on everyone's
nerves. But I supposed that there was a ritual that they would
observe before the boy would tell us anything, since they were
both Vietnamese in the presence of Americans, however much
they might hate one another.

Certainly, after the first hour, the boy looked tired. Probably
he had not slept for a long time. If he had been trying to get to

Saigon he had most likely been walking for days. Of course, if he were a Quai Dong guerrilla, it didn't matter; but I began to number the uses that a peasant might have for hand grenades, and especially for medicine, without being a Viet Cong. I could imagine several—the black market in Saigon for one—but it was none of my business, and I kept quiet. It didn't seem to be Nguyen's business either, for he had not asked the prisoner about it. He simply went down his original set of questions, as methodically as if he were performing a mass.

Buckley, however, was not taking it with Nguyen's equanimity. He dropped one half-smoked cigarette after another, ground them angrily under his heel, and told Nguyen to hurry up.

"We're wasting time!" he complained.

McGruder grunted and looked at the back of the boy's head. "He's afraid to hurt him," he said.

Nguyen denied it—he seemed to fear that accusation above all others—but he was silenced by a wave of Buckley's hand and told to continue in whatever way he thought was best.

"Only be quick," Buckley repeated. "We don't know when the guerrillas will attack again."

Buckley looked down at me and added that every minute that we lost might cost an American his life. I said nothing, and Nguyen turned back to the prisoner and began over again from the beginning, but he warned Buckley to be patient.

"He is very strong," he said, gazing at the boy's lowered face.

McGruder began to swear under his breath.

"I do not mean physical strength," Nguyen said, looking at McGruder with contempt and speaking in his slow but strangely fluent English, the tone of which seemed to aggravate McGruder even more than what Nguyen said. "I mean a stubborn spirit, which is much stronger. That is why you must not injure him again. Pain will not break his spirit. It will only kill his body. We must exhaust him, then he will be willing to betray his comrades."

"If I hit him," McGruder muttered, "he'll talk."

"No, he will only die, and thus escape us."

McGruder turned red and made a motion toward the fragile-looking Nguyen, but Buckley told him to keep away. Then he turned to Nguyen and asked him how much longer it would take.

"Two, maybe three days," Nguyen answered, studying the boy's face intently.

"But you said it would only be a day and a night!" Buckley shouted.

"I did not know then how strong he was," Nguyen said, straightening up and facing him.

Buckley ran his fingers through his hair and moved away from the light. "We can't wait that long," he said, shaking his head and shoving his hands into his hip pockets. "The major will never stand for it."

Again McGruder asked to be put in Nguyen's place. Buckley ignored him, lit another cigarette, and sat down. And then, without warning, he turned to me.

"What do you think?" he asked.

I shook my head, and told him that it was none of my business.

"I'm only asking your opinion."

"I don't have one," I replied, suddenly hating Buckley for trying to draw me into his game again, whatever it was going to be. Silence was my only defense. I refused to say anything more. Buckley glanced up at the boy's head, then he looked back at me and shrugged, as if to say that he had done his part and given me my chance and that now anything that happened to the boy would be my fault, not his.

"Do what you can, Nguyen," he said, and settled back against the wall.

McGruder moved quietly away from the light, apparently satisfied from the tone of Buckley's voice that his time would come, and Nguyen began his interrupted questions from the beginning. Now I understood more of his method, and I feared the room in a way that I had not before. Nguyen was not angry at anything that the boy might say—the answers themselves became meaningless when they had been repeated a hundred times. Even the words lost their accustomed sense and were reduced to nonsense syllables, like a chant in an alien tongue. Nguyen asked him, for the hundredth time and with no change whatever in the expression of his voice, where he had found the dead soldier. And the boy answered, for the hundredth time, "On the road to Weichu."

"There are no dead soldiers there."

"He was in a ditch."

"Why did you take the grenades?"

"To protect myself."

"Where did you get the medicine?"

"From the dead soldier."

"Soldiers of the Democratic Republic of North Vietnam do not carry penicillin and morphine!"

"This one did."

Nguyen stopped. Slowly his hand came up, and the boy said, "This one did, *sir*."

"Where were you taking your supplies?"

"I was going to Saigon, to my sister.

"The Weichu Road does not go to Saigon."

"There was fighting on the other side of the hills. I was afraid to go that way."

"You will tell me now where you were instructed to meet your comrades!"

"I am alone, sir. I was only going to my sister."

Then Nguyen, without allowing a second's rest to mark the completion of the cycle of questions, asked again where he had gotten the grenades. The boy answered as he had always answered, and the rhythm of the questions was repeated. It was maddening to listen to, and I tried to ignore it, for I saw now that Nguyen's purpose was not intelligence, but simple exhaustion. He would wear the boy down until he was too weak to give any answer at all. Then, I supposed, he would have a way of extracting whatever he wanted from him. They would beat the boy's mind into a shapeless mass, and in it, like splinters of broken glass, they would find what they had been looking for. But the end was a long way off, and it was obvious that someone would have to relieve Nguyen from time to time. The strain was more than one man could bear—and with a sudden halt in my thoughts I realized why I had been taken from the stockade into that room, for I, who had escaped a military prison because I spoke two thousand words of Vietnamese, was Nguyen's replacement.

I got up instantly and crossed the room. "Am I supposed to interrogate him?" I asked Buckley.

He looked up at me and seemed pleased, as if he had known that I would come to ask him that question, sooner or later. "Not entirely," he answered, and moved over to offer me a place to sit down next to him.

"I won't question the boy," I said. I warned him that I'd go back to the stockade first. The hut looked less like a reprieve than it had at the beginning. I didn't know if they could do anything more than send me back to the stockade, but I was ready to risk it.

To my surprise Buckley gave me a friendly look and told me to sit down. When I did, he lowered his voice and spoke under the steady droning of Nguyen's questions.

"Can you understand what they're saying to each other?" he asked.

I listened for a moment. "Yes," I said reluctantly, "I can."

Buckley was pleased with me then. "Good. All I want you to

do for the present is listen to what they say. Don't let a word slip by, not one word." He squinted up into the light and said, "We'd be fools to trust Nguyen."

"They're only repeating the same thing," I said. "It's meaningless."

"I don't care. We'll let him do it his way for now; but they're both Vietnamese and they'll try to stick together."

"I doubt it," I murmured, yet there was no way for me to know whether Nguyen was in earnest with his interrogation or not, since I had never seen an interrogation before and had no idea how one was carried on. I glanced at Buckley. Something had changed in the room. It had somehow become smaller. It seemed to give me less room in which to hide. Gradually I realized that the cost of my simple act of crossing from one wall to the other had been the loss of my immunity. I had wanted only to defend myself, and to warn Buckley that I would not interrogate the boy, but something had gone wrong. Perhaps, if I did what Buckley wanted, I would gain a degree of power. But I did not want the power. I wanted only to stay clear. Cowley was scowling at me from across the room, and Buckley was smiling, as if he understood perfectly what was in my mind and had been counting on it. Now he thought that I was his man.

"If Nguyen doesn't break him soon," he said, "we may have to do this by ourselves."

Buckley watched the two figures who stood under the light, but he was leaning so close to me that our shoulders touched. Some treacherous idea was fixed in his mind. That much was clear to me, and I drew away from him. But it was not clear to me how I was supposed to convince him that he was wrong. The only way for me to stay clear now was to stop the interrogation, but I had no way of doing it. Perhaps Buckley was right and Nguyen was protecting the boy. It meant nothing to me in either case, and that, at any other time, should have been enough to keep me out of it—but it was not difficult to see that if Buckley lost confidence in Nguyen entirely he would be left with no one to carry on the interrogation but myself, unless he gave the boy to McGruder. I glanced at Buckley's face. His eyes were fixed on the boy, waiting, and it was then that I realized that it was he, and not I, who had gained a degree of power. I was deep in the trap with him now, with no way out.

But of course there was no need for apprehension. Thus far everything was under control.

Another hour passed. The voices of Nguyen and the boy went on with the deadly regularity of a ticking clock. McGruder sat on the cot along the back wall, apparently passive, with his head covered by his hands and only his knuckles visible. Nguyen stood in front of the table with his back to us, his round shoulders and his short-cropped head in the light, and went on with his even and methodical questioning as though he were conscious of no threat to his position. The walls of the tin hut creaked in the heat. The boy's voice was a weak whisper, into which Nguyen jabbed each question before he could recover his breath from the last answer. The boy was allowed no rest, and he seemed to be losing ground. The torture was mental, a slow dulling of the senses. I found myself becoming fascinated by it; then, looking up, I saw that Russell was no longer in the room.

"He's outside," Buckley said, "standing guard duty."

"Why?" I asked, getting off the cot.

Buckley looked at me, and shrugged. "We have a prisoner," he said.

"There's a fence around the motor pool, and there's barbed wire around the entire compound. Nobody's going to get away."

"It's normal security. Why does it bother you so much?" Then he added, with a grin, "You should be used to barbed wire by now."

I walked to the door, but I did not open it, nor could I look out. There were no windows in the hut, not even an air vent through which I might have seen the sky, or the stars, if it was already night. We were entirely sealed in. The heat was suddenly unbearable. I wanted badly to see what was outside, for in that closed place I seemed unable to trust my memory of what I had left behind. I thought of the beach, but it was far away, beyond reach. I hated the thought of sentries outside the door, though I had never felt it so strongly before. But then I saw that Buckley was watching me with too much interest, and I moved away from the door.

Suddenly I heard Cowley shout, "Look out!" Instantly there was a loud crash behind me and a wild cry of anger.

When I turned around I saw the prisoner lying on his back in the dirt six feet from the table. McGruder, who had knocked his cot over to get at him, was standing alone under the light, panting, as if he couldn't breathe.

"He'll talk now, by God," he whispered.

Nguyen had been thrown aside, but he was already accusing McGruder at the top of his lungs. "You are a fool, you are a fool, Sergeant McGruder!" he yelled, losing his self-control. "You are a barbarian!"

"You're chicken-livered," McGruder grunted. "I swear to God I'll kill him if you don't get it over with."

"And do you think you can make him talk then?" Nguyen shouted.

McGruder turned slowly away from the boy and Nguyen backed out of his reach. Buckley stood up. For the first time since the interrogation began he looked calm and untroubled. He quietly told McGruder to get out of the hut. "If you attack the prisoner again," he said, "I'll have you put in detention."

To my surprise McGruder turned his back and went outside without a word. There was a flash of sunlight when he opened the door, and I saw that it was not yet night.

"Kreuger," Buckley said, without looking at me, "see if the prisoner is all right."

I should not have moved, but I had been conditioned too thoroughly in the stockade not to obey—at least once—and I went past Cowley, who had jumped to his feet when McGruder hit the boy and was standing in a corner, ready to fight his way out of the room if he had to. When I bent over the boy I saw that his eyes were open but dazed.

Nguyen leaned over my shoulder. His face was inexpressive again, as if nothing had happened. He reached down and took the boy by the chin and turned his head sharply from side to side. A thick swelling was rising on his left temple, but it was not bleeding.

"He is all right," Nguyen said quietly, and helped me pull him to his feet. The boy weighed less than a girl, and I pulled too hard and nearly upset him. Nguyen took him away from me and dragged him back under the light, but when he released him his knees buckled and he collapsed on the floor. We picked him up again, but he couldn't stand by himself. Nguyen finally left him sitting in the dirt with his head leaning to one side, and looked up at Buckley. "You see that we cannot go on," he said bitterly.

"Stand him up," Buckley ordered.

"It is no use if he cannot speak," Nguyen answered.

Buckley turned around. "All right," he said, and rubbed his hand across his mouth, "bring a medic."

I didn't look at anyone in the room. Not even the boy. My only instinct was to keep my head down, no matter what happened.

Finally it was Cowley who spoke up. "They're all down in the stockade giving shots."

"Get one up here then," Buckley answered impatiently.

Cowley hesitated. "It's outside the gate," he said.

"Damn it, I don't care where it is! I gave you an order! Do you know who you're talking to? I want a medic in here, and I want him fast!"

Cowley left without another word, and Buckley controlled himself. The three of us remained in silence, staring at the prisoner's face, waiting for a sign of life. Somehow I did not expect Cowley to come back—if I had gone I would not have come back—but he did. I suppose that he could think of no way of getting out either. He brought Finley with him. Cowley remained next to the door and Finley looked around the room, still blinded by the sun's light, as if he saw none of us.

"Revive him," Buckley said, pointing to the boy who still sat in the dirt with his back slumped against one of the heavy legs of the table.

Finley glanced at me, but when he received no sign of recognition he knelt beside the prisoner and began to examine his mouth and jaw, where he could see the dried blood.

That irritated Buckley. "It's his forehead that's hurt," he snapped.

Finley saw his error then, and he left the boy's mouth alone and cleaned and bandaged his temple. Then he gave him a shot of something that looked like water, but which made his head begin to roll from side to side.

"All right," Buckley said, "can he stand up?"

"Yes sir, I guess so," Finley answered, stepping back cautiously, as though the floor were mined.

Again the boy was pulled to his feet. This time he kept his balance, although his eyes were open abnormally wide and his breathing was shallow and hard. Then the drug seemed to wear off and his head fell into its lowered position once more. All that I could see was the pressure bandage on his temple and his eyes, which were blinking rapidly, as if he were dizzy or afraid. He looked smaller, as if something had broken inside him, but he stayed on his feet.

"Get back to work," Buckley ordered, and returned to his cot, where he picked up the cigarette that he had carefully laid aside when McGruder had knocked the boy down. "You may find the prisoner more willing to talk now," he added, and leaned back against the wall to watch.

Buckley looked satisfied, as though things had finally taken a turn for the better. Nguyen didn't say a word to any of us. He simply began his interrupted questions again. The only difference was that now there was a new sense of urgency in his voice, as if he too felt that his time was running out.

At first the boy did not answer, for the rhythm of the interrogation had been broken. McGruder's fist had allowed him to rest. Only when Nguyen's voice fell across his face like a whiplash, again and again, without mercy, did his broken lips open and begin to form the ritual phrases once more. He spoke now as if he were in a trance, but after a few moments his answers and Nguyen's questions slowly fell back into their accustomed pattern.

The sound of it was worse now than before, when it had looked as if it would go on undisturbed for days. Now we could see that it was only an interlude, and that at the end of it the boy would be hurt again. Yet the combined sound of their voices was almost worse than the sight of the boy's damaged head lying face down in the dirt. McGruder's attack had freed us from the sounds of the interrogation, if only for a moment. Now the deadening murmur of it filled the room again—and I wondered, with a dropping in the pit of my stomach, how many times the prisoner could recover and go on.

Finley moved noiselessly around the room, keeping his back near the wall and staying out of the circle of light where Nguyen worked the boy. He sat down next to me on my cot, where I had taken refuge when the interrogation got under way again. Soon Cowley joined us, and the three of us sat together. Cowley was very quiet now, and seemed to be waiting only to see what direction things would go. Finley glanced about the room nervously. "What's this all about?" he whispered.

"Nothing," I said; then I added, "Guerrillas—they think the kid was on his way to meet the guerrillas with supplies. Nguyen's trying to find out where."

"Oh," Finley answered, as if it made sense to him, then he stared up at the boy and at the ugly string of grenades that McGruder had left on the table under the light. "Is he really a guerrilla?"

I shrugged. "Most likely."

Finley said that he had never seen a guerrilla before. He studied the fragile neck and shoulders of the boy.

I was sick of Finley. His innocence was worse than McGruder's sadism. I stood up and moved deliberately toward the door.

All that I wanted now was to get out. Nothing else mattered. I saw that Cowley had been right; they had used us because we were convicts and they thought we had no choice. But they were wrong. We had nothing more to fear and, being outsiders, nothing whatever to gain from the interrogation. They did not understand that only men who still had something to hope for

could be made to do such things. They could send me back to the
stockade, under the harmless muzzle of Russell's carbine, as they
had brought me to the room. Cowley and the medic could take
care of themselves.

I was past Nguyen and the boy, who faced each other under
the hard light, chanting their litany of question and answer as if
they could keep it up for weeks. Then I was beyond Buckley,
who made no move to stop me, and I held the door knob. To my
relief it turned in my hand. I stepped out into the heat and the
blinding sunlight without looking back, and turned away toward
the jeep and the open gate.

And then I saw the barbed wire. Russell and three new guards
were pulling it up throat-high around all sides of the hut. Now
there was a third ring of barbed wire, and we were alone inside
of it. In the sunlight it looked black, like a barren hedge of
thorns, but metal, impassable. Only a six-foot zone of free ground
remained between it and the tin walls. McGruder was there,
sitting to my right with his back against the shed, regarding his
heavy boots, waiting with doglike tenacity. Outside the fence I
saw Russell watching me. Four carbines were stacked within his
reach, with fixed bayonets, ready; and far away, through the coils
of the second fence at the motor pool, were the distant tents of
the stockade and the guard towers, shimmering patiently in the
heat.

TROOP WITHDRAWAL— THE INITIAL STEP

Thomas Parker

The position that Specialist 4 Wetzel had assumed in a morning formation in Southeast Asia was not one covered in Army Regulation 122–156, "Dismounted Drill," Section 2, "Inspections and Formations." It was, in fact, a position not covered in any Army Regulation and was therefore unauthorized, an infraction of the military rules for body member placement. Wetzel's legs were not shoulder-width apart "at ease," nor were they together from crotch to heel at "attention," with the toes canted outwards forming an angle of not more than forty-five degrees. Only a single leg of Wetzel's touched the ground at all, while the other was elevated flamingo-like behind him. And each time inspecting officer First Lieutenant Ernest ·Bauer clicked his heels in a smart left face in front of one of the men standing at "attention" in Wetzel's platoon, Wetzel clapped his hands in a short burst of praise. Men to his right and left glanced at Wetzel out of the corners of their eyes, some with disdain, others with amusement, all, however, wondering what 1st Lt Bauer's reaction would be to Wetzel's nonmilitary behavior, to such an undisguised flouting of an officer's authority by an enlisted man.

Wetzel himself wondered how Bauer would react. Along with the clapping and his lack of "attention," would Bauer also ignore the tarnished brass belt buckle, the boots that had taken on the color of the hundreds of things that Wetzel had kicked, tripped over, and stepped into since the last inspection; would Bauer, for his own sake, for his own protection, pass Wetzel by without a word? It was a fair possibility. Wetzel had calculated that, despite Bauer's learning disabilities, by this, the third week of Bauer's conditioning, he would have caught on. The officer clicked his heels in front of Wetzel, looked him over, and, with a

queasy smile, clicked his heels again and went on to the next
man. Wetzel was pleased; it seemed that his Pavlovian experiment with Bauer was finally succeeding.

Lately, Bauer had been struck down by an epidemic of shots.
Following some reprimand to Sp4 Wetzel, who was in charge of
Company Personnel, his official shot record would be lost and he
would once again have to undergo the full battery of inoculations specified in AR 134–161, "Health in the Sub-Tropics." In
the last month alone, Bauer had had sufficient immunization to
guarantee the enduring good health of a sperm whale.

Wetzel's antagonism toward Bauer was not an immature one.
It had been nurtured over the past year, growing through in-
fancy, childhood, and adolescence, and finally reaching adult-
hood as their fifth month together in Vietnam was about to end.
It was an antagonism which germinated from Wetzel's experiences with Bauer at Fort Polk, Louisiana, where the two of them
had gone through Basic Combat Training together, forced by
circumstance to be "buddies," communally eating sand and dirt,
drinking rain, sleeping on rocks, and following impossible trails
at double time to get to useless objectives, where, if they got
there fast enough, they could take a five-minute-long "ten-minute
break," to sit in the snow and smoke and fart to keep each other
warm.

About three weeks into Basic, Wetzel realized with impassive
understanding that he and Bauer were star-crossed. There, in an
olive-drab mural of arms and legs, he among 250 men would run
a hundred yards into the hand-to-hand combat sand pit, where,
by the rules, the arbitrary man standing to his left would be his
opponent for the lesson. Wetzel would turn and, without a single
prayed-for exception, there would be Bauer glaring at him, froth-
ing from the run, eager to try out a new twist of the rear-
takedown-and-strangle. When Wetzel was the "aggressor," he
took it very easy, dummying the kidney punches, letting the
"enemy" fall gently to the ground, and then applying a minimum amount of pressure to the throat and larynx. But then
Bauer was the aggressor, smashing his fist into Wetzel's kidneys,
taking him down so Wetzel would hit the sand like a sack of
ballast, and applying sufficient pressure to the throat and larynx
so that Wetzel's eyes would bug, his lips would begin to turn
purple and the color would disappear from beneath his fingernails.

Also, in bayonet drill, prefaced by a card shuffle of 250 men
counting off, calling out numbers, where men whose numbers
equaled twice plus six the square root of each other became

partners, it was always Bauer's number that would fit Wetzel's equation. Wetzel, when he performed as aggressor in the long-thrust-hold-and-parry-horizontal-butt-stroke, thrust short, parried half-heartedly, and the horizontal swing of his weapon was a good two feet away from Bauer's head. Bauer, true to form, as aggressor, made incisions into Wetzel's web-belt, parried so zealously that Wetzel's weapon dropped from his hands to the ground, and performed a horizontal-butt-stroke with such gusto that the sand embedded in the heel of Bauer's stock would scratch Wetzel's nose.

But the greatest single contribution to Wetzel's growing antagonism toward Bauer was made by their Mexican drill instructor—a man whose name started with "F" and ended with "o," whose name no living man could pronounce, but whose name was shortened and simplified out of desperation by the men in his platoon to Sergeant Frito—who matched Bauer and Wetzel as bunkmates and buddies. It was a match that forced complete responsibility for the other man, a match which entailed making bunks together and making sure your buddy was dressed in time and wearing the right gear. It was a perverse marriage between men who never shared anything sacred in their nine weeks together other than air, water, and cigarettes and the fact that neither of them had been circumcised.

It became increasingly evident to Wetzel as Basic painfully dragged on, that Bauer had something going with Frito. Whenever anything had to be done for your buddy, Wetzel seemed to be doing it: cleaning Bauer's weapon, taking notes for classes Bauer missed, making Bauer's bunk, polishing Bauer's brass. Bauer cleaned his own weapon only once during Basic and that was in front of the entire company as a demonstration. "It was," said Sgt Frito, "the cleanest weapon in five platoons."

During range fire for record, Bauer was in sick bay, but nevertheless led the company qualifying as "expert." While it was unlikely that squinty-eyed Sgt Frito could even see as far as 350 meters, much less hit a target the size of a large man perched at that distance, it was nevertheless true, unless there was something that Frito had going with the cardboard silhouette as well.

So it seemed to Wetzel that truly, Bauer's trophy for soldier of the training cycle, Bauer's medal for M-16 firing, and Bauer's commission had been a mistake, the result of logical fallacy like so much else he knew existed in the Army. While death may have been a great leveler, leveling all men to zero, the Army leveled live men to an IQ of 85. Halfway through Basic, Wetzel resigned himself to sailing forever in Bauer's torpid wake, at least while they were both in uniform:

It came as no surprise to Wetzel then, when he was finally sent to Vietnam after two months of typing school at Fort Tara, Virginia, where, when he entered the course he could type seventy-plus words per minute and, upon leaving, was cut to a more moderate thirty-minus words per minute—under the theory that typing so fast demoralizes the other men—that he and Bauer were to be in the same company. For his efforts with Sgt Frito and whoever else's palm he greased in OCS, Private Bauer became 2nd Lt Bauer, and then miraculously, 1st Lt Bauer, stationed with a hospital company of almost a thousand men.

On the outside, Bauer had driven truck for a large fruit concern and had recently made the transition from fresh to quick-frozen produce. It was a status job, a bigger truck, ten feet longer, a foot wider, and the latest in cabin design. When he stopped at cafés with the new truck, he took little or no shit from anyone except maybe the Mayflower guys. Even then it was all in good fun, although Bauer once had his nose broken by a stainless-steel cream pitcher being used as brass knuckles by a guy with a small laundry truck who didn't seem to give a damn what anyone was driving. This code violation was a mystery to Bauer, who, without ever considering what it meant, thought that fair was only fair.

Because of his specialized background, Bauer was made Ground Transportation Officer in the company, a job that involved trucks and similar vehicles. Since the hospital was a permanent Army hospital near Saigon, the only real ground transportation that Bauer was called on to regulate was an eight-times daily bus to the city and an occasional ambulance to pick up American survivors who were injured in terrorist attacks. Usually however, the attacks were thorough and there were no survivors. At that point, the Vietnamese police would deliver to the hospital any bodies that seemed American. It was a "hands-across-the-sea" program that Bauer himself had instituted. There were only problems when it was impossible to tell whether the victims were Vietnamese or American or when they were not quite dead. Bauer put a thirty-mile-an-hour governor on the ambulance so that it would take just about a half-hour to make it into the city, and by that time, things would have, in his own words, "worked out one way or another."

All in all, Bauer didn't mind the war much. It was a way of

passing the day. Enlisted men assigned under him kissed-ass and
he responded by giving freely of absurdly long passes, which
Wetzel, in Personnel, would find reasons to tear up and then
send the men back to Bauer for others. In this way they would
miss at least one bus, although sometimes Bauer would run an
unscheduled charter for his men alone, which Wetzel, in Personnel, would find out about and feel obligated to mention to
Colonel Schooner, who, in turn, would be duty-bound to mention it back to Lt Bauer. It was then that Bauer would mete out
what he considered just punishment and Wetzel, as a result,
would spend series of weekends on KP and consecutive nights as
Charge of Quarters. The fabled shit rolled downhill from rank to
rank until it hit Wetzel, who, in Personnel, having no one under
him, did what he could for vengeance and protection, destroying
Bauer's official shot record, and then, as a dutiful Sp4, notifying
the proper medical authorities.

On the other hand, Wetzel *did* mind the war.
Before he was drafted he had been working as an accountant
in a branch bank in San Francisco, where, other than an occasional holdup which would cut into his two-hour lunch break, he
led a quiet, safe, and unobtrusive life. In Vietnam, what quietness there came to him was inner, his unobtrusiveness was the
result of his rank, and safety was a thing of the past.
And then there was the problem of the sounds. He had very
poor filtering devices and the constant going off of claymore
mines, rockets, and other forms of ammo would get on his nerves,
and often, before a day would end in the building where he went
over officers' and enlisted men's records, he would stutter and
show other visceral signs of psychic disorder.
In his room in Saigon atop a small barbershop, Sp4 Wetzel lay
on his bed listening to the rockets and claymore mines go off. It
was a drag, he realized, more than a drag, a colossal mistake for
him to be here. He would have to leave at the soonest time
possible. Why, he wondered, didn't he leave right now? The
answer he came to, he had arrived at before and before that: he
lay too close to the half-inspired middle of mankind. He was
neither smart enough nor stupid enough to desert; and also, he
didn't have the guts.
On his bureau in olive-drab cans marked with black letters
which read, "10 Weight US Army Oil," "20 Weight US Army
Oil," "30 Weight US Army Oil," and "10x30 Weight US Army
Multi-purpose Oil," Wetzel kept his different blends of grass.
The fact that he turned-on did not necessarily distinguish him

from the thousands of other enlisted men in Vietnam who did also. For Wetzel though, the grass provided neither a good stoning nor an orgiastic trip. It was merely a component in his survival kit, used to abstract, to make things disappear, things which ordinarily imposed themselves on his being with the bluntness of telephone poles. It worked: it kept him from harm and didn't seem to be doing him any harm.

It was anyway only the officers, medical and otherwise, who feared the stuff, and they would drink themselves into a puking stupor every day, sometimes so far gone by noon that they would disappear into their posh quarters, leaving the enlisted men in the hospital to perform reasonably delicate operations and to zip up the plastic bags that contained the newly dead patients. Wetzel could only guess how many of them weren't really dead when they were zipped. The fresh corpses simply didn't show the life-signs that the enlisted men were taught to look for: a certain level of heartbeat, breathing, pulse, the ability to cloud mirrors, etc. Zip! Off to the States, dog tags hanging from the zipper tabs on the outside, the name inked-in on the chest of the returnee. An early-out Wetzel realized one day in the zipping room—a thought.

Wetzel, along with every other man in the entire United States Army, was allotted by Army Regulation 14–198, "The Billeting of Troops," Section 1, Paragraph 2, a minimum of 300 cubic feet of living space, which, when broken down, yielded approximately 6 feet by 6 feet by 8 feet. He did, in fact, have at least that much living space in the five-hundred-man barracks, but other than make his bunk there the first day he got to Vietnam, the 300 cubic feet went almost completely unused. Like all the other enlisted men in the company who had space allotted and a bunk assigned them in the barracks, Wetzel didn't live there. Only when it rained, when it was impossible for him to maneuver his motor scooter through the shell-pocked streets from the hospital compound to Saigon, would he have to spend a night; and then it would be a night completely alone, for Wetzel was the only man not to qualify for Bauer's emergency transportation to the city. The last bus would leave Wetzel in the barracks among millions of cubic feet of space.

Appropriations for the maintenance and upkeep of the barracks, Wetzel found out one day reading Colonel Schooner's memo to First Army Command, was over $800,000 a year. This included the substantial maintenance and upkeep of Captain Ellsworth, Officer-in-charge—daily changing of sheets, Vietnamese maid service, and what seemed to Wetzel an inordinate amount (3 miles) of mosquito netting. Once a month a barracks inspection with all five hundred men present would be held and Colonel Schooner, nearly blind in both eyes but much in need of a year's active service for retirement points, would walk through followed by a retinue that included all the field-grade officers in the company along with a certain first sergeant named Horzkok.

"Horzkok," the colonel would ask, "are these men getting their sheets changed?"

"Yes, sir," Horzkok would reply, writing something down on a clipboard whose top sheet hadn't changed since Wetzel had been in the company.

"Horzkok, are the maids coming in daily?"

"Yes, sir."

"What about the netting? Do you need more netting?"

"Probably more netting, sir."

The colonel grinned and winked at Horzkok.

And so the retinue would eventually make their way past Wetzel's bunk, grown men, some of them making more than a thousand dollars a month, inspecting a barracks that no one lived in, checking to make sure that all the special niceties in these barracks for the hospital personnel, who lived twenty miles away in hovels and brothels, were being carried out.

In the beginning of his Vietnam stay, all that made life bearable for Wetzel were the menial tasks he performed while working in Company Personnel. There he could create his own order; there, all his antagonists existed only in paper files, on green and yellow cards, and on sheets of paper stapled to forms that, Wetzel realized one afternoon, in a company of a thousand men, only *he* understood. In realizing this, he realized also in a clouded way that whatever power he as an Sp4 had lay in this sole understanding of the forms.

In these first few months, Wetzel did little with his recognition until one night in his Saigon room after some moderate smoking, the idea came to him in a raw but almost crystalline form. As Wetzel looked up to study the contours of his thatched ceiling, Bauer appeared out of the smoke of Wetzel's burnt-down joint, the genie of Wetzel's high. But this ethereal Bauer was not the singular Bauer of the past; rather, Bauer took on the face and dimension of all the men in Wetzel's basic platoon, all the typical American fighting men that Wetzel had known. Here was Bauer with his Army sense of fairness and morality, his self-righteousness; of a certain breed of man, Bauer became their everyman. As the smoke dispersed and the ceiling came back into focus, Wetzel remembered the forms.

Why not, he wondered? Why not, if Bauer is indeed what I see him as, why not de-form him, re-form him, change his being, make him into a more agreeable human? Or why not change his duty station? But then Wetzel realized that by making small changes on Bauer's forms he would be just playing with him. It would be no different than destroying his shot record. It was in this second, as Wetzel recognized the pettiness of merely toying with Bauer's file, that the missing card meshed with the computer tabs in Wetzel's brain and lodged itself resolutely there, leaving nothing else to be considered. Why not plainly murder Bauer, eliminate him entirely, take him out of the war? After all, it would be simply a matter of form, of a form, to wound Bauer in action and have him captured, to make him a hero, a coward, to ship an unidentified body with Bauer's name on the chest along with a copy of Bauer's dog tags, which Wetzel could cut with the machine in his office, back to the States. All the Army would need would be the correct forms and the body would be buried in some military cemetery and his insurance policy paid.

What it came to with the imposition of the reality of the next morning was that Bauer was far more than just Bauer, and to eliminate him would be the inital step. It would be ample, sufficient, for Wetzel to know that while Bauer was harassing him in some formation, that the Army was concurrently paying off $10,000 to Bauer's beneficiary and inactivating his file in St. Louis—where it is said (and probably lied) that every man's record exists in duplicate.

If every day Wetzel weren't witness to the same idiocies of men whose actions were outlined by the cumbersome regulations—the brains behind the men who had given up their own—if every day he didn't feel that the Army, with him included, was digging deeper and deeper into the soggy Asian soil, if a hundred other things he had witnessed, noted, and forgotten hadn't happened, the idea would have never entered his head. But lately, as he sensed things getting worse around him, he turned-on with greater frequency and was beginning to stutter.

Somewhere also, Wetzel knew, if he kept after it, he would run down the regulation that would simply provide for his own release, the one that would send him legally back to the States. There, if things were not truly better, at least there was a semblance of order and peace and the Bauers were back on their trucks and not directly, at least, foisting their guerrilla tactics, their self-respected killer instincts, on those that had no desire for or interest in them. Wetzel didn't have it in for Teamsters or even Bauer anymore, really. Only symbolically did his war concern these people.

The morning following Bauer's nocturnal visit, his tragic story began to take form. Wetzel never felt as justified, as sure, in anything else he had ever begun. Using the regulation method, he changed Bauer's record to show that the Ground Transportation Officer had orders releasing him from the hospital company and transferring him to a small infantry unit a few hundred miles north of Saigon, where daily confrontations with the enemy produced a high rate of casualties. Now it was simply a matter of how and when it would happen. Would Bauer be a hero or a coward when he died? It was a decision that Wetzel could make without any more real concern than flipping a coin. He decided to wait before he actually killed Bauer off. Let him get used to his new surroundings, he thought. Let him get the feel of his new duty station before he died defending or running away from it.

Wetzel cut a set of the phony orders on the office mimeo machine and distributed copies to all officers that were in some manner concerned, but not in any position to care or to do anything about them. One thing was definite: everyone believed printed orders, and orders anyhow, were orders. Among the recipients would be the United States Army Records Center in St. Louis, Missouri.

The hospital mail clerk hoisted the bag with the bogus orders from the office floor. It seemed to Wetzel that the first budging of the huge boulder that he himself had been called on to push was, that second, taking place. Now it was merely a matter of momentum. As in any large organization, minor errors would become major errors, would become glaring errors, would become more than errors, lofting themselves into the fields of absurdity until finally a frantic hush-hush would become their epitaph.

Wetzel felt as he watched the mail clerk leave Personnel and make his way to Captain Ellsworth's bunker to pick up the never-existent barracks mail that his decision to end Bauer's involvement in Vietnam, even in an advisory capacity, was doing more for his private anti-war effort than if he himself had deserted, gone on extensive AWOL, or lied his way into the hospital with phony meningitis symptoms. It was to be something finally done; in his life, something he embarked on that soon would be completed, something he could actually be proud of, Bauer's paper-death. Through his mind flashed an image of Bauer doing a short-thrust-vertical-butt-stroke. "You're a grand old flag, Bauer, but you're a big boy now."

Wetzel did wonder, weeks before and even now, who was he, Wetzel, to be deciding the number and frequency of Bauer's inoculations and now his death. His own was not a history of unblemished service in the progress of mankind. Hadn't he frittered away a quarter of a century in self-indulgent sloth and leisure? In ways, didn't he share Bauer's guilt; was there really that much difference between negative action and inaction, Wetzel wondered.

For an accountant, he had done very little accounting in his lifetime, none actually until he was hit with the reality of the sounds of mines and rockets. But Wetzel also realized the afternoon the orders were sent, his past counted for nothing. One felt experience, one significant understanding in a lifetime, sometime, and you're on your way; and all that could be said about it was, if it happened, it happened. And now Wetzel felt that he was nearing the point of its happening.

If it was Bauer who had provided the emotion for Wetzel's homicide plan, it was the zipping room that contributed reason. Whenever anyone was zipped, Wetzel had to bring down the ex-man's 201 personal file to the zipping room and check his dog tags with his file for spelling, blood type, religion, and serial number. If any one of these things was off, Wetzel would have to cut a new set, then bang them up a little for authenticity and hang them on the special hooks at the top of the zipper. Accounts checked this way: St. Louis was happy, Colonel Schooner had no reason to be unhappy. But even when things ran smoothly in the zipping room, Wetzel was unhappy about the entire situation; more than unhappy. Each trip to the room took him further and further away from believing that he actually saw what he saw. The eerie, overlit room, with its plastic cleanliness and its antiseptic pink and black bodies made imperfect by bullet holes and missing chunks, became unreal to him; part of a white light-show that he was forced to participate in and then leave, spent and drawn, as if he had danced there too long. When Bauer was in the room, as he often was, overseeing a delivery, Wetzel's anxieties became directed and plain to him: clearly Bauer was in some way responsible.

The door to Personnel opened. Bauer stood in the doorway for a second, attempting, what seemed to Wetzel, a certain effect, and then walked in. Wetzel stood up, mentally discovered, his thoughts detonated and scattered. Immediately as he was faced with the man, Wetzel was sorry that he was so mercilessly, so whimsically, so self-righteously plotting his demise. It was impossible in the intimate situation of two men standing right next to each other without weapons for Wetzel not to bridge the span between men, and, for an instant, make himself that other man. But his feeling changed the second he saw the glint in Bauer's eye. This was not the glint that would save Bauer from death. Had he come with sorrow, with reverence, with a question or a runny nose, with anything other than the look of a man thinking that what he was doing was unquestionably justified, Bauer might have been saved, Wetzel might still have relented and had him transferred back to the hospital company.

"What's this dickin' around in formation, Wetzel? I want to know about that. I let it go today. You know why?"

Sure. Wetzel knew why. It was the shots. Bauer was actually tired of the shots, the side effects, the vaccinations that must have pocked his arms like craters. Bauer had ground the gears in his sturdy but simple brain and had finally made the connection between the shots and Wetzel.

"Well, Wetzel, I'll tell you why. Your attitude here is the shits. It demoralizes, it pisses-off the men. They look at you and figure, 'Why not, if Wetzel can do it, why not me?' And when there's a war going on, there isn't any room for that sort of crap. So today I decided I wouldn't draw attention to you by yelling in front of a whole platoon, but believe me, you better change your whole way of life around here. I'm telling you that personally, here and now, so that you know I'm not just jerking you around as an example. It's you and you alone I'm going to get, unless you change that high-and-mighty garbage of yours. Believe me, Wetzel, I'll have you out of this cozy office, working your ass off permanently for me, if you don't cut the shit. Do you understand that, Wetzel? Understand?"

The man would have to die, Wetzel then decided with all his heart. Bauer had just turned Wetzel's half-formed, fairly definite whim into an irrevocable mission. He had to see Bauer's file sent away, he had to see the look on Bauer's face on payday when he didn't get his cash to buy his prophylactics, beer, and ugly trinkets. Revenge asserted itself back into Wetzel's plan. He now knew that, in order to stay in Personnel in the the weeks pending the final processes of Bauer's demise, he would have to be careful, that he would have to stay away from Bauer's shot record altogether. It was unfortunate, but a necessity. It was something in Bauer's tone that indicated this to him, something that tipped him off to the fact that Bauer would literally kill him if there was a way of making it seem in the line of duty.

"Wetzel, I asked you a question. When an officer asks you a question, you answer. Do you understand *that*, Wetzel?"

It was then, at that very instant, the second that Wetzel was to come out with his servile apology to keep him safe in his job in Personnel, as Wetzel understood the meanness of means and the glory of ends, that the hospital compound was hit soundly, initially, and accidentally by a squadron of American planes launched from the carrier *Wendell Willkie* to fly cover for some Marines about to walk into the range of at least a half-dozen machine guns guarding VC mortar implacements, a few miles from the non-city side of the hospital.

The plan to paint the roofs of the various buildings that made up the compound white with huge red crosses like the other hospitals in Southeast Asia had failed when 1st Sgt Horzkok had ordered the wrong color paint from Supply. Colonel Schooner, in an attempt to cover up for Horzkok's error, pointed out at a high-level staff meeting that the crosses were not necessary. The hospital had excellent natural camouflage; having been built by a youthful and recently drafted group of Engineers, it was a masterpiece of integrated structure and terrain. It was impossible, the colonel assured his men, to spot the sprawling bunkers from the air or even from any distance on land. Colonel Schooner had called it right, but unfortunately the perfect camouflage was not working in his favor.

The entire out-patient clinic was destroyed with the first impact. With the second went the enlisted men's barracks. The building made a decent little puff and then, after a few seconds of limbo, burned itself to the ground; just minutes before, all the sheets had been changed. The zipping area was hit and the building in which Wetzel and Bauer stood facing each other with hate, then with questioning, and finally—and Wetzel noted it distinctly in Bauer's face—with fear, collapsed around them. Filing cabinets vomited out drawers full of papers and then the cabinets themselves fell. The wooden roof collapsed, raining down thin slats and shingling, and finally, the sides, no longer feeling any responsibility for the roof, bowed and quit. In the middle of the tangle of typewriters, paper, and Army Regulation pamphlets, Bauer and Wetzel lay pinned beneath a bookshelf, bodies crossed. Wetzel had hit the ground first, covering his head, having attended that particular class in Basic, and Bauer followed,

not having attended the class but having been told about it later
by buddy Wetzel.

"Get the hell off of me, Bauer." Bauer didn't respond. Wetzel
heard further impacts off in the distance. Possibly by now Radio
Operator Keyes, whose knowledge of international code was limited to a few words and catch phrases, would have awakened and
shot a quick message to the United States Navy or the United
States something to ask for a bombing halt.

"Come on, Bauer, get the hell off!" Still no answer, but then
Wetzel heard a moan. Bauer was alive! Big deal. Of course Bauer
was alive. All that had actually landed on him were some AR
pamplets and a bookshelf which had fallen on Wetzel a few days
before when he had attempted to move it and the regulations
outside the building.

Wetzel managed to crawl out from under the Ground Transportation Officer. Off in the distance he could see a fire in one of
the wards, backlighting crafty Marines as they snuck up on the
unsuspecting VC. There were bursts of machine-gun fire, lots of
lights from flares, tracers, and flames and huge explosions from
someone's heavy artillery. The war arena had invaded the sanc-
tity of the hospital compound. Bauer pulled himself up next to
Wetzel, looking out to the left and the right as he did.

"Jesus! Come on, Wetzel. We got to do something. We can't
just stand here. Follow me to that fire!"

Wetzel ran behind the man. As he ran, all he felt was the
movement of his legs and his face heating from the blaze he
neared. Bauer spotted some men in beds behind the flames and
ran through to them. Wetzel didn't have time to decide, running
through a few steps behind him. If he had stopped for just a
second, he would have never done it. In the pulsating orange
light, he saw Bauer pick up a man from one of the beds and run
out of the building with him. Wetzel looked around, picked
someone up himself, felt the weight on his shoulders, ran with it,
was outside, and dumped it off. He started back in after another,
but this time he stopped for a second and thought. He hesitated
at the edge of the flames. In the meanwhile Bauer had torn
through and dumped another body.

"See what you can do for these men, Wetzel. I'm going back
for another."

It was the perfect reason not even to think about going back
in, realized Wetzel. Bauer had given an order and now the idiot
was running back in himself. Wetzel looked down at the men on
the ground in front of him; all three of them were dead. The one
Bauer was running in to get would probably be dead also. But

Bauer couldn't know that; he was this second too busy being a hero. Wetzel wondered, how many rights did Bauer have to do to make up for his wrongs? What went on in that plodding mind that could transform Bauer from what he ordinarily was to the man who just ran back into a burning building to save what he thought was someone's life. As Wetzel looked again at the men on the ground and heard the machine-gun fire of the Marines or the VC, he realized that it was Bauer's wrongs that, by contrast, would put him in a position to make his rights seem great. If Bauer really thought about the humanity he was lugging out of the fire, he wouldn't be here in the first place: not in this hospital, in this fire, in this war or this Army. It hit Wetzel that way, but he knew it wasn't that simple, although he wished it was.

The fire went on for most of the day and into the night before it was finally put out by equipment that Bauer, in his official capacity, commissioned from Saigon, where it was always vitally needed. The equipment was not returned the next day or the day following. Wetzel knew it would go the way of all equipment that had been borrowed by the hospital. During an inspection, Colonel Schooner would spot it, declare it obsolete, and insist it be dismantled for parts.

Personnel was rebuilt in a day. It took three days for Wetzel to straighten out all the records. In that time he re-resolved that Bauer would have to die, but it became increasingly clear, as Wetzel relived the moments of Bauer's running into the burning ward, that to have him die a coward would be a lie. It was an option that circumstance had stolen from him. It bothered him to have to admit this. What death, then, would he himself have to die? What sort of man was he, Wetzel, who would choose cowardice over almost anything else dangerous or painful? He thought and all that came to him was that the heroes must be the men who didn't attach any worth to life—what did that make them: stupid, insensitive, unappreciative, or great, vital, keyed even more to life because they were that much more closer to death? Whatever, the world needed these men; Wetzel decided that he was not one of them. Most people, though, were or wanted to be heroes.

After Bauer's file had been located and carefully arranged, Wetzel made his way to the zipping room, carrying with him the file along with a newly minted copy of Bauer's dog tags. A large hole in the room's ceiling, still not repaired from the attack, admitted the sun and rinsed everything in the room in natural light. Boxes of the zippered plastic bags sat on one side of the room on shelves labeled "small," "medium," and "large." One entire wall of the spacious chamber held the deep drawers that contained the bodies that had been recently zipped. Because the bodies would never spend more than a day in the hospital before being lifted off by helicopters to landing strips where airplanes would take them back to the States, these drawers were not refrigerated. In the latest *Army Digest*, Wetzel read in an article entitled, "The Wonders of Body Evacuation," that the body of a United States serviceman killed in Vietnam could be evacuated from a given battlefield and be back in the States in less than twenty-four hours. Implicit in the article was the message that the Army profited doubly by this efficiency: first, by not having to refrigerate the filing cabinets which held the bodies and, second, by always having empty drawers in the case of a major enemy offense.

On a smaller wall, though, there was a group of the drawers that were refrigerated. In these drawers doctors would keep such perishables as sandwiches spread with mayonnaise, beer, mixer, etc. These would usually surround the "no-names" that were also in the drawers and were bodies being held for positive identification. Occasionally, during a rush, semi-positive identifications were made by Colonel Schooner or some other high-ranking officer, and the bodies would be zipped and shipped, telegrams sent and policies paid. All in all, it was a lot cheaper than expanded refrigeration.

Wetzel opened one of these drawers. A man lay on his back in a torn and burned fatigue uniform. His face had been scarred to a charcoal anonymity and next to his left arm was some onion dip with a few pieces of potato-chip shrapnel in the center of the bowl. The no-name's uniform had no identifying patches other than the one which read "US Army," black on green so that he couldn't be spotted by the enemy during nightfall. There were no dog tags; they had probably been destroyed in the same fire that the man had died in, obliterated in the heat.

The second before he decided anything, Wetzel noticed in the sunlight how very calm the no-name looked; the pressure was off. The only thing left for him to do was to lie there and eventually decompose. Compose, decompose, he thought; no matter, there was work to be done. "Well, Bauer, it may be better than you deserve; I'm not really sure. But I'll do my best for you." He wrote Bauer's name on the man's chest with the regulation pen, zipped him in the plastic bag on which he lay, and, with his own heart beating with notable panic, transferred him to a slot in the non-refrigerated section. In less than two hours there would be another lift-off; in less than ten the body would be on its way back to the States. Bauer, as his file had indicated, had no living family, no loved ones. The beneficiary on his Army insurance policy was a Teamsters local in Detroit, who, when they found out about Brother Bauer's demise, would cancel his card, take the $10,000, and have a wake with the corpse in absentia. Wetzel affixed Bauer's dog tags to the bag.

Then he went back to Personnel and cut orders to the unit that Bauer was supposedly transferred to, to drop Bauer's name from the morning report and all other rosters. To the Army Records Center in St. Louis and to the Pentagon, Wetzel sent the following letter:

> Sirs:
>
> *1st Lt Ernest L. Bauer, 0967543, a short time in my command as Unit Transportation Officer, was fatally wounded when trying to drive a burning truck away from our ammunition dump. Through his courageous action, the lives of our entire company are in his debt.*
>
> *I therefore recommend that Lt Bauer receive commendation for his valor, hopefully in the form of the Distinguished Service Cross. Lt Bauer lives in our minds as an example to us all.*
>
> WILFRED KRIEG, MAJ, INF-USRA *045328*
> *6789th Inf Reg, Quo Hop, SEA*

Major Krieg, Wetzel had learned in the *Vietnam Newsletter*, had been recently captured by the VC, so there was little or no official way to check the story out. Besides, there was no time to check stories out. In the meanwhile, Wetzel knew that with the receipt of his letter, Personnel at Quo Hop would be desperately dummying-up records to show that Bauer *had* been there. It was far better than trying to deny it. If they did, there would be investigations, the Inspector General would insist on auditing all the reports filed in the time of Bauer's supposed presence. It was better, far better, to change a few records, to forge Bauer's signature in a few places. Wetzel also sent Quo Hop a belated copy of Bauer's phony original orders, those that transferred him there in the first place. With them, Quo Hop would have nothing to worry about. It was now only a matter of hours before the Teamsters local would be notified.

With the death of Bauer completed, Wetzel, who had been short of breath ever since he had lifted the no-name from the "pending" to the "out" file, sat and slowly mused over what he

had done. And indeed, it had been done. In its execution, he
realized its infallibility. The huge wheels, though held on by
plastic cotter pins, would run true; turning and churning, they
would soon eliminate a member. Somewhere in St. Louis, Bauer's
duplicate file would be pulled and put into another container;
somewhere in the Pentagon, the decision was being made about
Bauer's decoration. Wetzel had done what the negotiators had
been trying to do. And he did it without violence, without more
destruction, and, the second he actually zipped the bag, without
any personal hate.

He wondered: if one man could be so easily eliminated, what
about a platoon of men, a company, an entire regiment? It would
be a graceful and honorable withdrawal. The Army had actually
provided the framework for it to be done, what with each man's
complex file, the mass of orders and orders countermanding orders, the regulations that by their mere volume would have to
lead to a notable contradiction—a massive one that could bring
the Leviathan crashing from the sea. He would have to study it
all more carefully before he went on.

In the rearranging of the files, Wetzel did run into the regulation that earlier he had expended so much energy looking for,
the one which quite clearly outlined his way back to the States. It
would work if he changed a few things on his own file. Other
than that, it involved having a stateside contact locate an old
man dying in a hospital and having the man claim that Wetzel
was his son, his only family. The Red Cross would be notified
and, in turn, would notify Personnel in Southeast Asia for verification. If the stories checked, in less than twenty-four hours,
Wetzel could be at the old man's bedside. And possibly the man
would grab at the last of life—and the choice of the old man
would have to be wisely made—leaving Wetzel at his bedside for
the duration of his active obligation. It would be time well-spent,
Wetzel conjectured; he would give an old man, who may well
have been in a war himself, some solace by telling him that,
indeed, he was dying in vain, but that we all did. "The world
didn't improve between our wars, old man, it just got a little
more complicated."

But Wetzel decided to forgo this loophole. He was onto something bigger, something far more worthwhile. Now, as he read
through the regulations to see what else there was to do, he
anxiously awaited the initial correspondence that would be crossing the Personnel desk. It was inevitable that the note would
come from St. Louis, a response to Bauer's urgent request. It

would state as succinctly as possible, composed and typed by someone in Personnel:

Dear 1st Lt Bauer:

The reason that you were not paid on 1 Jul68 was because you were killed in action a month preceding your request. You have been awarded the Purple Heart and the Distinguished Service Cross for your heroic service.

Further explanation of this matter will be found in AR 167–18, Sec. 3, para 4, "Payment Procedures." Any further correspondence should be taken up with:

AM-AGAP, 67543
APO San Francisco

Sp5 Giles Blanchey
Personnel Specialist

DOSSY O

Clarence Major

Shit! I don't feel good notime, baby, not here in all dis mess, and ain't no sense in me trying to pretend that I understand why I'm here or trying to bullshit somebody into thinking I know what all these generals mean when they demand "large scale fighting" or that I understand and sympathize with a mammyfucker like Sergeant Moke; yeah, the fathead rube with the sweat rings reliably around his ass, his shirt collar, his nose, and his redneck; me and Cocaine call him Hootenanny the Flagwaver. I get so pissing disgusted I don't even like to talk; for days baby I don't say shit to none of these lame peckerwoods these Discipline-drag-legs walking around here acting like they got as much invested here as some of them cats so waybackintheshadows you never see, hear their names whose for real da boss; yeah, all kinds of battle-fatigue monkeys strolling around here, bad shots hitting psychological maggie drawers all day long; I just get tired *tired* I keep a big funky headache all the time: lately I ain't said nothing to nobody but Dossy O, that's Cocaine which is the way my man keeps hisself together. I can't blame anybody here for getting high; if you felt like a battering ram, somebody's monkey-time doodlesquat which is what they had our man Bob Churchill into until we pulled his coat told him damn baby how long you gone be a chump we been checking you out ever since we landed . . . I think the deep furrow of our message got to him. Sergeant Dossy O Bud Cocaine Lemon a little bitty dude but wide with big muscles coming at you from behind thick horn-rimmed glasses is my ace boon coon! Me and Bob Churchy sometimes call him Hopperlone Cane, or just plain Hophead or Hopstick or Hoss like keeping each other in stitches is one means of surviving this hubba-hubba flagwaving get-them-first thing when I first shipped into this regiment my thoughts started moving along the lines of

getting out. I heard so many brothers quiet as its kept get washed
up and put in prison for just thinking the way I thought to say
the least. I laid in my sack night after night weighing the crucial
matter fearfully carefully. I thought about it for possibly 24
hundred hours a day through tough extended trips into self; I
knew a Vietnamese faker, a real expert, had an in with a lot of
black market people a lot of Victor Charlies I suspected he was
from Hanoi though he denied it said he was a former officer in
the Army of the Republic, even claimed he was tight with several
very powerful smooth persons in Saigon who could get me
straight into China with absolutely no hassle crossing the Bamboo Curtain but how do you know a little grinning buckteeth
sapsucker like dat ain't trying to murphy you? You just don't. He
seemed very sure he could ease me like a breeze for the right
bread of course right into Sweden where I could get political and
military immunity just oodles of it I never told anybody what
was on my mind during the few days I met with him except right
after the last time I met with him I found Bud under the half
roof of a hut in a captured village. He was nodding, his gear
disposed around him. I sat down, and eased mine off; we had
extra heavy loads being the only two Medical Tech Assistants in
the unit it was always good to rest all dat shit. When I first
started wearing it the straps ate belligerently into my shoulder
blades now its O.K. I'm just like a jinxed jackass I can't even
think about it no more Bud told me that day: "I'd be the last cat
to tell you not to do it if I had the nerve—I'd get my simple-
minded ass outta this muckety-muck jive Sylvester's whipping on
me! But I think about my baby brother at home growing up in a
bullshit city like Chicago and he ain't got nobody to look up to
but me you dig; so I kinda owe it to the dude to make it back
there; to answer as many questions for him as I can if I didn't
stay high baby I'd have probably run up to Captain George Rat
Cheese Zedtwitz heself a long time ago and put a birthday cake
full of surprises into his hands; and the same goes for 2nd Lieutenant Sal Magoo Ramono and faggot 1st Lieutenant John Madison Avenue Brinkerhoff too!" "Yeah," I said. *That* rap by Bud
put my mind on strike to demand of my heart a logical enough
reason to want to go back to the States; I couldn't get any
homespun shit together on this score so I got some honorary
convictions slightly boosted by logical respect for death you dig
'cause anything as torrid as getting-your-hat right in the middle
of military commitment is a highly repeat highly dangerous activity so dis is why I'm still in Captain Sedtwitz's regiment still
responsible to 2nd Lieutenant Sal Ramono still have to chance a

look at Hootenanny's nasty red face every day this is why too I never feel really gooooood you know deep down good never. It's been three days now since we had any action and that was only a kind of routine thing where we kinda dashed in and finished taking the beauty out of a couple of old harmless men and about six children they were turned over to Master Serg Dokus Mokus for delivery to Battalion prison control detachment some five kilometers behind us because no helicopter from the unit nor higher up from Company Command could be sent in well you know what happened to them Dokus who was returned by helicopter the next morning said "By God, them crazy VCs ain't got a bit of sense: they plum ran away from me and I had to shoot 'em." Later after Captain Zedtwitz and his fun flunkies had the incident report written up and everybody tough theoretically had forgotten it Dossy O asked Rube Moke, "Did you shoot 'em in the back?" and Mississippi Moke said: "Listen, you little sawed-off nigger, I don't have to explain a dagblasted thing to the likes of you! You uppity nigras think you own the world! All the godblasted fuss you people raise back home proves that you're not true Americans and ain't got no respect for law and order if it was up to me I wouldn't have none of you defending the country you don't love it I would—" Coke cut him off: "You would jump into a tub of Cap'n Rat Cheese's shit and eat it if he commanded you to wouldn't you? You big muckety-muck slab of—" WOOPH! Fathead Moke's fist put a spell on Hoss who quickly recovered his dignity from the ground obviously still quite dizzy and tired but tried to get to Mississippi when Cap'n Ratty Cheese came up from a nap in the surviving basement of what was once a well-built Indo-China house never touched by the French, who were here before we were, trying to do something like what we're trying to do. When Cheese came to the surface we were all about to take sides and waltz a war dance. There's just no way on earth I can elevate a killer like Stars and Stripes Moke-anny to the level of a human divine creature when I think back on the drama of his battlefield history and how he's so tolerated by these upstanding officers and his fella countrymen how he gets Affirms on requests a boot'd have a bitch of a time copping; I remember dat time Bud and I accidented into the Butcher himself and his running ace Smith engaged in a act of their common sadism and killing that day the antiaircraft TAT TAT TAT TAT TAT TAT ratratratratrat-rat-rat-rat shit sounding everywhere along the parallel we'd just reached can't remember which one like that's a month ago which now seems a year back in all this contradiction you notice I even stop trying

to talk proper shit whatda fuck difference do it makes dats what I
ask! Anyway, the Air Force drivers were laying eggs all over the
designated VC installations zone we wuz s'pose to move in on
and sop up being grunts which is what you do while you shit
that's the way they seed us this action was not far from the Ho
Chi Minh Trail, if memory ain't failed me. Dossy had busted a
cap and got heself together never touched shit til Sam got him
under all dis pressure he was ready to walk right in and fuckup
Mississippi Moke if he could catch him that's why we'd come shit
I can't remember boo koos of kilometers 'fore we began to really
hear the mortar shells singing in them curves they take, the
perfection of US electric magic! You sometimes had to just stand-
back and look up there in amazement at those US Discipline-
Conformity cats and say Wow! they really could workout
takecareofbusiness their particular kind, you dig; even if the war
wasn't honorable like the Trojan War where a good cause was at
the center where pussy always is suppose to be anyway now these
flying Trojan Horses with all their traditional help had us and
the Army of The Republic of Vietnam, which Coke Bud L.
called "Marvin," while the rest of the USA Army settled for a less
remote corruption "Arvn." Anyway mortar shells kept on tinging
the sky all morning as we waited in our DMZ foxholes busting
blood rivers into lives already trapped deep in hot frigid death
cracking our eardrums while most of us applauded the numbing
skill of the US drivers. For days man after a deal like that we'd
go to sleep with our ears skunky from the decimation of it so
when the pilots split back to the US birdman (aircraft carrier)
we'd hubba-hubba ah ambitious cadence in to mopup the rotten
eggs and this particular time is when Wallace Sylvester Mokus
and Smitty turned my stomach so profoundly I gag everytime I
see 'em I could never before eat with 'em in my eyesight but
afterwards it became impossible to look at him I never would
have believed Moke'd cry though that same day it was just as we
were about to go in for the mopup when the last bomber aircraft
was splitting that we heard the one just before it crash into the
cables on the carrier and the boltering killed the pilot instantly
that got Moke's tears I heard that the Cap'n patted him on the
back like he was a baby and Madison Avenue tongue in cheek
said looking at the Cap'n: "The best soldier we have in this
outfit, sir!" And ol stonewall agreed with him. I know nobody on
earth would believe such an unmilitary act and statement coming from an officer I found it hard to swallow 'cause I never for a
moment thought Georgia Cap'n Sedtwitz could ever pat anybody
on the back anyway.

ILLUMINATION ROUNDS

Michael Herr

We were all strapped into the seats of the Chinook, fifty of us, and something, someone, was hitting it from the outside with an enormous hammer. *How do they do that,* I thought, *we're a thousand feet in the air!* But it had to be that, over and over, shaking the helicopter, making it dip and turn in a horrible out-of-control motion that took me in the stomach. I had to laugh, it was so exciting, it was the thing I had wanted, almost what I had wanted except for that wrenching, resonant metal-echo; I could hear it even above the noise of the rotor blades. And they were going to fix that, I knew they would make it stop. They had to, it was going to make me sick.

They were all replacements going in to mop up after the big battles on Hills 875 and 876, the battles that had already taken on the name of one great battle, the Battle of Dak To. And I was new, brand-new, three days incountry, embarrassed about my boots because they were so new. And across from me, ten feet away, a boy tried to jump out of the straps and then jerked forward and hung there, his rifle barrel caught in the red plastic webbing of the seat-back. As the chopper rose again and turned, his weight went back hard against the webbing and a dark spot the size of a baby's hand showed in the center of his fatigue jacket. And it grew—I knew what it was, but not really—it got up to his armpits and then started down his sleeves and up over his shoulders at the same time. It went all across his waist and down his legs, covering the canvas on his boots until they were dark like everything else he wore, and it was running in slow, heavy drops off his fingertips. I thought I could hear the drops hitting the metal strip on the chopper floor. Hey! . . . oh, but this isn't anything at all, it's not real, it's just some *thing* they're going through that isn't real. One of the door gunners was heaped up on the floor like a cloth dummy. His hand had the bloody raw look of a pound of liver fresh from the butcher paper. We touched down on the same LZ we had left just a few minutes before, but I didn't know it until one of the guys shook my shoulder, and then I couldn't stand up. All I could feel of my legs was their shaking, and the guy thought I'd been hit and helped me up. The chopper had taken eight hits, there was shattered plastic all over the floor, a dying pilot up front, and the boy was hanging forward in the straps again; he was dead, but not (I knew) really dead.

It took me a month to lose that feeling of being a spectator to something that was part game, part show. That first afternoon, before I'd boarded the Chinook, a black sergeant had tried to keep me from going. He told me I was too new to go near the kind of shit they were throwing around up in those hills. ("You a reporter?" he'd asked, and I'd said, "No, a writer," dumbass and pompous, and he'd laughed and said, "Careful. You can't use no eraser up where you wanna go.") He'd pointed to the bodies of all the dead Americans lined in two long rows near the chopper pad, so many that they could not even cover all of them decently. But they were not real then, and taught me nothing. The Chinook had come in, blowing my helmet off, and I grabbed it up and joined the replacements waiting to board. "Okay, man," the sergeant said. "You gotta go, you gotta go. All's I can say is, I hope you get a clean wound."

The battle for Hill 875 was over, and some survivors were being brought in by Chinook to the landing strip at Dak To. The 173rd Airborne had taken over 400 casualties, nearly 200 killed, most of them on the previous afternoon and in the fighting that had gone on all through the night. It was very cold and wet up there, and some Red Cross girls had been sent up from Pleiku to comfort the survivors. As the troops filed out of the helicopters, the girls waved and smiled at them from behind their serving tables. "Hi soldier! What's your name?" "Where you from, soldier?" "I'll bet some hot coffee would hit the spot about now."

And the men from the 173rd just kept walking without answering, staring straight ahead, their eyes rimmed with red from fatigue, their faces pinched and aged with all that had happened during the night. One of them dropped out of line and said something to a loud, fat girl who wore a Peanuts sweatshirt under her fatigue blouse, and she started to cry. The rest just walked past the girls and the large, olive-drab coffee urns. They had no idea of where they were.

At one time they would have lighted your cigarette for you on the terrace of the Continental Hotel. But those days are almost twenty years gone, and anyway, who really misses them? Now there is a crazy American who looks like George Orwell, and he is always sleeping off his drinks in one of the wicker chairs there, slumped against a table, starting up with violence, shouting and then going back to sleep. He makes everyone nervous, especially the waiters: the old ones who had served the French and the Japanese and the first American journalists and O.S.S. types ("Those noisy bastards at the Continental," Graham Greene called them.) and the really young ones who bussed the tables and pimped in a modest way. The little elevator boy still greets the guests each morning with a quiet "*Ça va?*", but he is seldom answered, and the old baggage man (he also brings us grass) will sit in the lobby and say, "How are you tomorrow?"

"The Ballad of Billy Joe" plays from speakers mounted on the terrace's corner columns, but the air seems too heavy to carry the sound right, and it hangs in the corners. There is an exhausted, drunk master sergeant from the First Infantry Division who has bought a flute from the old man in khaki shorts and pith helmet who sells instruments along Tu Do Street. The old man will lean over the butt-strewn flower boxes that line the terrace and play "Frère Jacques" on a wooden stringed instrument. The sergeant has bought the flute, and he is playing it quietly, pensively, badly.

The tables are crowded with American civilian construction engineers, men getting $30,000 a year from their jobs on government contracts and matching that easily on the black market. Their faces have the look of aerial photos of silicone pits, all hung with loose flesh and standing veins. Their mistresses were among the prettiest, saddest girls in Vietnam. I always wondered what they had looked like before they'd made their arrangements with the engineers. You'd see them at the tables there, smiling their hard, empty smiles into those rangy, brutal, scared faces. No wonder those men all looked alike to the Vietnamese; after a while, they all looked alike to me. Out on the Bien Hoa Highway, north of Saigon, there is a monument to the Vietnamese war dead, and it is one of the few graceful things left in the country. It is a modest pagoda set above the road and approached by long flights of gently rising steps. One Sunday, I saw a bunch of these engineers gunning their Harleys up those steps, laughing and shouting in the afternoon sun. The Vietnamese had a special name for them to distinguish them from all other Americans; it translated out to something like "The Terrible Ones," although I'm told that this doesn't even approximate the odium carried in the original.

There was a young sergeant in the Special Forces, stationed at the C Detachment in Can Tho that served as the SF headquarters for IV Corps. In all, he had spent thirty-six months in Vietnam. This was his third extended tour, and he planned to come back again as soon as he possibly could after this current hitch was finished. During his last tour, he had lost a finger and part of a thumb in a firefight, and he had been generally shot up enough times for the three Purple Hearts which mean that you don't have to fight in Vietnam anymore. After all that, I guess they thought of him as a combat liability, but he was such a hard-charger that they gave him the EM Club to manage. He ran it well and seemed happy, except that he had gained a lot of weight in the duty, and it set him apart from the rest of the men. He loved to horse around with the Vietnamese in the compound, leaping on them from behind, leaning heavily on them, shoving them around and pulling their ears, sometimes punching them a little hard in the stomach, smiling a stiff small smile that was meant to tell them all that he was just being playful. The Vietnamese would smile too, until he turned to walk away. He loved the Vietnamese, he said, he really *knew* them after three years. As far as he was concerned, there was no place in the world as fine as Vietnam. And back home in North Carolina, he had a large, glass-covered display case in which he kept his medals and decorations and citations, the photographs taken during three tours and countless battles, letters from past commanders, a few souvenirs. The case stood in the center of the living room, he said, and every night his wife and three kids would move the kitchen table out in front of it and eat their dinner there.

At eight hundred feet we knew we were being shot at. Something hit the underside of the chopper but did not penetrate it. They weren't firing tracers, but we saw the brilliant flickering blips of light below, and the pilot circled and came down very fast, working the button that released fire from the flex guns mounted on either side of the Huey. Every fifth round was a tracer, and they sailed out and down, incomparably graceful, closer and closer, until they met the tiny point of light coming from the jungle. The ground fire stopped, and we went on to land at Vinh Long, where the pilot yawned and said, "I think I'll go to bed early tonight and see if I can wake up with any enthusiasm for this war."

A twenty-four-year-old Special Forces captain was telling me about it. "I went out and killed one VC and liberated a prisoner. Next day the major called me in and told me that I'd killed fourteen VC and liberated six prisoners. You want to see the medal?"

There was a little air-conditioned restaurant on the corner of Le Loi and Tu Do, across from the Continental Hotel and the old opera house which now served as the Vietnamese Lower House. Some of us called it the Graham Greene Milk Bar (a scene in "The Quiet American" had taken place there), but its name was Givral. Every morning, they baked their own *baguettes* and *criossants*, and the coffee wasn't too bad. Sometimes I'd meet there with a friend of mine for breakfast.

He was a Belgian, a tall, slow-moving man of thirty who'd been born in the Congo. He professed to know and love war, and he affected the mercenary sensibility. He'd been photographing the Vietnam thing for seven or eight years now, and once in a while he'd go over to Laos and run around the jungles there with the government, searching for the dreaded Pathet Lao, which he pronounced "Paddy Lao." Other people's stories of Laos always made it sound like a lotus-land where no one wanted to hurt anyone, but he said that whenever he went on ops there he always kept a grenade taped to his belly because he was a Catholic and knew what the Paddy Lao would do to him if he were captured. But he was a little crazy that way, and tended to dramatize his war stories.

He always wore dark glasses, probably even during operations. His pictures sold to the wire services, and I saw a few of them in the American news magazines. He was very kind in a gruff, off-hand sort of way; kindness embarrassed him, and he was so graceless among people, so eager to shock, that he couldn't understand why so many of us liked him. Irony was the effect he worked for in conversation, that and a sense of how exquisite the war could be when all of its machinery was running right. He was explaining the finish of an operation he'd just been on in War Zone C, above Cu Chi.

"There were a lot of dead VC," he said. "Dozens and dozens of them! A lot of them were from that same village that has been giving you so much trouble lately. VC from top to bottom—

Michael, in that village the fucking *ducks* are VC. So the American commander had twenty or thirty of the dead flown up in a sling-load and dropped into the village. I should say it was a drop of at least two hundred feet, all those dead Vietcongs, right in the middle of the village."

He smiled (I couldn't see his eyes).

"Ah, Psywar!" he said, kissing off the tips of his fingers.

Bob Stokes of *Newsweek* told me this: In the big Marine hospital in Danang, they have what is called the "White Lie Ward," where they bring some of the worst cases, the ones that can be saved but who will never be the same again. A young Marine was carried in, still unconscious and full of morphine, and his legs were gone. As he was being carried into the ward, he came to briefly and saw a Catholic chaplain standing over him.

"Father," he said, "am I all right?"

The chaplain didn't know what to say. "You'll have to talk about that with the doctors, son."

"Father, are my legs okay?"

"Yes," the chaplain said. "Sure."

By the next afternoon the shock had worn off, and the boy knew all about it. He was lying on his cot when the chaplain came by.

"Father," the Marine said, "I'd like to ask you for something."

"What, son?"

"I'd like to have that cross." And he pointed to the tiny silver insignia on the chaplain's lapel.

"Of course," the chaplain said. "But why?"

"Well, it was the first thing I saw when I came to yesterday, and I'd like to have it."

The chaplain removed the cross and handed it to him. The Marine held it tightly in his fist and looked at the chaplain.

"You lied to me, Father," he said. "You cocksucker. You lied to me."

His name was Davies, and he was a gunner with a helicopter group based at Tan Son Nhut airport. On paper, by the regulations, he was billeted in one of the big "hotel" BEQs in Cholon, but he only kept his things there. He actually lived in a small two-story Vietnamese house deeper inside of Cholon, as far from the papers and the regulations as he could get. Every morning he took an Army bus with wire-grill windows out to the base and flew missions, mostly around War Zone C, along the Cambodian border, and most nights he returned to the house in Cholon where he lived with his "wife" (he'd found her in one of the bars) and some other Vietnamese who were said to be the girl's family. Her mamma-san and her brother were always there, living on the first floor, and there were others who came and went. He seldom saw the brother, but every few days he would find a pile of labels and brand names torn from cardboard cartons, American products that the brother wanted from the PX.

The first time I saw him he was sitting alone at a table on the Continental terrace, drinking a beer. He had a full, drooping moustache and sharp, sad eyes, and he was wearing a denim workshirt and wheat jeans. He also carried a Leica and a copy of *Ramparts Magazine,* and I just assumed at first that he was a correspondent. I didn't know then that you could buy *Ramparts* at the PX, and after I'd borrowed and returned it, we began to talk. It was the issue that featured left-wing Catholics like Jesus Christ and Fulton Sheen on the cover. *"Catholique?"* one of the bar girls said later that night. *"Moi aussi,"* and she kept the magazine. That was when we were walking around Cholon in the rain trying to find Hoa, his wife. Mamma-san had told us that she'd gone to the movies with some girl friends, but Davies knew what she was doing.

"I hate that shit," he said. "It's so uncool."

"Well, don't put up with it."

"Yeah."

Davies' house was down a long narrow alley that became nothing more than a warren at the end, smelling of camphor-smoke and fish, crowded but clean. He would not speak to Mamma-san, and we walked straight up to the second floor. It was one long room that had a sleeping area screened off in an arrangement of filmy curtains. At the top of the stairs there was a large poster of Lenny Bruce, and beneath it, in a shrine effect, was a low table with a Buddha and lighted incense on it.

"Lenny," Davies said.

Most of one wall was covered with a collage that Davies had done with the help of some friends. It included photos of burning monks, stacked Vietcong dead, wounded Marines screaming and weeping, Cardinal Spellman waving from a chopper, Ronald Reagan, his face halved and separated by a stalk of cannabis; pictures of John Lennon peering through wire-rimmed glasses, Mick Jagger, Jimi Hendrix, Dylan, Eldridge Cleaver, Rap Brown; coffins draped with American flags whose stars were replaced by swastikas and dollar signs; odd parts clipped from *Playboy* pictures, newspaper headlines (Farmers Butcher Hogs to Protest Pork Price Dip), photo captions (President Jokes with Newsmen), beautiful girls holding flowers, showers of peace symbols; Ky standing at attention and saluting, a small mushroom cloud forming where his genitalia should have been; a map of the Western United States with the shape of Vietnam reversed and fitted over California; and one large, long figure that began at the bottom with shiny leather boots and rouged knees and ascended in a microskirt, bare breasts, graceful shoulders, and a long neck, topped by the burned, blackened face of a dead Vietnamese woman.

By the time Davies' friends showed up, we were already stoned. We could hear them below, laughing and rapping with Mamma, and then they came up the stairs, three blacks and two white guys.

"It sure do smell *peculiar* up here," one of them said.

"Hi, you freaky li'l fuckers."

"This grass is Number Ten," Davies said. "Every time I smoke this grass over here it gives me a bad trip."

"Ain' nuthin' th' matter with that grass," someone said. "It ain' the grass."

"Where's Hoa?"

"Yeah, Davies, where's your ole lady at?"

"She's out hustling Saigon tea, and I'm fucking sick of it." He tried to look really angry, but he only looked unhappy.

One of them handed off a joint and stretched out. "Hairy day today," he said.

"Where'd you fly?"

"Bu Dop."

"Bu Dop!" one of the spades said, and he started to move toward the joint, jiving and working his shoulders, bobbing his head. "Bu Dop, budop, bu dop dop *dop!*"

"Funky funky Bu Dop."

"Hey, man, can you O.D. on grass?"

"I dunno, baby. Maybe we could get jobs at the Aberdeen Proving Grounds smokin' dope for Uncle Sugar."

"Wow, I'm stoned. Hey, Davies, you stoned?"

"Yeah," Davies said.

It started to rain again, so hard that you couldn't hear drops, only the full force of the water pouring down on the metal roof. We smoked a little more, and then the others started to leave. Davies looked like he was sleeping with his eyes open.

"That goddam pig," he said. "Fuckin' whore. Man, I'm paying out all this bread for the house, and those people downstairs. I don't even know who they are, for Christ's sake. I'm really . . . I'm getting sick of it."

"You're pretty short now," someone said. "Why don't you cut out?"

"You mean just split?"

"Why not?"

Davies was quiet for a long time.

"Yeah," he finally said. "This is bad. This is really bad. I think I'm going to get out of here."

A bird colonel, commanding a brigade of the 4th Infantry Division: "I'll bet you always wondered why we call 'em Dinks up in this part of the country. I thought of it myself. I'll tell you, I never *did* like hearing them called Charlie. See, I had an uncle named Charlie, and I liked him, too. No, Charlie was just too damn good for the little bastards. So I just thought, What are they *really* like? and I came up with rinky-dink. Suits 'em just perfect, Rinky-Dink, 'cause that's what they are. 'Cept that was too long, so we cut it down some. And that's why we call 'em Dinks."

One morning before dawn, Ed Fouhy, a former Saigon bureau chief for CBS, went out to the 8th Aerial Port at Tan Son Nhut to catch the early military flight to Danang. They boarded as the sun came up, and Fouhy strapped in next to a kid in rumpled fatigues, one of those soldiers you see whose weariness has gone far beyond physical exhaustion, into that state where no amount of sleep will give them the kind of rest they need. Every torpid movement they make tells you that they are tired, that they'll stay tired until their tours are up and the big bird flies them back to the World. Their eyes are dim with it, their faces almost puffy, and when they smile, you have to accept it as a token.

There was a standard question you could use to open a conversation with troops, and Fouhy tried it. "How long you been in-country?" he asked.

The kid half-lifted his head; that question could *not* be serious. The weight was really on him, and the words came slowly:

"All . . . fuckin' . . . day," he said.

"You guys ought do a story on me suntahm," the kid said. He was a helicopter gunner, six-three with an enormous head that sat in bad proportion to the rest of his body and a line of picket teeth that were always on show in a wet, uneven smile. Every few seconds he would have to wipe his mouth with the back of his hand, and when he talked to you his face was always an inch from yours, so that I had to take my glasses off to keep them dry.

He was from Kilgore, Texas, and he was on his seventeenth consecutive month in-country.

"Why should we do a story about you?"

" 'Cause I'm so fuckin' good," he said, " 'n' that ain' no shit, neither. Got me one hunnert 'n' fifty-se'en gooks kilt. 'N' fifty caribou." He grinned and stanched the saliva for a second. "Them're all certified," he added.

The chopper touched down at Ba Xoi and we got off, not unhappy about leaving him. "Lis'n," he said, laughing, "you git up onna ridgeline, see y' keep yer head down. Y'heah?"

"Say, how'd you get to be a co-respondent an' come ovah to this raggedy-ass motherfucker?"

He was a really big spade, rough-looking even when he smiled, and he wore a gold nose-bead fastened through his left nostril. I told him that the nose-bead blew my mind, and he said that was all right, it blew everybody's mind. We were sitting by the chopper pad of an LZ above Kontum. He was trying to get to Dak To, I was heading for Pleiku, and we both wanted to get out of there before nightfall. We took turns running out to the pad to check the choppers that kept coming in and taking off, neither of us were having any luck, and after we'd talked for an hour he laid a joint on me and we smoked.

"I been heah mo'n eight months now," he said. "I bet I been in mo'n twenny firefights. An' I ain' hardly fired back once."

"How come?"

"Shee-it, I go firin' back, I might kill one a th' Brothers, you dig it?"

I nodded, no Vietcong ever called *me* honky, and he told me that in his company alone there were more than a dozen Black Panthers, and that he was one of them. I didn't say anything, and then he said that he wasn't just a Panther; he was an agent for the Panthers, sent over here to recruit. I asked him what kind of luck he'd been having, and he said fine, real fine. There was a fierce wind blowing across the LZ, and the joint didn't last very long.

"Hey baby," he said. "That was jes' some jive I tole you. Shit, I ain' no Panther. I'se jes' fuckin' with you, see what you'd say."

"But the Panthers have guys over here. I've met some."

"Tha' could be," he said, and he laughed.

A Huey came in, and he jogged out to see where it was headed. It was going to Dak To, and he came back to get his gear. "Later, baby," he said. "An' luck." He jumped into the chopper, and as it rose from the strip he leaned out and laughed, bringing his arm up and bending it back toward him, palm out and the fist clenched tightly in the Sign.

One day I went out with the ARVN on an operation in the rice paddies above Vinh Long, forty terrified Vietnamese troops and five Americans, all packed into three Hueys that dropped us up to our hips in paddy muck. I had never been in a rice paddy before. We spread out and moved toward the marshy swale that led to the jungle. We were still twenty feet from the first cover, a low paddy wall, when we took fire from the treeline. It was probably the working half of a crossfire that had somehow gone wrong. It caught one of the ARVN in the head, and he dropped back into the water and disappeared. We made it to the wall with two casualties. There was no way of stopping their fire, no room to send out a flanking party, so gunships were called in and we crouched behind the wall and waited. There was a lot of fire coming from the trees, but we were all right as long as we kept down. And I was thinking, Oh man, so this is a rice paddy, yes, wow! when I suddenly heard an electric guitar shooting right up into my ear and a mean, rapturous black voice singing, coaxing, "Now c'mon baby, stop actin' so crazy," and when I got it all together I turned to see a grinning black corporal hunched over a cassette recorder. "Might's well," he said. "We ain' goin *no*-where till them gunships come."

That's the story of the first time I ever heard Jimi Hendrix, but in a war where a lot of people talked about Aretha's "Satisfaction" the way other people speak of Brahms' Fourth, it was more than a story; it was Credentials. "Say, that Jimi Hendrix is my main man," someone would say. "He has *def*initely got his shit together!" Hendrix had once been in the 101st Airborne, and the Airborne in Vietnam was full of wiggy-brilliant spades like him, really mean and really good, guys who always took care of you when things got bad. That music meant a lot to them. I never once heard it played over the Armed Forces Radio Network.

The sergeant had lain out near the clearing for almost two hours with a wounded medic. He had called over and over for a Medevac, but none had come. Finally, a chopper from another outfit, an LOH, appeared, and he was able to reach it by radio. The pilot told him that he'd have to wait for one of his own ships, they weren't coming down, and the sergeant told the pilot that if he did not land for them he was going to open fire on them from the ground and fucking well *bring* him down. So they were picked up that way, but there were repercussions.

The commander's code name was Mal Hombre, and he reached the sergeant later that afternoon from a place with the call signal Violent Meals.

"God *damn* it, Sergeant," he said through the static. "I thought you were a professional soldier."

"I waited as long as I could, sir. Any longer, I was gonna lose my man."

"This outfit is perfectly capable of taking care of its own dirty laundry. Is that clear, Sergeant?"

"Colonel, since when is a wounded trooper 'dirty laundry'?"

"At ease, Sergeant," Mal Hombre said, and radio contact was broken.

There was a spec 4 in the Special Forces at Can Tho, a shy Indian boy from Chinle, Arizona, with large, wet eyes the color of ripe olives and a quiet way of speaking, a really nice way of putting things, kind to everyone without ever being stupid or soft about it. On the night that the compound and the airstrip were hit, he came and asked me if there was a chaplain anywhere around. He wasn't very religious, he said, but he was worried about tonight. He'd just volunteered for a "suicide squad," two jeeps that were going to drive across the airstrip with mortars and a recoilless rifle. It looked bad, I had to admit it; there were so few of us in the compound that they'd had to put me on the reaction force. It might be bad. He just had a feeling about it, he'd seen what always happened to guys whenever they got that feeling, at least he *thought* it was that feeling, a bad one, the worst he'd ever had.

I told him that the only chaplains I could think of would be in the town, and we both knew that the town was cut off.

"Oh," he said. "Look then. If I get it tonight . . ."

"It'll be okay."

"Listen, though. If it happens . . . I think it's going to . . . Will you make sure the colonel tells my folks I was looking for a chaplain, anyway?"

I promised, and the jeeps loaded and drove off. I heard later that there had been a brief firefight, but that no one had been hurt. They didn't have to use the recoilless. They all drove back into the compound two hours later. The next morning at breakfast, he sat at another table, saying a lot of loud, brutal things about the gooks, and he wouldn't look at me. But at noon he came over and squeezed my arm and smiled, his eyes fixed somewhere just to the right of my own.

For two days now, ever since the Tet Offensive had begun, they had been coming by the hundreds to the province hospital at Can Tho. They were usually either very young or very old or women, and their wounds were often horrible. The more lightly wounded were being treated quickly in the hospital yard, and the more serious cases were simply placed in one of the corridors to die. There were just too many of them to treat, the doctors had worked without a break, and now, on the second afternoon, the Vietcong began shelling the hospital.

One of the Vietnamese nurses handed me a cold can of beer and asked me to take it down the hall, where one of the Army surgeons was operating. The door of the room was ajar, and I walked right in. I probably should have looked first. A little girl was lying on the table, looking with wide dry eyes at the wall. Her left leg was gone, and a sharp piece of bone about six inches long extended from the exposed stump. The leg itself was on the floor, half wrapped in a piece of paper. The doctor was a major, and he'd been working alone. He could not have looked worse if he'd lain all night in a trough of blood. His hands were so slippery that I had to hold the can to his mouth for him and tip it up as his head went back. I couldn't look at the girl.

"Is it all right?" he said quietly.

"It's okay now. I expect I'll be sick as hell later on."

He placed his hand on the girl's forehead and said, "Hello, little darling." He thanked me for bringing the beer. He probably thought that he was smiling. But nothing changed anywhere in his face. He'd been working this way for nearly twenty hours.

The courtyard of the American compound in Hue was filled with puddles from the rain, and the canvas tops of the jeeps and trucks sagged with the weight of the water. It was the fifth day of the fighting, and everyone was still amazed that the NVA or the Cong had not hit the compound on the first night. An enormous white goose had come into the compound that night, and now his wings were heavy with the oil that had formed on the surface of the puddles. Every time a vehicle entered the yard he would beat his wings in a fury and scream, but he never left the compound and, as far as I knew, no one ever ate him.

Nearly two hundred of us were sleeping in the two small rooms that had been the compound's dining quarters. The Army was not happy about having to billet all of the Marines that were coming through, and they were absolutely furious about all of the correspondents who were hanging around, waiting until the fighting moved north across the river, into the Citadel. You were lucky to find space enough on the floor to lie down on, luckier if you found an empty stretcher to sleep on, and luckiest of all if the stretcher was new. All night long the few unbroken windows would rattle from the airstrikes across the river, and a mortar pit just outside fired incessantly. At two or three in the morning, Marines would come in from their patrols. They'd cross the room, not much caring whether they stepped on anyone or not. They'd turn their radios on and shout across the room to one another. "Really, can't you fellows show a bit more consideration?" a British correspondent said, and their laughter woke anyone who was not already up.

One morning there was a fire in the prison camp across the road from the compound. We saw the black smoke rising over the barbed wire that topped the camp wall and heard automatic weapons' fire. The prison was full of captured NVA and Vietcong or Vietcong suspects; the guards said that the fire had been started to cover an escape. The ARVN and a few Americans were shooting blindly into the flames, and the bodies were burning where they fell. Civilian dead lay out on the sidewalks only a block from the compound, and the park that ran along the Perfume River was littered with dead. It was cold during those days, the sun never came out once, but the rain did things to the corpses that were worse in their way than anything the sun could have done. It was on one of those days that I realized that the only corpse I could not bear to look at would be the one I would never have to see.

Between the smoke and the mist and the flying dust inside the Citadel, it was hard to call that hour between light and darkness a true dusk, but it was the time when a lot of us would open our C-rations. We were only meters away from the worst of the fighting, not more than a Vietnamese city block in distance, and yet civilians kept appearing, smiling, shrugging, trying to get back to their homes. The Marines would try to menace them away at riflepoint, shouting, "Di, di, *di* you sorry-ass motherfuckers, go on, get the hell away from here!" and the refugees would smile, half-bowing, and flit up one of the shattered streets. A little boy of about ten came up to a bunch of Marines from Charlie Company. He was laughing and moving his head from side to side in a funny way. The fierceness in his eyes should have told everyone what it was, but it had never occurred to most of the Grunts that a Vietnamese child could be driven mad, too, and by the time they understood it the boy had begun to go for their eyes and tear at their fatigues, spooking everyone, putting everyone really up-tight, until one of the spades grabbed him from behind and held his arms. "C'mon, poor l'il baby, 'fore one of these Grunt mothers shoots you," he said, and carried the boy to where the corpsmen were.

On the worst days, no one expected to get through it alive. A despair set in among the members of the battalion that the older ones, the veterans of two other wars, had never seen before. Once or twice, when the men from graves registration took the personal effects from the packs and pockets of dead Marines, they would find letters from home that had been delivered days before and were still unopened.

We were running some wounded onto the back of a half-ton truck, and one young Marine kept crying from his stretcher. His sergeant held both of his hands, and the Marine kept saying, "Shit, sarge, I ain' gone make it. Oh damn, I'm gone die, ain't I?" "No, you ain't gonna die, for Christ's sake," the sergeant said. "Oh yeah, sarge, yeah, I am." "Crowley," the sergeant said, "you ain't hurt that bad. I want you to just shut the fuck up. You ain't done a thing 'cept bitch ever since we got to this fuckin' Hue City." But the sergeant didn't really know. The kid had been hit in the throat, and you couldn't tell about those. Throat wounds were bad. Everyone was afraid of throat wounds.

We lucked out on our connections. At the battalion aid-station in Hue we got a chopper that carried us and a dozen dead Marines to the base at Phubai, and three minutes after we arrived there we caught a C-130 to Danang. Hitching in from the airfield, we found a Psyops official who felt sorry for us and drove us all the way to the Press Center. As we came through the gate we could see that the net was up and that the daily volley ball game between the Marines assigned to the Press Center was in progress.

"Where the hell have *you* guys been?" one of them said. We looked pretty wretched.

The inside of the dining room was freezing with air-conditioning. I sat at a table and ordered a hamburger and a Remy Martin from one of the peasant girls who worked the tables. I sat there for a couple of hours, and ordered four more hamburgers and at least a dozen brandies. (I had no idea of it until the check came.) It was not possible, it was just not possible to have been where we'd been before and to be where we were now, all in the same afternoon. One of the correspondents who had come back with me sat at another table, also by himself, and we just looked at each other, shook our heads, and laughed. I went to my room and took my boots and fatigues off, putting them under the bed where I wouldn't have to look at them. I went into the bathroom and turned on the shower. The water was hot, incredibly hot, for a moment I thought I'd gone insane from it, and I sat down on the concrete floor for a long time, shaving there, soaping myself over and over. I was using up all the hot water, I knew that, but I couldn't get interested in it. I dressed and went back to the dining room. The net was down now, and one of the Marines said hello and asked me what the movie was going to be that night. I ordered a steak and another string of brandies. Then I went to bed and smoked a joint. I was going back in the morning, I knew that, it was understood. But why was it understood? All of my stuff was in order, ready for the five o'clock wakeup. I finished the joint and shuddered off into sleep.

Major Trong bounced around in the seat of his jeep as it drove us over the debris scattered across the streets of Hue. His face seemed completely expressionless as we passed the crowds of Vietnamese stumbling over the fallen beams and powdered brick of their homes, but his eyes were covered by dark glasses, and it was impossible to know what he was feeling. He did not look like a victor; he was so small and limp in his seat, I was sure he was going to fly out of the jeep. His driver was a sergeant named Dang, one of the biggest Vietnamese I'd ever seen, and his English was better than the major's. The jeep would stall on rubble heaps from time to time, and Dang would turn to us and smile an apology. We were on our way to the Imperial Palace.

A month earlier, the palace grounds had been covered with dozens of NVA dead and the burned-over leavings of three weeks' siege and defense. There had been some reluctance about bombing the palace, but a lot of the bombing nearby had done heavy damage, and there had been some shelling, too. The large bronze urns were dented beyond restoring, and the rains poured through a hole in the roof of the throne room, soaking the two small thrones where the old Annamese royalty had sat. In the great hall (great when you scaled it down to the Vietnamese) the red lacquerwork on the upper walls was badly chipped, and a heavy dust covered everything. The crown of the main gate had collapsed, and in the garden the broken branches of the old cay-dai trees lay like the forms of giant insects seared in a fire, wispy, delicate, dead. It was rumored during those days that the palace was being held by a unit of student volunteers who had taken the invasion of Hue as a sign and had rushed to join the North Vietnamese. The final assault had been a privilege reserved for a battalion of elite South Vietnamese Rangers called the Hoc Bao, the Black Panthers, but once the walls had been taken and the grounds entered, there was no one left inside except for the dead. They bobbed in the moat and littered all the approaches. The Marines moved in then, and empty ration cans and muddied sheets from the *Stars and Stripes* were added to the litter. A fat Marine had his picture taken pissing into the locked-open mouth of a decomposing North Vietnamese soldier.

"No good," Major Trong said. "No good. Fight here very hard, very bad."

I'd been talking to Sergeant Dang about the palace and about the line of emperors. He seemed to know a lot about it. We stalled one last time at the foot of a moat bridge, and I asked him the name of the last of the emperors to have occupied the throne. He smiled and shrugged, not so much as though he didn't know, but as though the answer didn't much matter.

"Major Trong is Emperor now," he said, and gunned the jeep into the palace grounds.

The Intel report lay closed on the green field table, and someone had scrawled "What does it all mean?" across the cover sheet. There wasn't much doubt about who had done that; the S-2 was a known ironist. There were so many like him, really young captains and majors who had the wit to cut back their despair, a wedge to set against the bitterness. What got to them sooner or later was an inability to reconcile their love of service with their contempt for the war, and a lot of them finally had to resign their commissions, leave the profession.

We were sitting in the tent waiting for the rain to stop, the major, five Grunts, and myself. The rains were constant now, ending what had been a dry monsoon season, and you could look through the tent flap and think about the Marines up there patrolling the hills. Someone came in to report that one of the patrols had discovered a small arms cache.

"An arms cache!" the major said. "What happened was, one of the Grunts was out there running around, and he tripped and fell down. That's about the only way we ever find any of this shit."

He was twenty-nine, young in rank, and this was his second tour. The time before, he had been a captain commanding a regular Marine company. He knew all about Grunts and patrols, arms caches and the value of most Intelligence.

It was cold, even in the tent, and the enlisted Marines seemed uncomfortable about lying around with a stranger, a correspondent there. The major was a cool head, they knew that; there wasn't going to be any kind of hassle until the rain stopped. They talked quietly among themselves at the far end of the tent, away from the light of the lantern. Reports kept coming in: reports from the Vietnamese, from recon, from Division, situation reports, casualty reports, three casualty reports in twenty minutes. The major looked them all over.

"Did you know that a dead Marine costs $18,000?" he said. The Grunts all turned around and looked at us. They knew how the major had meant that because they knew the major. They were just seeing about me.

The rain stopped, and they left. Outside, the air was still cool, but heavy, too, as though a terrible heat was coming on. The major and I stood by the tent and watched while an F-4 flew nose-down, released its load against the base of a hill, leveled, and flew upward again.

"I've been having this dream," the major said. "I've had it two times now. I'm in a big examination room back at Quantico. They're handing out questionnaires for an aptitude test. I take one and look at it, and the first question says, 'How many kinds of animals can you kill with your hands?' "

We could see rain falling in a sheet about a kilometer away. Judging by the wind, the major gave it three minutes before it reached us.

"After the first tour, I'd have the goddamndest nightmares. You know, the works. Bloody stuff, bad fights, guys dying, *me* dying . . . I thought they were the worst," he said, "but I sort of miss them now."

THE AMBUSH

Asa Baber

Here at Camp Pendleton it is summer even in winter and I dream of the grasshoppers. Here in sunny money land I listen to the singing and I wait to break, to crack like a cup and spill my soul. If I was not plunking my white-haired librarian it would be unbearable. She saves me as she straddles me. Do not be too superior, brothers, for you have not seen it all yet. Sometimes I think I have seen it all. Everything opens up and makes terrible sense and I want to die then.

Now out of Laos it has become a clean world again. The smells are gone. Even my rotting feet stay away from my nose. The malaria has retreated to my gall bladder, there to sleep. My brain is slowing down. They give me pills for that. I understand all the words spoken around me. There is no excuse for my sorrow except that I have heard the world crying and I have seen the strange alliances of nations and I think we are all filled with bile. When the doctors talk to me I say all this but they do not understand it.

There are cypress trees outside my window and across the road there is an artificial lake. The Engineers use that lake to build water obstacles and bridges. At dawn the sun lifts over the avocado orchards and gilts Vandergrift Boulevard. Then I can see the artillery trucks headed out towards Roblar Road and the firing ranges. All day the choppers and OE's fly over the hospital. They are noisy but they cannot stop the singing.

My room is in one of the white frame huts built at the beginning of World War II. It has venetian blinds that make prison shadows and a white rail bed and a print of a Utrillo on the wall. I do not know how a print like that found its way into a Marine Corps hospital. I hope it came with the room because I am sure many men have died in this room and it would be better to die looking at that street scene with the red splotch of paint on all that white. I do not plan to die here except on the bad days when the fever comes back and the dysentery hits again. When I cannot eat anything and my bowels pass water and blood I look at the Utrillo and think about dying.

They are very kind when they question me. I tell them it is screwed up over there. They will only listen to what they want to hear, both the Navy doctors and our own G-2. I try to tell them about the tangled things, that the French are strong with patrol leaders down to platoon level, that Russian civilian pilots are flying the airlift Ilyushins, that the North Vietnamese run the Fire Direction Centers. They listen to me and say yes yes we know all that. They know because they read reports. But it makes it a crazy war when you are over there.

Even Major Kline came by to see me. He lied to General Grider the night we were called out. Sutton and Devereux and I were lined up taking shots. They were pumping exotic vaccines into both my arms. Major Kline told the General we had been on a twelve hour alert. Yes sir they are ready yes sir the last shots of a series yes sir. Devereux got mad and said the last of a series like a one game World Series. The General knew somebody was lying but there was nothing he could do. We flew to Okinawa without calling anyone or saying goodby. I do not like Major Kline and he does not like me, but he owes me something and he knows it.

The grasshoppers come when I sleep. They have the heads of dolphins and they buzz like locusts. They come from left to right across my dreams and always they chant we're coming to get you we're coming to get you. Then I try to wake up but I am too heavy for myself and I have to keep on dreaming while the grasshoppers hurt me. Sometimes I wake up screaming when I see Sutton with his non-head or Devereux with his wet intestines or Boun Kong in his burning skin.

I met my librarian when I was screaming one morning. It is better to sleep during the day because it is easier to wake up. She had brought books in a cart. She thought I was still asleep and she bent over me saying there there it's all right. I kept screaming so that she would not go away. She bent very close and I put my hands on her breasts. They felt like warm doves. She was not sure about me and she backed away. She was angry when she knew I was awake and she would not give me any books to read. Now she gives me all the books I want. She smells of quince and sharp things. She has blue eyes. She is only ten years older than I am but she has white hair.

What I want most is to have MatchKo scrubbing me. She knew all my tight nerves and muscles. Sutton loved her like he loved all the Okinawa whores. He was very immature about sex. He was always buying little personal presents for MatchKo. That last night at the baths he bought her a pearl and silver holly-leaf pin. He tried to bring it in to her while she was bathing me. She was pulling on me with the vibrator and oil and I was up in all my six by six glory. Sutton could not believe she would cheat on him. Not his MatchKo. His MatchKo of the rabbit warren and rice fields, his gold-toothed contortionist who had paid for her hut with God knows how many copulations. He stood there frozen and fearful while she manipulated me and winked at him. He threw the pin at her and ran out. He went north of Kadena to the native whorehouse area where no American should go. He was caught and tied by his feet to the back bumper of a taxi and dragged for miles with his head bouncing on the road. They dumped his body on a street in Naha. There was nothing left of his head but pulp. I saw it the next morning after Devereux and I spent the night looking for him.

Sutton was good in his job but stupid in life. He was one of the oldest Captains in the Marine Corps. They could not afford to get rid of him. He had all the languages they needed. He had French and Mandarin and Japanese. He knew some of the Meo dialect. If he had lived it might have helped us.

One of the doctors asked me if Sutton was queer. I said he was no more queer than some of the others. He wanted us to go to the baths and be rubbed down by MatchKo. He had lost a wife because he could make love only with whores. But that did not make him so different. There is a myth that the military is a masculine profession. I do not buy that. It is a profession where men dress for other men. Spit polish and web gear and linseed oil and starch and bleach. For my white-haired librarian I will clean and comb myself. For a commanding officer I will not go to much trouble. Sutton was sloppy in inspections but he dressed well when he went whoring. I do not think he was queer.

When Sutton was killed I was made c.o. of the Interrogation Team. We were attached to Task Force 116. We thought we were going into southern Laos. The panhandle area near Mahaxay and Tchepone covered Route Nationale 9. We had black and white lists and air recon maps. We were sent to Vientiane instead.

My room is as white as noise. The sheets and the bandages are white. I would like to see a calendar. It is either the end of

February or the beginning of March. February is a cheating month so I hope it has finished. I do not think I will die this year because it is an odd year, 1961. I will die in an even year like my father and my grandfather.

The red-headed doctor asked me if I wanted to go back to Laos when I got better. He was not serious. I wanted to tell him how soft and fine a country it is with its rain forests dark and green all year. The tree trunks are branchless. They are topped with lianas that hold ferns and orchids and wild figs. Walking through these forests, you cannot see the sun. Flying over, you cannot see the forest floor. There are groves of small softwoods mixed with wild ginger, rhododendron and bamboo. There are coconut and areca palms and bananas. These forests shelter tigers, panthers, elephants, deer. When there is a war, our newspapers call these forests "jungles."

I cannot tell the doctor what it is like there because his spirit is not with me. If I could go back without bearing arms or a colonial message, I would.

I often see the *phi* of Sutton and Devereux and Boun Kong. They are wandering the earth and they will always be with me. They are also back in Laos in the Meo country. They are harvesting the poppies now. They are lucky; a *phi* can be two places at once. The plants are waist high now, in full bloom of rose or white or blue or mauve. I would like to be back at the harvest before the pale-green stems of the poppies are cut. The women go to the fields before the dew lifts. They collect the sap and dry it and wrap it in banana leaves. The brown blocks of raw opium are sold for very little in Xieng Khouang Province, and for a lot in Saigon.

The *phi* are strong spirits. They must always be honored. They are in the trees and mountains and rivers. They are in every human being and every dead person. I think it was Sutton's *phi* that came as a goat to warn us.

Go north of Vientiane on the Royal Road, Route Coloniale 13. For twenty miles there are flat paddies and thickets and the sky is open. Then you climb to Ban Namone as the road circles and becomes covered with forest. Here are the lowland people. They are not good fighters. Pull them into combat and they will shoot their rifles into the air. To teach them to shoot to kill, you must set up targets, let them fire one shot at the target, walk them to the target and show them the bullet hole, go back and shoot one shot again. Their houses are on stilts. Pigs and chickens live under them. The men sleep most of the day and the women grow only enough rice to survive. These lowland dwellers will be the last people to fight for anything. They are the first people the Americans tried to indoctrinate.

After Ban Namone comes the valley of Vang Vieng. Here the road starts to climb steeply, through Ban Pha Tang, Ban Thieng, Muong Kassy. At Sala Phou Khoun, the road to the Plain of Jars goes east, Route Nationale 7.

All of these roads were built under the supervision of the French. The French also collected taxes and rice and salt and women under their "Protectorate" which lasted for many generations. The French set the image for the white man. A white man is a Frenchman, a colonialist. A white man is diseased, as anything white in Asia must be diseased, whether it is spoiled buffalo meat or moldy fruit or human flesh.

In the mountains near the Plain of Jars live the fighters, the Meo. They build their houses on the ground. They are great hunters and riflemen and horsemen. They live off the land. They eat corn, cabbage, eggplant, onions, and the produce of their hunt. They live long lives doctored by the gall of bear and python, marrow of tiger, deer's soft horn. Devereux had worked with the Meo before Dien Bien Phu when he was attached to the French. He wanted to get back to them and he got permission for the two of us to go. We had to travel in civvies and an unmarked quarter-ton and we had to take a government driver. His name was Boun Kong. He drank *choum*, a rice wine, through a straw while he drove. He strapped a transistor radio to the emergency brake and gave us a bumpy rock and roll concert.

After the turn at Sala Phou Khoun we were in no-man's land. We drank the wine. Devereux even stopped calling me lieutenant. I think it was the last happy time of my life.

When Boun Kong saw the goat he stopped the jeep. He was drunk and he tried to back the jeep while staring at the goat. It was a very dignified goat and it walked slowly across the road without looking at us. Devereux yelled allons allons and Boun Kong backed the jeep even farther saying c'est impossible c'est impossible c'est La Morte. Devereux stood up in the back seat and slapped Boun Kong on the ears. I jumped out and ran at the goat. That is when they hit us. They probably thought I had seen them.

There was the great horrible compression of air and dust and noise. I don't think they used any launchers or grenades. They wanted the jeep. But they had .50's and their own Chinese weapons and they aimed high to spare the chassis. We hadn't come all the way into their setup. They had gotten behind us. They opened up a little too early. Everything hit Devereux's belly. He folded and fell out. I ran into the brush. I am ashamed I ran, but there was not anything I could do. Sometimes the doctors push me on this. They think I wanted to be a hero. Boun Kong tried to be a hero. He wanted to throw the extra jerry-can of gas at them. It bounced against his leg as he carried it a few steps down the road. The bullets were cracking and spitting around him. I rolled on down the slope and heard an explosion. Then there was that deep silence after battle when the eardrum vibrates and the balance slowly returns. I kept my head down. I heard one of them sweeping through the grass. He stopped near me but he did not shoot. I raised my head and he looked at me. He was a white man, perhaps French or Russian. He fired a few shots down the gulley and climbed back to his platoon of gooks. They wanted the jeep. They took it.

I crawled back to the road. Boun Kong was still burning. Devereux's guts were in his hands. He had died looking surprised. I went into the brush. I did not start to walk back until it was night. I did not use the road because I was afraid of it. It took me three days before I reached the road north of Vientiane.

Here in Camp Pendleton the blinds are raised each day and the sunlight comes into this bleached vanilla room. There are deer running through the sage in the canyons near San Clemente. You can walk the firebreaks on the ridgeline and hunt the deer. I will not ever be a good hunter again because my hands shake now. The doctors give me pills for it and say I will get over it. I do not think so. My hands shake because I have to fight the grasshoppers and listen to the singing. That makes me tired. The singing is always in the back of my head. I do not know what song they are singing. It is a march with a steady rhythm and stamping feet and many voices. It is not pleasant and sometimes they stop singing and they shout.

GONE ARE THE MEN

Thomas A. West, Jr.

1.

I hadn't realized how far it was. My lungs, forced as they were, longed for a cigarette—yet I didn't smoke. Fear? Definitely. Fear of incoming rounds and gooks we never laid eyes on, and a sense that something was wrong, something in the air. Call it intuition if you want. Hell, I can't spell it out. The heights were slightly dizzier, the winds more bold, the rocks treacherous. Harder to scramble over. I turned once for a breather, looked down and thought I saw my bunker. Suddenly I longed for an apartment, a woman, a joint, and some music. Way down, miles into the bowl below, the regimental tents stood, and beyond them the endless forest. And above it all was a low fleet of gray clouds which seemed anchored to the horizon. I shuddered and continued on toward the ridge near Charlie Company, where they held chapel in between barrages. Before I realized it, I was humming "Onward Christian Soldiers."

2.

Yes   well
when I was in the service
I marched up tight   with boots
and belt so bright they'd wink
like polished coins when the sun
hit   Jesus
I was sharp
as the bayonet I cleaned
and   we marched or stood
at attention all together now full of

brotherhood   dreaming
    orange juice and teats
or we waited. Chow lines   mess
halls   four a.m.   feel like
pieces of shit on a shingle on a
grease-trap tray   dreaming
buses   trains   anything to home
duffel bags
(full field pack)
fifty pounds
(add nine, lock and load, one round
ball ammunition
                        ready on the range
lieutenant halsey?)

3.

There weren't many men there, on the reserve slope. Maybe
thirty, thirty-five. The chaplain's voice, buffeted by strong
breezes, said "You belong to God," but the word "God" emerged
"Gawd" and it grated on with the pulling taut of a rusted screen
door spring.

I wasn't sure the chaplain knew what he was talking about.
"You belong to Gawd . . . from The Beginning you were His,
and to the End."

Yes. Well.

"You *are* His, He *will* be with you. Therefore, men, commend
your soul, your heart, your body to Gawd, in the name of The
Father, The Son and The Holy Ghost Amen now let us pray."

A few lowered their heads. They knelt down slowly, as if
gently pushed, but movements were interrupted by the struggling
with weapons, helmets—the shedding of armor like surrendered
knights. Several of us stood, listening or not listening at all but
staring out at the landscape.

"The Lord is my Shepherd, I shall not want.
"He maketh me to lie down in green pastures . . ."

4.

folded civvies crammed after folding
jammed in an overnight bag
gone
gone are the sleek upholstered cars
    and skirts hiked up on

summer nights waiting for flicked off
headlights
gone are the dusty loafers   snack bars
text books   gone
are the cities and the soft hands
held while snow settled sleepily
on paths   on campus paths
gone

5.

What was I waiting for? Why was I suddenly so up-tight? Did
the others feel it too? I looked at many faces. They had no
expression at all. Eyes glazed. They were not looking at the
chaplain any more than they were listening to Psalm Twenty-
three. It was then I sensed I was in the midst of the dead. Expected jaws to drop, skin and flesh to fall from the faces. Like
praying mantises, their hands up in front of their shaven skulls,
they begged for life with brittle bones.

The chaplain continued while skies darkened. The sun was
still up, but it should have been eclipsed. The Plague should
have struck, withering bodies of Christians in their bunkers, casting down lords in battle tents below.

6.

Men.
Men have brains
            (your rifle number   soldier)
                    5720126   sir
            (your serial number   soldier)
                    US 51040194   sir
            (your general orders   soldier
            (your ass
            (your
Yes Sir   Yes Sir   Yes Sir
(Tod day we are goin to dis
            cuss the no men clay tshor
            of th M-16)
Yes Corporal
What's your philosophy Corporal
            (screw or get screwed mister)

7.

The chaplain's voice droned nonsense syllables and at the end
of each string he named the Trinity, and then he began all over

again. Was it Latin now? I didn't know and didn't give a flying crap in hell. Yet I still strained to hear. All I got was "goodness," "mercy," and "life." I thought, sure they will, chaplain. Sure they will.

His face froze. He stared out of hollow black sockets under black brows. The eyes, somehow were still there.

"Hit it!" someone yelled.

I went crashing down, remembering only that I was struck before the earth exploded.

8.

Men have brains
I knew a sergeant overseas
drank like a dehydrated horse
lost on a salt flat   down in
death valley
sat fat and sour on his sleeping
bag   said as he rocked
like a little old maid on the edge
of her last veranda
    Holy Cow
    Kiss My Ass
    Piss on it
Oh he'd try to say more yes
but he gave up (unconditionally) to
    Holee Cow
    Kisssh my Asssh
    Pisssh on it
Men have brains
scrambled egg brains under
glass   kiss my
under steel pots   piss
on it all well   they think
of time and grade   men do   and
point systems
rotation to the station to the states

memorizes numbers   a man does
addresses of lost friends
in civilian clothes in towns
outside cities sprawled near bases
Gone is the hair
Gone are the bell-bottoms
nehru jackets   levis

9.

Rounds screeched against air. In urgent cacophonies came great blocks of splitting sound, as if trucks the size of ships unloaded lumber, sliding it down from skies, and packs of plywood like huge blank playing cards collapsed all about us.

Someone had flung me down, and I pulled my knees up, covered my head with my arms and hands as if they could ward off searing steel, and the weird thing was, I tried burying fingers into my helmet. Well, I thought: I was nothing more than a deformed Spartan baby, snatched from my mother's womb by military hands only to be shoved back in at the age of twenty-three (I will fear no evil), and I shook, unable or unwilling to be a whole man. Prayed to Sweet Mother of Holy God I could work my way back into life. I shook and then began to cry.

As far as I know, the others didn't hear me, they being as deafened as I was. What stopped me was a thud against my right arm. It was harsh, yet soft—a nudging which slid off and landed by my side. But I couldn't open my eyes, my precious eyes, and I was terrified to expose my good face, my important brain. I wanted to feel, remember, study some more, do things for the whole fucking world.

Yet in my gut I was riding a nightmare. I tasted red, saw noise, heard black. Suddenly I felt like joining the fun. Hell, I craved to sit up, have a joint, sing, watch shells crash, wanted to encourage them on, think them down the clouds and laugh at their moanings; as if *they* could mourn death, as if *they* could cry their metal souls out before they hit.

The barrage kept up, got madder. Teachers, police, army officers, all those in authority slammed doors in my face, swore at me from behind them, opened them suddenly or kicked them open with a rush of air, threw dirt in my eyes, spit blood and swore and slammed doors again. You know, there are shells and shells. Some mince and whine like fags on a well-lit street; others shuffle like gamblers at cards before they stare you down, draw and fire point-blank, and some pull up their skirts, old ladies hustling through corridors filled with dry autumn leaves, and some like wounded warriors drag themselves across the field of sky and crumple at our feet.

10.

(all right you guys
this is a gas mask

                    someday   it might
                    save your ass
        Wake up, wake that man up, sergeant)

        Lectures after chow after calisthenics
        after forced marches

        Men
        Pull triggers
        Bruise shoulders
        Feel helmet liners rapped with swagger sticks
        cut and trimmed by sergeant's knives
                        (watch the mess sergeant
                        he has long fingernails   I hear)
        Men
        oil stocks   swab barrels   click
        trigger housing groups   shut
        and snap bolts that sound like
            steel doors closing
                        close with the enemy
                        your mission is to
                        close with the enemy
                            and destroy him

                        11.

    I think I said aloud, "I will fear no evil," only I wondered if
that's what I really said because I was drowned out by the
tumult. Then I saw great halls around me, lined with sandbags
as far as I could see. Rats in packs swarmed and scurried over the
bags. One of them glared at me at eye level. I saw its fur being
ruffled by gales of howling, wind-tunnel air.
    The incoming stuff stopped. I remember thinking someone
had turned on the lights.

                        12.

        yes
        well
        a man who majored in humanities
        and i
            followed all the rules
        why not   to the beat of a drum
                YOUR LEAFT   YOUR LEAFT   YOUR LEAFT
        in the cold cold bivouac

(gone are the beds) (gone are the picnics)
the forest calls to men who squat over
pits and
shit

> YOUR LEAFT   YOUR LEAFT   YOUR LEAFT
> JO-DY LOOKS FROM THE WINDOW SILL
> SHE WON'T DO IT BUT HER SISTER WILL
> SOUND OFF   SOUND OFF
> SOUND OFF   1-2-3-4-1-2   3-4

Men
Sweat men dry men   easy flowing march men
shouldering thick rifles
dying for one lousy smoke
take ten in olive drab
class A pass
my ass

> I GOT A GAL HER NAME IS SUE

Streets are lit for men at night
        (and now the lighting of the lamps)
who swagger with their caps squared
and pants bloused
weekend polish sings reflections of horsechestnuts
I wouldn't mind
playing marbles in the dust
        or playing soldiers: tin   lead iron
hell, rugs were softer
even attic floors   soft, soft
softer than this goddam earth

13.

I waited.

What was the thing that had weighed against me? I uncovered my face slowly, looked, and there was a hand belonging to a man I'd never seen, but he stared into my eyes with the same intensity as the rat. It was like I was staring into my own eyes. He was maybe twenty, freshly shaven for Chapel on the Hill. Only one smudge of dirt was on his chin. He looked like he wanted to talk to me, mouth open, about to say something. I thought, probably he was the one who pushed me down, saved my life.

I got up. Saw the damage. His head was connected to his shoulders by two large strands of red muscle. I vomited. Next thing I knew I heard a man wailing like a baby. Not crying, but leading up to it. I had to see. I knew it was someone hurt really bad, but I had to go see him. It was a sergeant and his legs were gone.

14.

> Men
> At ease, Rest,
> Smoke if you have 'em   inhale
> memories   breathe
> country   desert   forest   city air
> it's all the same now
> off we go
> overseas   FECOM

15.

The chaplain came. We made way for him, slowly, all of us moving in a dream-dance, a sleep-walking on stage. Moving back, then converging on the legless man, in this drama without an audience.

The chaplain came. He held the sergeant's head as it made its baby sounds, as it realized what had happened, its mouth growing larger, larger. Once, his right reached out, pleading, as hands can do, begging with a life all its own.

"It's all right, son." But the chaplain's face was a bitter mask and he must have known how stupid-ass his words were. "We'll take care of you—" Then he shouted at the clouds: "WHY THIS." As he cradled the body, he suddenly pulled away from it, and I thought he had gone mad because he let the sergeant drop and he desperately fumbled for a weapon lying on a rock ledge. The chaplain fired pointblank at the dying man's head, which caved in. Arms heaved outward, hands fisted, went limp. Why, one of us demanded. Legless men can live. But the chaplain rolled the sergeant over. In his back was a hole the size of a football. Then he dropped the weapon. Nobody said a word as he began walking down the slope in a trance.

By this time another sergeant took charge. His hollerings jarred us out of our dream. "MOVE" he yelled, then cursed us with every oath he knew from five thousand years of history and forty thousand wars. His voice was on the edge of hysteria, and tears streamed down his flushed cheeks. I remember him screaming for medics and calling down the wrath of every god on every officer who was responsible for holding chapel on a reverse slope on the MLR. Some of us, myself included, still dazed, ears still ringing from the bursting shells, were shoved by the sergeant who kicked one guy in the ass because he didn't have his weapon.

16.

APO what? Division   Regiment   Bat-alllllion
Companeeee   Platooooon
    REPORT
        Fourt platoon all pres'nt'n accounted *for*
     Third Platoon five men missing
    Second Platoon twelve men killed
   First Platoon: i'm it,   sarge
Got hit up the ridge
Didn't even see 'em
Broad daylight too

               Dear Son
               when do you think you'll
                 be coming home
               I remember how it was
               you and me
               out hunting in the dawn
Didn't even see 'em, sarge
               you outshot me in the dawn
               but then   my eyes got bad
               ever since I got hit   at
               Salerno on the beaches did
               I ever tell you about that
               Son?
The whole place opened up on us   sarge
Don't think we zapped even one of 'em

               Darling
               Please come home
               I miss you so
               I love you so
There's a tag on a boot
sticking out from a poncho
and there are tags on boots
sticking out from ponchos
on a truck on a half-track
in a helicopter

17.

More curious than concerned about the chaplain, I followed him, found him sitting on a boulder, looking out at the ridges. I

didn't think he realized I was there, but he said, "Did you know,
friend, we are hurtling through space at forty thousand miles an
hour. Through space. Space does not react, friend. It does not
weep, nor laugh nor sigh nor yawn nor preach. It has received
the bodies of men as it will receive yours and mine, without a
single thought as to what we did on this planet; not a solitary
thought about how we felt, how we loved—hated—nothing. We
are, friend—I was taught this—resurrected in body as well as
spirit. Who thought that one up, friend?"

Clearly, he was through.

I saluted. I don't know why. Chauvinism. May be we are all
hung over from Walter Mitty and Lord Cardigan. I walked back
toward my bunker. I grew aware of a gentle rain, then. Perhaps,
if it rained hard enough and long enough, it would some day
wash away all the blood on all the ridges.

18.

Men
Men have hearts
    have brains
    have guts

YOUR LEAFT   YOUR LEAFT   YOUR LEAFT

"Hear the pitter-patter
  of little feet
It's the First Cav Division
  in full re-treat

We're movin' on
O we're movin' on

So we get a little shy
When they cry Banzai

We're movin' on."

PORTRAIT: MY AMERICAN MAN, FALL, 1966

Paul Friedman

It should be Sunday. My American Man would be on the couch
in the living room with his shoes off and his feet up after a late
breakfast of bacon and eggs and toast and coffee. The newspapers
should be scattered. Everything's fine, a full stomach, and hours
to look forward to, of peace. He's just seen Lindsay on T.V. It's
quite a thing when you stop and think about it, being mayor. A
man in a position like that could really do something if he
wanted, not that politicians ever wanted to really do anything
except stay in office. That goes for all of them, they're all the
same. Steal a dollar and you go to jail, steal a million and you go
to Congress, that's the way it is, face it, it's a well known fact.
Take Johnson. He made a speech in Toledo yesterday. Now they
just got done with a race riot there, the Secret Service told Johnson not to go to Toledo, it was too dangerous there they said, so
what's Johnson say in his speech when he gets to Toledo: that
things have never been better. Politicians sure must think people
are stupid. Over the noise of the kitchen faucet the phone was
ringing. It would either be for Adele, her mother, or Jerry—
What would you think of my growing a beard, Dad? Dye your
hair, grow a beard, what do I have to say about anything— Don't
politicians give the public credit for any intelligence? Adele's
voice. This would be good for half an hour. Who the hell knew
what this war was about? You're not for it, by the same token
you're not against it because you don't like bucking your own
government. I was down at Times Square when some of those
peace kids were having a demonstration. Picketing, waving signs,
not all kids, either. Terrible, terrible, this man next to me kept
saying. They ought to take those people out, line them up
against a wall and shoot them. You think the Commies would

treat them any better? They love the Commies so much let's give
them a taste of their own medicine. I have strong feelings on this
subject but I'm pulled two ways. You don't want to be pushed
around, but you don't want to blow up the world either, so you
fight with one hand tied behind your back, it's crazy. I might
only be a postal employee, basically I'm an uneducated person,
but I'm not blind, I see the mess. It's everywhere. Just look at the
niggers, they're rioting every week, who ever heard of this kind of
stuff happening in America? There, that. Calling them that, I
know its wrong. Now either I shouldn't call them that or I
should and I shouldn't feel bad about it, but neither's the case.
Things were never better, things were never more screwed up,
that's what Johnson should have said. Jerry's only twenty but he
says some bright things. The kid has insights. Your whole thing,
Dad, the kid says, is you believe in stereotypes when you talk
about Negroes in general, but when you meet a Negro, one
Negro, then you see him as a person, as an individual. That's one
thing, Dad, you see Negroes as individuals. Well of course, what
do you expect, what am I, Governor of Alabama, am I a Southern sheriff? Haven't I known the colored all my life? Wasn't my
boss for two years, Frank Philips, colored? Of course I see them as
individuals. I just say one thing, they've got to help themselves,
the government can't do it all for them. The Jet game would be
coming on soon from Shea Stadium. Adele, how much longer you
going to be on that phone? Why couldn't they stay in their own
neighborhoods? They weren't like the Mets, this year they
weren't clowns. Joe Namath. Four hundred grand. Who the hell
knew how much money that was? With a bum knee. Four hundred grand. How could any man be worth that kind of money?
They're taking the silver out of dimes because there's not much
money around and they give this guy almost half a million bucks
to throw a football. The Black Muslims, what was that nonsense
he'd heard, their master plan: to have hundreds of thousands of
babies, go on relief, drain the budget that way, and then use the
money to buy some of the Southern states and hand it all over to
Castro's Cuba. Crazy foolishness, but these days you couldn't be
sure. You ever see a politician die young, why should they? Post
Office clerks die young. The kid says the government tries to keep
the war impersonal. For instance, dropping bombs: pilots don't
see the people they kill; it's impersonal, and that's the way the
government likes it. How about hand to hand combat, Jerry?
Sure, Dad, if a guy takes a shot at you you're going to shoot back,
that's not the point. Why do they blindfold a guy when he goes
before a firing squad? To show mercy, so he won't see the bullets

coming? No. If you want to show mercy you don't kill the guy.
The blindfold's there so the guy who does the shooting won't
have to look at the eyes of the guy who's being shot, the blindfold
makes it easier on the executioner, it all stays impersonal. Maybe
Jerry's right, I don't know. I remember the good old days when
the bad guys were bad and you were glad you killed them. The
Nazis, the Japs. Now you drop bombs and you hope you don't
kill people, that's too deep for me. My mother-in-law's eighty-
nine, it's time, what's she waiting for? Remember when the
Giants and Dodgers were still in New York, those were the days,
complications. You hated the Giants and loved Brooklyn. The
Bums. Take Branch Rickey, tight-fisted, he didn't smoke, he
didn't drink, but he knew how to make a baseball team. Campy
catching, Hodges at first, Robinson second, Reese short, and Billy
Coxe third. On Friday night you couldn't get a seat in Ebbets
Field if your life depended on it. Furillo in right, the Reading
Rifle, he's a delicatessen man now, that's the last I heard. Duke
Snider center. The Duke of Flatbush. But they could never get
anyone for left. That's a truism of life I guess, nothing's perfect.
Either you don't have a good left fielder or you can't beat the
Yanks, there's got to be something. Abrams, Hermanski, Andy
Pafko, Sandy Amoros, a whole slew of them but they could never
get that third outfielder. That rotten so-and-so O'Malley: taking
them out of Brooklyn, anything for a buck, the almighty dollar.
Robinson came up in 1947, Dixie Walker was on the team then,
the People's Choice, he played right field like he owned it. But
Dixie had to go—so they traded him to Pittsburgh. Nothing's as
simple as it seems, the older I get the more convinced I become of
that, it's never all on the surface. We've all got our peculiarities.
Take me. For years I was a fanatic about cleaning my fingernails.
I don't know why. Then I started collecting the dirt, saving it.
I'd just been transferred from the floor over at the G.P.O. to the
stamp window. Naturally I started handling a lot of money and
you'd be surprised how dirty money is. I started hoarding that
dirt. I got a coffee tin and kept it in the bottom drawer of my
desk at home and every night I'd clean my fingernails and drop
those tiny specks of dirt in there. Pretty soon just collecting the
day's accumulation wasn't enough. I started carrying around an
envelope and two, three, four times a day I'd go to the john,
clean my nails, put the dirt in the envelope, and then at night
empty the dirt from the envelope into the coffee tin. I came home
one night and there was Adele holding the can in her hand. She
waited a minute, then said, What in God's name is this, I found
it in the bottom drawer when I was cleaning out your desk, it

stinks to high heaven. I didn't know what to say. Special soil to grow cucumbers in, I said, I've been saving it. I always could think on my feet. Then I started for the bathroom to wash up but before I got there Adele exploded, What kind of secrets are you keeping from me, you've got almost two pounds of filth hidden away in one of my Maxwell House coffee cans, why? Adele, I don't want to talk about it. What else could I say to her? I started for the bathroom again but she kept on yelling and screaming so I finally blurted out, Okay, you're right, I am keeping something from you. She got pale. Now you figure out what it is that I'm hiding, Adele, because I'm not going to tell you. As far as I'm concerned the matter's closed and I don't want to hear another word about it. Right after that I stopped collecting dirt. We never spoke about it again. Adele probably still wonders what it was all about. So do I. If Jerry would take my advice he'd become a politician, there's no better racket in the world. The Post Office is a pretty good job. Today especially, for a young man, I can't see anything the matter with it. You don't kill yourself, there's security, good vacation. Back during the Depression the Post Office clerk was king. Working steady, bringing home a salary every two weeks. Then, when a top clerk was drawing a big twenty-one hundred a year, Roosevelt gave a ten percent across-the-board cut. I never had any use for Roosevelt after that. The war broke out, people started getting rich . . . Four terms, the man was power crazy. It just went to show you how important a union could be, even one like the Post Office union, which by law isn't allowed to strike. If we'd had a union back in those days he'd never have gotten away with that cut. No two ways about it, today it's a damn good job for a young man, particularly if he knows the right politician and gets himself fixed up with a steady day tour. Not that it's any picnic serving the public all day long. Like the time I was working over at Empire and an old lady came in and asked for a Lincoln stamp. This was when first-class mail was still three cents so I gave her the Lincoln three and she shoved it right back at me and says she doesn't want that stamp, it isn't a good likeness. I've got a line out to the street, it's almost time to close the window, this is how you get ulcers. What do you mean it's not a good likeness? It's a poor replica, that's what I mean, young man, and don't be fresh. Isn't there a stamp where Mr. Lincoln's clean-shaven? Lady— Watch your tone of voice with me, young man. Hey, Mr. Philips. I don't say another word, I just wait for the Assistant Superintendent to come over. What's the trouble, he asks. When she sees that he's colored the old lady says, My God, what's the country coming to, then turns around and walks out. The next customer says to me, you get people like that often? All day long, mister, all day long. I'll tell you one thing, there are better ways to spend your life than selling stamps, so what's Jerry want to do: quit school and join the Army. Sure, great idea, go to Vietnam and get killed. With your beard. Why do you always twist around what I say, Dad. I don't want to join the Army—I don't want so spend my life selling stamps either—I just want to get away from school for a while, I'd like to join the Merchant Marine, that's not joining the Army, is it? Okay, fine, when the Vietcong's sending torpedoes at your ship you tell them you're not in the Army, you tell them you're in the Merchant Marine and see how much it helps. If some of us had the same chances we give our kids . . . Well, what's the sense in thinking about that. I try to listen to classical music on WNYC sometimes, not to impress anyone, I only do it when I'm alone, it's just for my own enjoyment. But it's no go, after a couple of minutes my mind starts to wander, I'm yawning, pretty soon I'm not even listening. Okay, you are what you are, I am what I am: a slob; I admit it, I'm not ashamed of it. There's this thing Jerry keeps raving about, this poem, *The Waste Land*, it's so wonderful, so great, it opened his eyes . . . I took a look at it and I couldn't make heads or tails out of it. This is what they teach you in college? It's symbolic, he tells me. Symbolic, that's a newfangled word they're using in school these days. College graduates, they can't add or spell, but symbolic stuff, that they understand. What nonsense. You have dreams, Dad? Yeah. Are there things in your dreams that don't make sense? Yeah. Now do you think they don't make sense because they don't have any meaning or because you don't understand what they mean, in other words because they're symbolic? That stopped me. He's some kid. What do you mean? You know what I mean, he said. Imagine, a kid with a head like that and he wants to quit school. What I wouldn't give to be an educated man. You're an adult and you have to sit and watch Westerns. Don't watch, they say. Sure, fine, I just plunked down four hundred and fifty bucks for a new color set and now I won't watch. They sure must think people are stupid. Every day another ten, twenty American kids are getting killed. They got Cuba and it's not hurting us, that's the way I look at it. De Gaulle's crazy, maybe, I'm no expert, I didn't go to college, but it looks to me like France isn't doing so bad with him. More money for taxes, everything's sky high, you'll die before you get a doctor to come to your house on the weekend: things were never better, Johnson says. Our parents worked in sweatshops, they didn't know the language, there wasn't any Relief—okay, you finally show me that it's different with the colored, they were slaves, this, that, they need special help, I'm finally convinced: the War on Poverty, Head Start, fine, good, I'm all for it—so now there's no money, there's a war in Vietnam. Maybe I'm stupid but it seems to me we got a war in Bedford-Stuyvesant. You take your life in your hands any time you go by there. Let's get that cleared up. The way I feel about it we didn't lose anything on the moon, what's the big rush, if we don't get there next year I won't feel I missed much, but I'll tell you what I do miss, I miss being able to walk down my block at night and feel safe. Broadway's a honky-tonk. There's not a park in the city that's safe, muggings, thuggings. Sure, big deal, the mayor goes for a walk through Central Park and no one rapes him so he gets on T.V. and says the parks are safe. Listen, if fifty cops followed me around I'd feel safe walking through the park too. Goddam politicians, how dumb do they think we are? I had a dream. I was in a room with college kids, it was some kind of party. I don't know what I was doing there. All the people were talking, they seemed relaxed and comfortable. Then I saw Jerry and even though he's twenty and I'm fifty-four, somehow, in the dream, when he came over to talk to me he was the father and I was the son. Why aren't I like all these other people, I asked him. He's holding a mixed drink and smoking a pipe. Why should you be, he says. The smoke was coming out of his pipe and it was getting hard for me to see his face. Because I want to fit in. Just be yourself. Be myself, what do you mean, aren't I myself? How do I know, Jerry says, I'm not you. I don't understand, what do you mean, speak so I can understand you. How can you understand, Jerry says, you're still a child. He started to laugh at me. Then, a second before I woke up I heard what all the people were saying: Things have never been better, things have never been better, and they're all laughing. When I woke up I was shaking, terrified. I can't get rid of that dream, I just can't get rid of it. Hey, Adele, give us a break will you, enough's enough. Listen, I better hang up, Harry's pestering me for something to eat.

HE THAT DIED OF WEDNESDAY

W. C. Woods

When Emily left the red-brick building, she was in a State of Grace. The young man who had been her interim lover found that charming and amusing. Over the eleven months of their affair, he had often tapped a private reserve of irony about it—at least while he was down, which was the majority of the daylight hours. Drunk, or drifting toward an acid high, he lost such subtleties and became sentimental and horny: an impossible combination. If he couldn't manage an agreeable hour with her, he cursed; if he could, he cried. Sober, he was altogether the same man. He had once written a characterization of himself in the manner of Overbury, and he particularly guarded one sentence as a talisman to hold shares in every failure: "He says he loves his friends, but his friends call him a liar; he says he lies for love, but his lovers bear him none." Emily suspected every word was true.

The young man watched her step from the door of the church into the crew-cut green grass and walk toward the parking lot, where he had been patiently waiting in her car for forty-five minutes, body curled behind the wheel, feet slung awkwardly onto the wide dashboard, the heels of his sand-colored boots digging shallow cups into the olive vinyl. As Emily got to the car door, she quickly opened it for herself, because he was sure to be gaily grabby if she let him reach across to do it. The mean bastard had made it impossible for her to go to Communion with her parents last Easter by fooling with her after she had been to confession.

"Purified?" he asked cheerfully.

"Shut up." Emily was prim. Emily *was* purified? It almost astonished him to look at her at such moments, her skin somehow freshly pale, her lips tight over the locked gate of her teeth. He thought about the night before, and was boorishly charmed. He started the car.

"No, just sit here a minute," Emily ordered as he reached for the gearshift. "Turn off the motor. I want to talk."

"About what?" The young man was a little bored. He still held the lever.

"Are you up to a kind of biggish blow?"

He glanced over at her, irritated by the childish diminutive. "Yes, I'm up to a 'biggish' blow," he mimicked. "Shall I guess?"

"If you think that would be fun."

"You're pregnant. Or you've changed your mind again. Or maybe the war's over."

"Sort of. Stephen is home."

It was a biggish blow. The young man found and fondled a cigarette and frowned at the windshield wipers. "What are you going to do about it?" he asked, after a pause he judged long enough.

"I'm going back to him," Emily said.

"Oh? Do I get to see you on your lunch break, or what?"

"You got to see me today for the last time. I'm . . . I'm going back to him altogether, completely, don't you understand, *completely*." —Elaborately overexplaining, showing sad nerves.

"Why?" asked the young man, after a more genuine pause.

"Because I love him and I'm going to marry him," Emily said, with a touch of surprise. "I think I told you that a year ago, didn't I, right at the start?"

Her companion managed a shrug. He was beginning to feel sick and afraid. "Oh—well, I can't compete with a war hero."

Emily darkened. "He's *not* that. He didn't want anything to do with it, any more than either of us. He just got by, that's all."

"He went, though, didn't he? *I* managed not to." There was perhaps too much pride in his voice, or maybe the wrong kind. But Emily didn't hear it.

"I guess you'll just have to overlook some things for all the goodies, huh, Em?" the young man pushed on. "I mean, a football player in bed is worth any number of napalmed babies."

"Oh, shut up, for God's sake," Emily whispered softly, but there was an urgency in her tone that told him he had found the right tack. Because Emily—like most of the earnest young girls whose sensibilities are encoded into a political vocabulary which has no relation to their experiences—was foreplay-ardent in her social consciousness. With her, it was ban the bomb or burn the babies, and for such supercharged humanism there are no shades of grey. He had taught her that.

Helpless, she rested her face against his chest. He stroked her hair gently. He put his hand on her thigh, his fingertips brushing a white coin of flesh that rose through a rip in her worn black tights. Under the yellow beard that infected his jaw, her thick, soft black hair caped over her green sweater as she curled tensely against him. Holding her, he still felt some confidence that he would hold her again. It seemed to him that he had constructed her world too completely for her ever to willingly shatter it; and the strength of that construction lay in the innocence of its design. They had filtered through the dizzy snake dance of a score of picket lines together, they had sat and lain in all the places where young students sit and lie, they had, above all, done one excessive and extraordinary thing that might not be too easy for a man back from the war to understand, they had done that, and it gave him a sudden ugly comfort. And they had moved through love's arabesques in much the same way they occupied their political overworld. Sex had the same convenient wry tenderness as being sentimental about the Spanish Civil War.

"I told you," Emily suddenly insisted in a soupy voice, though he had not spoken, "I love him."

The young man pressed his tangled chin into the top of her head by way of a nod. "Yes, you told me. You told me at least once a week, sometimes at the goddamnedest times. Now you can tell him. He'll probably believe it."

"It's true."

Without warning, a thin clear pool of pure jealousy crested in him. "If it's true . . . ." he returned, and he opened a charge against her. He suggested to her the possibility that she might properly be called a slut, a whore, something of that sort—damning in the desperate, ugly fashion of a high-school boy whose steady let someone else paw her breasts at a party or a prom. He swiftly regretted doing it, because she would not care, and he was becoming argumentative, which was demeaning and therefore, for him, a bit attractive. And he was mishandling the tactic he had cut into so well for starters. Her grateful seizure of the new tack confirmed him.

"I never represented myself as anything else, if that's the way you want to look at it," Emily said proudly. "I'm not going to hide you from him. I'm not ashamed of anything."

"All right, you're not going to hide me from him. Are you going to hide you?"

"What do you mean?"

"You know damn well what I mean. He was wounded, wasn't he? It was in the paper, for Christ's sake."

"He knows how I feel about the war," Emily whispered. "He

knows that I've picketed and marched and stuff. He wouldn't
hold that against me."

"No, but that's different, and you know it. He would *hate* you
for the other. He was *wounded*, Emily!"

She shuddered. "Shut up. Shut up."

"Em. . . ."

"Drive me home."

The young man shrugged. "Let's get a beer." She nodded
mutely, but as they turned into the town ten minutes later, when
she saw he was heading the car down the street he lived on, she
insisted that they have their beers in a bar, and he could not
persuade her otherwise.

Stephen Wallace came home from the war in the fall of that
year. He was wearing his uniform as he stepped off the train. It
was not necessary. He had a suit in his B-4 bag, neatly pressed,
and a light-blue shirt somewhere in his duffel bag, sandwiched
between two poplin shirts, starched hard as Masonite, that went
with the Class A's he was wearing, a semidress uniform he had
hardly seen since he had left it in the capital city thirteen months
before. He also had a silk necktie of wide red-and-gold stripes in
the suitcase. He supposed he was wearing the uniform to please
his parents, who met him at the station, or Emily, who didn't.

"Tell us what each one means," his mother insisted as they
were driving home.

So Stephen began to describe his ribbons. They were a standard complement for a returning soldier whose chief, and not
insignificant, heroism had been daily competence. Over the row
was the silver and blue of the Combat Infantryman Badge, and
under it, fixed to the flap of the pocket with a certain display of
mockery, was the unadorned Maltese cross that indicated Stephen had only minimal competence with his personal weapon.
The badge made no allowance for the fact that he had acquired
a shotgun somewhere along the way, and had had much better
luck with that.

"That ribbon," his mother said after a while. "As a matter of
fact, I know what it means. I don't think you wrote us about that
one."

Stephen chose an answer as he watched the red and yellow hills
of trees stammer past the open windows of the car. "I didn't want
to worry you about it," he said finally, lamely.

"You never even wrote about it," his mother repeated.

"Well, we're home," his father contributed a few minutes
later. "How does it look?"

"Good. It looks good," Stephen said.

"What will you want special?" his mother asked him, as they all sat in the kitchen and she fried eggs and sausage.

"That's fine."

"No, I mean all the time."

Stephen smiled at her, knowing that she thought she meant for the rest of his life if he cared to sit forever and be served.

"An awful lot of creature comforts."

"You'll have them."

"I know."

"You look so well! You won't mind if we show you off in your uniform?"

"I'll pose for a few days," Stephen said, "but then we mothball it. Deal?" His parents smiled. "Well—where's Emily?" Stephen asked suddenly, but his father's question came as suddenly into his, and it seemed an honest collision of voices, not a kind strategy: "Did you see a lot of action, son?" Stephen considered, and was surprised. It surprised him every time he thought about it.

Actually—comparatively—he hadn't. It had been really bad only that once, but of course that was bad enough. It had been almost at the end of his tour. He was due to return to the capital at the end of the month to be processed until early September, when he would leave, leave this country, leave the service, leave the last two years somewhere in mid-ocean, perhaps, in much the same way a cicada deserts his shell.

That was an image he toyed with often. There was relief in packing the contents of the strange, numbing world he wandered in into a disposable metaphor that way. Sometimes at the base camp, wakeful in the hour before dawn, he would lie under the gauze of netting that shrouded his cot, watching the stars swim back into the deeps of space as a rim of light sharpened the tree line, and he would think about cracking out of the shell of his life. Already the things he had done—in other words, the man he had become—lay on him like a crust. In his mind, he pressed tentatively against it. He thought he could feel it give.

One morning, then, he awoke and knew that it was all almost over. He awoke the way he always did, a way that made him feel he had never really been asleep at all, but that separate areas of his body had simply gone interchangeably dormant; so that waking up was nothing more than a matter of again becoming acutely conscious of his body, bit by bit. He felt his jungle fatigues, the tiger suit, scrape against him, felt stale sweat along the length of his body and in its hollows return thin pools of salt to the molding cloth; that was what he felt first. Then he felt his hands curling and uncurling along the thick canvas belt at his waist, chewed fingertips tapping broken nails on the eyelets of the belt, dull rings of metal blind and swimming green with verdigris. He reached slowly up and felt his chin. The skin on his face was so unbearably tender that, when he touched the wire of the morning's beard, each hair awoke an unkind ache along his cheek, a subcutaneous horror.

It was not the last day. Life seldom offers that kind of drama. So it was not the last day. But it was close enough.

Noon found him sitting silently in a little clearing somewhere very far from the base camp. Around him quietly sat the other members of the long-range reconnaissance patrol, as motionless as still underbrush in their tiger suits; their faces smeared as black and green as their clothes; watches, weapons, and dog tags taped; all black and green; no jingle or glitter; pieces of this jungle no more incidental than a vine; only their eyes moving ceaselessly, restlessly under the shadows of their crushed and wadded Anzac hats.

An hour later, moving back, they were hit. They were hit worse than they had been hit in an entire year. Most were killed, and all who weren't were wounded, and none of the wounded were slightly wounded. So Stephen did not get home until late October. He spent some days in a field hospital in the country, and then some weeks in a bigger hospital in Japan, and finally they sent him home.

As he had promised he would, Stephen posed for three or four days. He even managed a small-town strut in honor of his mother's wrinkled face, crisp with pride before her canasta cronies. Then he sent his uniform off to be pressed, fixed its decorations back on it when it returned, and hung it in the back of his closet in a plastic bag sickly with the tang of paradichlorobenzene.

His old room gave him hours of amusement. He picked things up and put them back into the clear circles and squares marked into the thin wash of dust that framed them. He riffled the pages of books until he found the one in which he had drawn, down the margin of fifty pages, a crudely animated parachute descent. He tried on his old clothes and noted with satisfaction that the coats were tight across the shoulders and the pants were loose around the hips. He made a show of job-hunting, but he was in fact planning to take a disorderly and unpredestined trip for a month or so before he did anything else, because he had heard about Emily at last, at length, and he was defenselessly miserable. She had not met him, or called him, the day of his return. Her young man, on his way out, had done that much damage. And perhaps he had talked to Stephen himself. She was to wonder that often. In any case, her small vacillation had cost her the right she had to be the one to tell Stephen what she had done.

Stephen, for his part, had sharply determined not to call her: a sure short hourglass that he would. But when he had been home a week she called him, finally. He knew who it was from the reticence with which his mother summoned him to the phone. He answered in a balanced tone, modest, assured, without falsehood or rudeness. But Emily, though tinned by the wire, was breathless and girlish, and his heart crawled.

"May I see you?" she asked at once, saying nothing before, and nothing more after.

"Oh, Christ, I want to see you, Emily," Stephen muttered, "but I don't see the point."

"I wonder who told you."

"What does that matter? It wasn't you, and it should have been."

"It would have been."

"It wasn't."

"Just: can I see you," Emily repeated, almost harshly. "Don't torment me."

Stephen, to his distress, was starting to shudder. It saved him from dragging on, as a weaker, more cruel corner of his nature was tempted to. "Yes, all right. When?" He was unwilling to grant her a long pause. "Tonight?" he asked, mockingly. She caught the edge, dropped a lie. "I'm busy tonight." Exactly as though he had been the one who called. It was neatly done.

"Oh, well, of course, in that case—" Stephen tied off this disconnected babble: "Very well, I can come over now."

"All right," Emily said desperately, "but I won't screw for you. This afternoon."

"Wait until you're asked." He hung up, somewhat dizzy. A thin shaft quivered in his capacity for surprise. It wasn't the language. Emily had of her own accord taken to whispering really bawdy—yes, detailed—things to him in lusty moments of their months together two years ago, and they had been a sweet mirror for the dimensions of her ardor. But there was some cold presumption in her last remark, words clad in hooker's guile.

He moped about the house for a bit, though not to collect himself, for he had sense enough to know that the sight of her either would disarm him or it wouldn't; nor to compose a front, because he was not willing to believe on the strength of that one remark that Emily now dealt strictly in surfaces. Finally he dropped a fresh pack of cigarettes into his shirt pocket and got in his mother's car and drove to Emily's house. He played a rock station loud on the radio on the way over, to still the din in his mind, and loosen himself, and jam the flow of photographs and scents that his predatory memory was tossing up to him with disinterested malice.

He parked in front of her house, and was not out of the car when he saw her waiting inside the open doorway. It seemed to him that he went much too swiftly up the steps, and when he stepped inside the door, his neat lack of preparation flew back at him more painfully than the most carefully planned and quickly demolished strategy. He felt sick, and almost faint, as he bent his face toward her mouth, holding her body away and then against him, helplessly sensing that the action was stubbing his honor on his hunger. She was wearing an old shirt of his, and chopped-off white jeans, and her long hair was riven into her broad white collar by cool sweat. There at the foot of the stairs in the cold fall darkness.

"Why did you call me?" Stephen asked stupidly. He had thought the question, and he was entirely too distracted to do any better than simply repeat his thoughts as they came to him.

"Love you. Want you back. How's chances?" Emily whispered, her face lowered delicately. It seemed to him that her use of the clipped speech they had once affected together was as ill-thought as her telephone remark. How had she come to these churlish extremes?

"I don't know," Stephen said. "If you love me—if you want me back—why did you say that on the phone?"

"I don't know." Emily looked away. "I guess because you sounded mean on the phone."

"Didn't I—*don't* I—have a right to sound mean?" He at once disliked his question.

Emily looked back at him. In an instant, and only for an instant, her eyes were suddenly full of a prayer that he might have learned in the jungle how to be brave in the city. He did not miss it.

"Don't be short with me," Emily murmured. "Be mad or sad or whatever else you want, but don't—oh, *be* short with me. Be what you like. Do you want a sandwich or anything? How good you look. I mean how well you look."

Stephen looked away from her to steady himself. He took his hands from her shoulders. His eyes swept through the big, cool,

dark room at staggered intervals, in exact imitation of a target-
detection method he had learned in basic training. They paused
like bleary travelers at familiar objects. It was her parents' living
room, but it was Emily's domain, and the easy litter of her nature was scattered through it like a skin of years: a music book, a
stuffed black duck, crumpled gloves, a square mountain of massive high-school yearbooks crowding a bookshelf by the mantel,
edged with bric-a-brac and bound condensations of twenty years
of best sellers.

"No, I don't want a sandwich."

"Well—do you want to talk about it?" Emily's head was
cocked. It seemed coy to him. He missed her meaning deliberately.

"No, I just don't want a sandwich." And somehow that made
her wonder, for the first time, if he knew only about her affair.
Not about the other thing.

"I want you back," Emily repeated. "I want you back. I've left
. . . I'm . . . I'm not messed up anymore. In any way, Steve. I'm
my own me. I want you back."

"Like candy," Stephen teased gently.

"Yes or no?" Emily said, almost screaming it.

"Yes."

Stephen had taken a nature of more than average fineness off
to war, and it may be that he brought a nature of much more
than average fineness back. If anything, the shock of the last two
years of his life had refined his sensibilities, had sandblasted
them with duty and fear. He restored himself to Emily willingly,
apparently on the mere sight of her, and if his forgiveness might
have been thought prompted by loneliness and lust, it would
seem to have been free forgiveness all the same. It required no
major effort of will on his part to pass up the opportunities he
had for post-facto rebukes. Before he had had Emily, and now he
had Emily and her dreary history, such as he knew it, and knew
of it, but both were his to guard. They wandered their old
haunts and discovered new ones, made love with satisfactory
verve, talked together with small restraint. For Stephen, the only
difficulty with the whole thing at present was his tenacious sus-
picion that he was producing an off-Broadway play instead of
recovering a life. The answer to that was to be a fair director, a
good male lead, and be grateful that it wasn't a high-school
musical. And to let the rest fend for itself. Stephen had flesh and
ease and time. He was in no mood to quarrel. Among other

things, a fresh sexuality had been liberated in him. He became a bedroom aristocrat, which is rarely bad news.

Emily was less fortunate. Her recovery of him had been much too easy for her to be comfortable with it, so everything was shot with doubt for her. She had not expected a restoration of old magics, but she had not expected her smoothest wishes to run so smoothly, either. Soon she was consoling herself with a campaign of active doubt. And she could not shake the feeling that her silence on the critical confession her other young man had known she would have to make to Stephen made the form of their life only an overlay on chaos.

They were married the week before Christmas, and in the months that followed, in the often savage web they wove of each other's emotions, a curious if not unprecedented thing happened: they tripped heavily into something like love, as two people can who have sounded certain depths and survived various cruelties—lights and hammerings, human music—and come out alive, bewildered and blinking like blind men found by sun. This condition must have been bought by time; yet even for Stephen and Emily it had a kind of narrative suddenness. And it seemed solid, theirs.

They were living in the city now, in a small white apartment at the mid-slope of a steep hill, hemmed in by tall graceful old buildings. While Stephen loafed through a vague humanities course at a city college and taught a period of freshman English, Emily made their money as a secretary, and they stayed cool and fed and almost happy in their three rooms. The rooms were painted bone-white and hung with good prints and overcrowded with comfortable Salvation Army furniture. It was not too far from what Stephen had dreamed of in the jungle. It may be that it was a bit too close to what Emily had known with her other young man.

And so they endured, and even a bit better than endured. But something rather large was tearing at Emily, Stephen knew, something that had very profoundly to do with loving him, and maybe hating him. He could sense it always in the background of a curious conversation they often had. It was almost like a litany, and there was this pressure behind it. Emily began it with one question, sometimes at dinner, sometimes in bed, sometimes at dusk as they walked up the hill to their building, watching the walls go pink with twilight. She would ask, and Stephen would answer carefully, and each time a little differently, searching always for what Emily was trying to get at. But she could never find a way of saying whàt she wanted to say. It was not easy to watch her confusion. The question was: "What was it like to be wounded?"

The first time, Stephen had considered seriously and at length, and had tried to answer her. They were in bed. An electric heating unit spread a deep orange blanket of light over their bodies and over the crumpled sheets and cracked white plaster wall. The heating unit answered an aesthetic rather than a practical need. It was like making love in front of an open fire. As she asked him, her fingers lingered in turn on the several parts of his body that had been marked by metal.

He answered her by talking briefly about pain. He was as pragmatic as possible; he stayed away from theory. But finally there was no way to answer her question, and he turned to the wall and looked at the way the light from the heating unit had turned the white plaster pink in some places, it had turned networks of chips and cracks into deep red lakes and rivers. Fanciful Stephen looked for a long time at the world of that wall, and wondered if he could tell Emily about the cicada and the shell.

"Would you rather I hadn't mentioned that?" Emily asked him at last.

"No, it's just that I don't know how to answer it. I really don't. My father asked me how much action I had seen, and I didn't really know how to answer that. A guy I used to know at college asked me what it felt like to kill people, and that was only a little easier to answer."

Emily shuddered. "I don't ask you that. I'm sorry about the other." She touched him. "Does it ever hurt anymore?"

"No." He took her hand. "Don't talk."

"I won't ask you again."

"It's all right. Don't talk."

And so she didn't. And that was the first time.

That winter he began to have nightmares. Hard ones. They left him sick in the mornings, always grey and awake at dawn. He would wake himself up, not when they were at their worst, but when they were over, and gaze steadily at his sleeping wife as the light changed in the room and changed the tones of her skin. Emily slept quiet and still. Sometimes it seemed to him that he had a new wife with each changing of the light. He thought perhaps he could awaken her at different hours and have a different wife. At four, when the room was dark, she took shape only as an imprint on his eyes, pressed there by his straining to see her. He was careful not to touch her, and he breathed only through his mouth so as not to be robbed of a new creation by her familiar smell. At four, she would be the same girl should he awaken her. Dark, quiet, innocent, unwise. An hour later, when the grey tones had come, she would be perhaps more mysterious and gentle, a little cryptic, richer in history, even in breeding. When the room was full light, she might be something less: flesh heavier than her flesh, coarse in her sleeping movements, a maid, a waitress, full around the mouth, stupid, a little stupid.

Daylight never wakened Emily. Darkness rarely let her husband sleep. It was a hard time. Stephen sometimes thought it might cost him his maturity.

One night he woke up shaking with fear and confusion, and Emily had to repeat his name to him, over and over, and then hers, before he could stop. His body shook, and he heard his name, and hers, and felt her hands on him—but she was touching him much too gently!—but they were hands, her hands, and his name, her name, and gradually he rested and came awake.

"Christ, I'm sorry," Stephen said miserably.

She comforted him, a bit woodenly. And she turned her face away from him when she spoke. "Was it . . . was it about being wounded? Was that what you were dreaming about?"

Stephen said that it was. He was lying. He had been dreaming about his wife. He had seen her digging a flowerbed in some dark and shadowed garden. Emily, who had never held a trowel. But she was digging. And she had dislodged something, worked it free from the peaty clods of soil that moved under her fingers. She held it up: a waxen hand splayed bloodless through the blade of a bayonet gone red with rust.

"Steve, can I tell you something?" Emily asked. Stephen was sitting on the edge of the bed now, fishing in his rumpled shirt for a cigarette, his softening waist crowded by the tangle of wet sheets. "Yeah, sure," he said dully.

But instead she asked him the question again, she asked him again what it was like to be wounded. She looked back at him after she asked, and saw his face flare briefly into shadows and angles as he drew on his cigarette.

"You know I don't know how to tell you, Emily."

"But I wish you did. I wish you could," Emily whispered, and she was crying.

He put the burning cigarette carefully into the ashtray and put his arms around her and kissed her. "How many ways do you know of making love?"

Emily stopped crying. In fact, she managed a laugh. "Why?
Are you bored?" She frowned. Perhaps it was a mock frown. "Do
you think I'm holding out on you?"

"My own little diamond mine," Stephen muttered, not gently.
But Emily was becoming interested. "I don't know. I've never
counted. If you're including every variation and variable possible, you know, positions . . . intoxication . . . or not . . . the
color of the wallpaper . . . and is it raining outside, or maybe
we're out in the rain? . . . well . . . millions, I guess."

"I don't even know why I asked."

"I don't know. Three. Six. Maybe twenty. I really don't know
what you mean."

"I'm sorry I asked."

"*That's* a lie."

"Anyway," Stephen said, "it's a more interesting question, isn't
it?"

She started to smile as she realized what he meant. He moved
against her, and she caught him up, sweetly, and he her, timing
freed by dreams, full of nostalgia. In thirty-five minutes—
Stephen had been watching the clock—they knighted each other,
and Stephen lay by her a moment, then turned over and closed
his eyes and feigned sleep, or even went to sleep, still holding her
hand. Light from the street seeped through the venetian blinds
and banded his chest and neck, but his face was high on the
pillow, high in darkness. And Emily, lying quiet beside him,
finally knew that she would never have to tell him that, in the
year before, in the happy heat of her passion for her interim
young man, and for the cause of freedom and peace, and in the
service of a revolutionary people locked in a birth throe or a
death pang with the warlords of imperialism, she had gone so far
as to contribute money for guns, and from her own body, a tiny
bottle of blood to refresh the enemy who had almost killed the
man who was to be her husband.

So she lay still. And Stephen finally began a quiet rhythmic
breathing. He was asleep. And Emily, looking into his shadowed
face one more time before she settled into sleep herself, had no
reason to believe that he was dreaming.

THE CONGRESSMAN WHO LOVED FLAUBERT

Ward Just

1.

The deputation was there: twelve men in his outer office and he would have to see them. His own fault, if "fault" was the word. They'd called every day for a week, trying to arrange an appointment. Finally his assistant, Annette, put it to him: Please see them. Do it for me. Wein is an old friend, she'd said. It meant a lot to Wein to get his group before a congressman whose name was known, whose words had weight. LaRuth stood and stretched; his long arms reached for the ceiling. He was his statuesque best that day: dark suit, dark tie, white shirt, black beard neatly trimmed. No jewelry of any kind. He rang his secretary and told her to show them in, to give them thirty minutes and then ring again; the committee meeting was at eleven.

"What do they look like?"

"Scientists," she said. "They look just as you'd expect scientists to look. They're all thin. And none of them are smoking." LaRuth laughed. "They're pretty intense, Lou."

"Well, let's get on with it."

He met them at the door, as they shyly filed in. Wein and his committee were scientists against imperialism. They were physicists, biologists, linguists, and philosophers. They introduced themselves, and LaRuth wondered again what it was that a philosopher did in these times. It had to be a grim year for philosophy. The introductions done, LaRuth leaned back, a long leg hooked over the arm of his chair, and told them to go ahead.

They had prepared a congressional resolution, a sense-of-the-Congress resolution, which they wanted LaRuth to introduce. It was a message denouncing imperialism, and as LaRuth read it he was impressed by its eloquence. They had assembled hard facts:

so many tons of bombs dropped in Indochina, so many "facilities" built in Africa, so many American soldiers based in Europe, so many billions in corporate investment in Latin America. It was an excellent statement, not windy as so many of them are. He finished reading it, and turned to Wein.

"Congressman, we believe this is a matter of simple morality. Decency, if you will. There are parallels elsewhere, the most compelling being the extermination of American Indians. Try not to look on the war and the bombing from the perspective of a Westerner looking East but of an Easterner facing West." La-Ruth nodded. He recognized that it was the war that truly interested them. "The only place the analogy breaks down is that the Communists in Asia appear to be a good deal more resourceful and resilient than the Indians in America. Perhaps that is because there are so many more of them." Wein paused to smile. "But it is genocide either way. It is a stain on the American Congress not to raise a specific voice of protest, not only in Asia but in the other places where American policy is doing violence . . ."

LaRuth wondered if they knew the mechanics of moving a congressional resolution. They probably did; there was no need for a civics lecture. Wein was looking at him, waiting for a response. An intervention. "It's a very fine statement," LaRuth said.

"Everybody says that. And then they tell us to get the signatures and come back. We think this ought to be undertaken from the inside. In that way, when and if the resolution is passed, it will have more force. We think that a member of Congress should get out front on it."

An admirable toughness there, LaRuth thought. If he were Wein, that would be just about the way he'd put it.

"We've all the people you'd expect us to have." Very rapidly, Wein ticked off two dozen names, the regular antiwar contingent on the Democratic left. "What we need to move with this is not the traditional dove, but a more moderate man. A moderate man with a conscience." Wein smiled.

"Yes," LaRuth said.

"Someone like you."

LaRuth was silent a moment, then spoke rapidly. "My position is this. I'm not a member of the Foreign Affairs Committee or the Appropriations Committee or Armed Services or any of the others where . . . war legislation or defense matters are considered. I'm not involved in foreign relations, I'm in education. It's the Education and Labor Committee. No particular reason why those two subjects should be linked, but they are." LaRuth smiled. "That's Congress for you."

"It seems to us, Congressman, that the war—the leading edge of imperialism and violence—is tied to everything. Education is a mess because of the war. So is labor. And so forth. It's all part of the war. Avoid the war and you avoid all the other problems. The damn thing is like the Spanish Inquisition, if you lived in Torquemada's time, fifteenth-century Spain. If you did try to avoid it you were either a coward or a fool. That is meant respectfully."

"Well, it is nicely put. Respectfully."

"But you won't do it."

LaRuth shook his head. "You get more names, and I'll think about cosponsoring. But I won't front for it. I'm trying to pass an education bill right now. I can't get out front on the war, too. Important as it is. Eloquent as you are. There are other men in this House who can do the job better than I can."

"We're disappointed," Wein said.

"I could make you a long impressive speech." His eyes took in the others, sitting in chilly silence. "I could list all the reasons. But you know what they are, and it wouldn't do either of us any good. I wish you success."

"Spare us any more successes," Wein said. "Everyone wishes us success, but no one helps. We're like the troops in the trenches. The Administration tells them to go out and win the war. You five hundred thousand American boys, you teach the dirty Commies a lesson. Storm the hill, the Administration says. But the Administration is far away from the shooting. We're right behind you, they say. Safe in Washington."

"I don't deny it," LaRuth said mildly.

"I think there are special places in hell reserved for those who see the truth but will not act." LaRuth stiffened, but stayed silent. "These people are worse than the ones who love the war. You are more dangerous than the generals in the Pentagon, who at least are doing what they believe in. It is because of people like you that we are where we are."

Never justify, never explain, LaRuth thought; it was pointless anyway. They were pleased to think of him as a war criminal. A picture of a lurching tumbrel in Pennsylvania Avenue flashed through his mind, and was gone, an oddly comical image. LaRuth touched his beard and sat upright. "I'm sorry you feel that way. It isn't true, you know." One more number like that one, he thought suddenly, and he'd throw the lot of them out of his office.

But Wein would not let go. "We're beyond subtle distinctions, Mr. LaRuth. That is one of the delightful perceptions that the war has brought us. We can mumble all day. You can tell me about your responsibilities and your effectiveness, and how you don't want to damage it. You can talk politics and I can talk morals. But I took moral philosophy in college. An interesting academic exercise." LaRuth nodded; Wein was no fool. "Is it true you wrote your Ph.D. thesis on Flaubert?"

"I wrote it at the Sorbonne," LaRuth replied. "But that was almost twenty years ago. Before politics." LaRuth wanted to give them something to hang on to. They would appreciate the irony, and then they could see him as a fallen angel, a victim of the process; it was more interesting than seeing him as a war criminal.

"Well, it figures."

LaRuth was surprised. He turned to Wein. "How does it figure?"

"Flaubert was just as pessimistic and cynical as you are."

LaRuth had thirty minutes to review his presentation to the committee. This was the most important vote in his twelve years in Congress, a measure which, if they could steer it through the House, would release a billion dollars over three years' time to elementary schools throughout the country. The measure was based on a hellishly complicated formula which several legal experts regarded as unconstitutional; but one expert is always opposed by another when a billion dollars is involved. LaRuth had to nurse along the chairman, a volatile personality, a natural skeptic. Today he had to put his presentation in exquisite balance, giving here, taking there, assuring the committee that the Constitution would be observed, and that all regions would share equally.

It was not something that could be understood in a university, but LaRuth's twelve years in the House of Representatives would be justified if he could pass this bill. Twelve years, through three Presidents. He'd avoided philosophy and concentrated on detail, his own time in a third-rate grade school in a Southern mill town never far from his mind: that was the reference point. Not often that a man was privileged to witness the methodical destruction of children before the age of thirteen, before they had encountered genuinely soulless and terrible events; the war, for one. His bill would begin the process of revivifying education. It was one billion dollars' worth of life, and he'd see to it that some of the money leaked down to his own school. LaRuth was lucky, an escapee on scholarships, first to

Tulane and then to Paris, his world widened beyond measure; Flaubert gave him a taste for politics. *Madame Bovary* and *A Sentimental Education* were political novels, or so he'd argued at the Sorbonne; politics was nothing more or less than an understanding of ambition, and the moral and social conditions that produced it in its various forms. The House of Representatives: *un stade des arrivistes.* And now the press talked him up as a Southern Liberal, and the Northern Democrats came to him for help. Sometimes he gave it, sometimes he didn't. They could not understand the refusals—Lou, you won with 65 percent of the vote the last time out. What do you want, a coronation? They were critical that he would not get out front on the war, and would not vote against bills vital to Southern interests. (Whatever they were, now that the entire region was dominated by industrial combines whose headquarters were in New York or Chicago—and how's that for imperialism, Herr Wein?) They didn't, or couldn't, grasp the paper-thin depth of his support. The Birchers and the segs were everywhere, and each time he voted with the liberals in the House he'd hear from a few of them. *You are being watched.* He preferred a low silhouette. All those big liberals didn't understand that a man with enough money could still buy an election in his district; he told them that LaRuth compromised was better than no LaRuth at all. That line had worked well the first four or five years he'd been in Washington; it worked no longer. In these times, caution and realism were the refuge of a scoundrel.

The war, so remote in its details, poisoned everything. He read about it every day, and through a friend on the Foreign Affairs Committee saw some classified material. But he could not truly engage himself in it, because he hadn't seen it firsthand. He did not know it intimately. It was clear enough that it was a bad war, everyone knew that; but knowing it and feeling it were two different things. The year before he'd worked to promote a junket, a special subcommittee to investigate expenditures for education. There was plenty of scandalous rumor to justify the investigation. He tried to promote it in order to get a look at the place firsthand, on the ground. He wanted to look at the faces and the villages, to see the countryside which had been destroyed by the war, to observe the actual manner in which the war was being fought. But the chairman refused, he wanted no part of it; scandal or no scandal, it was not part of the committee's business. So the trip never happened. What the congressman knew about the war he read in newspapers and magazines and saw on television. But that did not help. LaRuth had done time as an infan-

tryman in Korea, and knew what killing was about; the box did
not make it as horrible as it was. The box romanticized it,
cleansed it of pain; one more false detail. Even the blood deceived, coming up pink and pretty on the television set. One
night he spent half of Cronkite fiddling with the color knob to
get a perfect red, to insist the blood look like *blood*.

More: early in his congressional career, LaRuth took pains to
explain his positions. He wanted his constituents to know what
he was doing and why, and two newsletters went out before the
leader of his state's delegation took him aside one day in the hall.
Huge arms around his shoulders, a whispered conference. Christ,
you are going to get killed, the man said. *Don't do that.* Don't
get yourself down on paper on every raggedy-ass bill that comes
before Congress. It makes you a few friends, who don't remember, and a lot of enemies, who do. Particularly in your district:
you are way ahead of those people in a lot of areas, but don't
advertise it. You've a fine future here; don't ruin it before you've
begun. LaRuth thought the advice was captious and irrespon-
sible and disregarded it. And very nearly lost reelection, after
some indiscretions to a newspaperman. *That* son of a bitch, who
violated every rule of confidence held sacred in the House of
Representatives.

His telephone rang. The secretary said it was Annette.

"How did it go?" Her voice was low, cautious.

"Like a dream," he said. "And thanks lots. I'm up there with
the generals as a war criminal. They think I make lampshades in
my spare time."

Coolly: "I take it you refused to help them."

"You take it right."

"They're very good people. Bill Wein is one of the most distinguished botanists in the country."

"Yes, he speaks very well. A sincere, intelligent, dedicated
provocateur. Got off some very nice lines, at least one reference to
Dante. A special place in hell is reserved for people like me, who
are worse than army generals."

"Well, that's one point of view."

"You know, I'm tired of arguing about the war. If Wein is so
goddamned concerned about the war and the corruption of the
American system, then why doesn't he give up the fat government contracts at that think tank he works for . . ."

"That's unfair, Lou!"

". . . why do they think that anyone who deals in the real
world is an automatic sellout? Creep. A resolution like that one,
even if passed, would have no effect. Zero effect. It would not be

binding, the thing's too vague. They'd sit up there and everyone would have a good gooey warm feeling, *and nothing would happen*. It's meaningless, except of course for the virtue. Virtue everywhere. Virtue triumphant. So I am supposed to put my neck on the line for something that's meaningless . . ." LaRuth realized he was near shouting, so he lowered his voice. "Meaningless," he said.

"You're so hostile," she said angrily. "Filled with hate. Contempt. Why do you hate everybody? You should've done what Wein wanted you to do."

He counted to five and was calm now, reasonable. His congressional baritone: "It's always helpful to have your political advice, Annette. Very helpful. I value it. Too bad you're not a politician yourself." She said nothing, he could hear her breathing. "I'll see you later," he said, and hung up.

LaRuth left his office, bound for the committee room. He'd gone off the handle, and was not sorry. But sometimes he indulged in just a bit much introspection and self-justification, endemic diseases in politicians. There were certain basic facts: his constituency supported the war, at the same time permitting him to oppose it so long as he did it quietly and in such a way that "the boys" were supported. Oppose the war, support the troops. A high-wire act—very Flaubertian, that situation; it put him in the absurd position of voting for military appropriations and speaking out against the war. Sorry, Annette; that's the way we think on Capitol Hill. It's a question of what you *vote* for. Forget the fancy words and phrases, it's a question of votes. Up, down, or "present." Vote against the appropriations and sly opponents at home would accuse him of "tying the hands" of American troops and thereby comforting the enemy. Blood on his fingers.

2.

LaRuth was forty; he had been in the House since the age of twenty-eight. Some of his colleagues had been there before he was born, moving now around the halls and the committee rooms as if they were extensions of antebellum county courthouses. They smelled of tobacco and whiskey and old wool, their faces dry as parchment. LaRuth was amused to watch them on the floor; they behaved as they would at a board meeting of a family business, attentive if they felt like it, disruptive if their mood was playful. They were forgiven; it was a question of age. The House was filled with old men, and its atmosphere was one of very great age. Deference was a way of life. LaRuth recalled a friend who aspired to a position of leadership. They put him through his paces, and for some reason he did not measure up; the friend was told he'd have to wait, it was not yet time. He'd been there eighteen years, and was only fifty-two. Fifty-two! Jack Kennedy was President at forty-three, and Thomas Jefferson had written the preamble when under thirty-five. But then, as one of the senior men put it, this particular fifty-two-year-old man had none of the durable qualities of Kennedy or Jefferson. That is, he did not have Kennedy's money or Jefferson's brains. Not that money counted for very much in the House of Representatives; pluto- crats belonged in the other body.

It was not a place for lost causes. There were too many conflict- ing interests, too much confusion, too many turns to the laby- rinth. Too many *people*: four hundred and thirty-five represen- tatives and about a quarter of them quite bright. Quite bright enough and knowledgeable enough to strangle embarrassing proposals, and take revenge as well. Everyone was threatened if the eccentrics got out of hand. The political coloration of the eccentric didn't matter. This was one reason why it was so diffi- cult to build an ideological record in the House. A man with ideology was wise to leave it before reaching a position of influ- ence, because by then he'd mastered the art of compromise, which had nothing to do with dogma or public acts of conscience. It had to do with simple effectiveness, the tact and strength with which a man dealt with legislation, inside committees, behind closed doors. That was where the work got done, and the credit passed around.

LaRuth, at forty, was on a knife's edge. Another two years and he'd be a man of influence, and therefore ineligible for any poli- tics outside the House—or not ineligible, but shopworn, no longer new, no longer fresh. He would be ill-suited, and there were other practical considerations as well, because who wanted to be a servant for twelve or fourteen years and then surrender an opportunity to be master? Not LaRuth. So the time for tem- porizing was nearly past. If he was going to forsake the House and reach for the Senate (a glamorous possibility), he had to do it soon.

LaRuth's closest friend in Congress was a man about his own age from a neighboring state. They'd come to the Hill in the same year, and for a time enjoyed publicity in the national press, where they could least afford it. *Two Young Liberals from the*

South, that sort of thing. Winston was then a bachelor, too, and for the first few years they shared a house in Cleveland Park. But it was awkward, there were too many women in and out of the place, and one groggy morning Winston had come upon LaRuth and a friend taking a shower together and that had torn it. They flipped for the house and LaRuth won, and Winston moved to grander quarters in Georgetown. They saw each other frequently, and laughed together about the curiosities of the American political system; Winston, a gentleman farmer from the plantation South, was a ranking member of the House Foreign Affairs Committee. The friendship was complicated because they were occasional rivals: who would represent the New South? They took to kidding each other's press notices: LaRuth was the "attractive liberal," Winston the "wealthy liberal." Thus, LaRuth became Liberal Lou and Winston was Wealthy Warren. To the extent that either of them had a national reputation, they were in the same category: they voted their consciences, but were not incautious.

It was natural for Wein and his committee of scientists to go directly to Winston after leaving LaRuth. The inevitable telephone call came the next day, Winston inviting LaRuth by for a drink around six; "small problem to discuss." Since leaving Cleveland Park, Warren Winston's life had become plump and graceful. Politically secure now, he had sold his big house back home and bought a small jewel of a place on Dumbarton Avenue, three bedrooms and a patio in back, a mirrored bar, and a sauna in the basement. Winston was drinking a gin and tonic by the pool when LaRuth walked in. The place was more elegant than he'd remmbered; the patio was now decorated with tiny boxbushes and a magnolia tree was in full cry.

They joked a bit, laughing over the new Southern manifesto floating around the floor of the House. They were trying to find a way to spike it without seeming to spike it. Winston mentioned the "small problem" after about thirty minutes of small talk.

"Lou, do you know a guy named Wein?"

"He's a friend of Annette's."

"He was in to see you, then."

"Yeah."

"And?"

"We didn't see eye to eye."

"You're being tight-lipped, Liberal Lou."

"I told him to piss off," LaRuth said. "He called me a war criminal, and then he called me a cynic. A pessimist, a cynic, and a war criminal. All this for some cream-puff resolution that will keep them damp in Cambridge and won't change a goddamned thing."

"You think it's *that* bad."

"Worse, maybe."

"I'm not sure. Not sure at all."

"Warren, *Christ.*"

"Look, doesn't it make any sense at all to get the position of the House on record? That can't fail to have some effect downtown, and it can't fail to have an effect in the country. It probably doesn't stand a chance of being passed, but the effort will cause some commotion. The coon'll be treed. Some attention paid. It's a good thing to get on the record, and I can see some points being made."

"What points? Where?"

"The newspapers, the box. Other places. It'd show that at least some of us are not content with things as they are. That we want to change . . ."

LaRuth listened carefully. It was obvious to him that Winston was trying out a speech; like a new suit of clothes, he took it out and tried it on, asking his friend about the color, the fit, the cut of it.

". . . the idea that change can come from within the system . . ."

"Aaaaaoh," LaRuth groaned.

"No?" Innocently.

"How about, *and so, my fellow Americans, ask not what you can do for* Wein, *but what* Wein *can do for you.* That thing is loose as a hound dog's tongue. Now tell me the true gen."

"Bettger's retiring."

"You don't say." LaRuth was surprised. Bettger was the state's senior senator, a living Southern legend.

"Cancer. No one knows about it. He'll announce retirement at the end of the month. It's my only chance for the next four years, maybe *ever.* There'll be half a dozen guys in the primary, but my chances are good. If I'm going to go for the Senate, it's got to be now. This thing of Wein's is a possible vehicle. I say possible. One way in. People want a national politician as a senator. It's not enough to've been a good congressman, or even a good governor. You need something more: when people see your face on the box they want to think *senatorial,* somehow. You don't agree?"

LaRuth was careful now. Winston was saying many of the things he himself had said. Of course he was right, a senator needed a national gloss. The old bulls didn't need it, but they were operating from a different tradition, pushing different buttons. But if you were a young man running statewide for the first time, you needed a different base. Out there in television land were all those followers without leaders. People were pulled by different strings now. The point was to identify which strings pulled strongest.

"I think Wein's crowd is a mistake. That resolution is a mistake. They'll kill you at home if you put your name to that thing."

"No, Lou. You do it a different way. With a little rewording, that resolution becomes a whole lot less scary; it becomes something straight out of Robert A. Taft. You *e-liminate* the fancy words and phrases. You steer *clear* of words like corrupt or genocide or violence. You and I, Lou, we know: our people *like* violence, it's part of our way of life. So you don't talk about violence, you talk about American traditions, like 'the American tradition of independence and individuality. Noninterference!' Now you are saying a couple of *other* things, when you're saying that, Lou. You dig? That's the way you get at imperialism. You don't call it imperialism because that word's got a bad sound. A foreign sound."

LaRuth laughed. Winston had it figured out. He had to get Wein to agree to the changes, but that should present no problem. Wealthy Warren was a persuasive man.

"Point is, I've got to look to people down there like I can make a difference . . ."

"I think you've just said the magic words."

"Like it?"

"I think so. Yeah, I think I do."

"*To make the difference. Winston for Senator.* A double line on the billboards, like this." Winston described two lines with his finger, and mulled the slogan again. "*To make the difference, Winston for Senator.* See, it doesn't matter what kind of difference. All people know is that they're fed to the teeth. *Fed up and mad at the way things are.* And they've got to believe that if they vote for you, in some unspecified way things will get better. Now I think the line about interference can do double duty. People are tired of being hassled, in all ways. Indochina, down home." Winston was a gifted mimic, and now he adopted a toothless expression, and hooked his thumbs into imaginary galluses. "Ah think I'll vote for that-there Winston. Prob'ly won't do any harm. Mot do some good. Mot mek a diff'rence."

"Shit, Warren."

"You give me a little help?"

"Sure."

"Sign the Wein thing?"

LaRuth thought a moment. "No," he said.

"What the hell, Lou? Why not? If it's rearranged the way I said. Look, Wein will be out of it. It'll be strictly a congressional thing."

"It doesn't mean anything."

"Means a whole lot to me."

"Well, that's different. That's political."

"If you went in too, it'd look a safer bet."

"All there'd be out of that is more gold-dust-twins copy. You don't want that."

"No, it'd be made clear that I'm managing it. I'm out front. I make all the statements, you're back in the woodwork. Far from harm's way, Lou." Winston took his glass and refilled it with gin and tonic. He carefully cut a lime and squeezed it into the glass. Winston looked the part, no doubt about that. Athlete's build, big, with sandy hair beginning to thin; he could pass for an astronaut.

"You've got to find some new names for the statement."

"Right on, brother. Too many Jews, too many foreigners. Why are there no scientists named Robert E. Lee or Thomas Jefferson? Talmadge, Bilbo." Winston sighed, and answered his own question. "The decline of the WASP. Look, Lou. The statement will be forgotten in six weeks, and that's fine with me. I just need it for a little national coverage at the beginning. Hell, it's not decisive. But it could make a difference."

"You're going to *open* the campaign with the statement?"

"You bet. Considerably revised. It'd be a help, Lou, if you'd go along. It would give them a chance to crank out some updated New South pieces. The networks would be giving that a run just as I announce for the Senate and my campaign begins. See, it's a natural. Bettger is Old South, I'm New. But we're friends and neighbors, and that's a fact. It gives them a dozen pegs to hang it on, and those bastards love *you*, with the black suits and the beard and that cracker accent. It's a natural, and it would mean a hell of a lot, a couple of minutes on national right at the beginning. I wouldn't forget it. I'd owe you a favor."

LaRuth was always startled by Winston's extensive knowledge of the press. He spoke of "pieces" and "pegs," A.M. and P.M. cycles, facts "cranked out" or "folded in," who was up and who was down at CBS, who was analyzing Congress for the editorial board of the Washington *Post*. Warren Winston was always accessible, good for a quote, day or night; and he was visible in Georgetown.

"Can you think about it by the end of the week?"

"Sure," LaRuth said.

He returned to the Hill, knowing that he thought better in his office. When there was any serious thinking to be done, he did it there, and often stayed late, after midnight. He'd mix a drink at the small bar in his office, and work. Sometimes Annette stayed with him, sometimes not. When LaRuth walked into his office she was still there, catching up, she said; but she knew he'd been with Winston.

"He's going to run for the Senate," LaRuth said.

"Warren?"

"That's what he says. He's going to front for Wein as well. That statement of Wein's—Warren's going to sign it. Wants me to sign it, too."

"Why you?"

"United front. It would help him out. No doubt about that. But it's a bad statement. Something tells me not to do it."

"Are you as mad as you look?"

He glanced at her and laughed. "Does it show?"

"To me it shows."

It was true; there was no way to avoid competition in politics. Politics was a matter of measurements, luck, and ambition, and he and Warren had run as an entry for so long that it disconcerted him to think of Senator Winston; Winston up one rung on the ladder. He was irritated that Winston had made the first move and made it effortlessly. It had nothing to do with his own career, but suddenly he felt a shadow on the future. Winston had seized the day all right, and the fact of it depressed him. His friend was clever and self-assured in his movements; he took risks; he relished the public part of politics. Winston was expert at delivering memorable speeches on the floor of the House; they were evidence of passion. For Winston, there was no confusion between the private and the public; it was all one. LaRuth thought that he had broadened and deepened in twelve years in the House, a man of realism, but not really a part of the apparatus. Now Winston had stolen the march, he was a decisive step ahead.

LaRuth may have made a mistake. He liked and understood the legislative process, transactions which were only briefly political. That is, they were not public. If a man kept himself straight at home, he could do what he liked in the House. So LaRuth had become a fixture in his district, announcing election plans every two years from the front porch of his family's small farmhouse, where he was born, where his mother lived still. The house was filled with political memorabilia; the parlor walls resembled huge bulletin boards, with framed photographs, testimonials, parchments, diplomas. His mother was so proud. His life seemed to vindicate her own, his successes hers; she'd told him so. His position in the U.S. Congress was precious, and not lightly discarded. The cold age of the place had given him a distrust of anything spectacular or . . . capricious. The House: no place for lost causes.

Annette was looking at him, hands on hips, smiling sardonically. He'd taken off his ocat, and was now in shirt-sleeves. She told him lightly that he shouldn't feel badly, that if *he* ran for the Senate he'd have to shave off his beard. Buy new clothes. Become prolix, and professionally optimistic. But, as a purchase on the future, his signature . . .

"Might. Might not," he said.

"Why not?"

"I've never done that here."

"Are you refusing to sign because you don't want to, or because you're piqued at Warren? I mean, Senator Winston."

He looked at her. "A little of both."

"Well, that's foolish. You ought to sort out your motives."

"That can come later. That's my business."

"No. Warren's going to want to know why you're not down the line with him. You're pretty good friends. He's going to want to know *why*."

"It's taken me twelve years to build what credit I've got in this place. I'm trusted. The speaker trusts me. The chairman trusts me."

". . . little children see you on the street. Gloryosky! There goes trustworthy Lou LaRuth . . ."

"Attractive, liberal," he said, laughing. "Well, it's true. This resolution, if it ever gets that far, is a ball-buster. It could distract the House for a month and revive the whole issue. Because it's been quiet we've been able to get on with our work, I mean the serious business. Not to get pompous about it."

"War's pretty important," she said.

"Well, is it now? You tell me how important it is." He put his drink on the desk blotter, and loomed over her. "Better yet, you tell me how this resolution will solve the problem. God forbid there should be any solutions, though. Moral commitments. Statements. Resolutions. They're the great things, aren't they? Fuck solutions." Thoroughly angry now, he turned away and

filled the glasses. He put some ice and whiskey in hers, and a
premixed martini in his own.

"What harm would it do?"

"Divert a lot of energy. Big play to the galleries for a week or
two. Until everyone got tired. The statement itself? No harm at
all. Good statement, well done. No harm, unless you consider
perpetuating an illusion some kind of harm."

"A lot of people live by illusions, *and what's wrong with getting this House on record?*"

"But it won't be gotten on record. That's the point. The thing
will be killed. It'll just make everybody nervous and divide the
place more than it's divided already."

"I'd think about it," she said.

"Yeah, I will. I'll tell you something. I'll probably end up
signing the goddamned thing. It'll do Warren some good. Then
I'll do what I can to see that it's buried, although God knows we
won't lack for gravediggers. And then go back to my own work
on the school bill."

"I think that's better." She smiled. "One call, by the way. The
chairman. He wants you to call first thing in the morning."

"What did he say it's about?"

"The school bill, dear."

Oh shit, LaRuth thought.

"There's a snag," she said.

"Did he say what it was?"

"I don't think he wants to vote for it anymore."

3.

Winston was after him, trying to force a commitment, but La-
Ruth was preoccupied with the school bill, which was becoming
unstuck. It was one of the unpredictable things that happen;
there was no explanation for it. But the atmosphere had subtly
changed and support was evaporating. The members wavered,
the chairman was suddenly morose and uncertain; he thought it
might be better to delay. LaRuth convinced him that was an
unwise course, and had set about repairing damage. This was
plumbing, pure and simple, talking with members, speaking to
their fears. LaRuth called it negative advocacy, but it often
worked. Between conferences the next day, LaRuth found time
to see a high-school history class, students from his alma mater.
They were touring Washington and wanted to talk to him about
Congress. The teacher, sloe-eyed, stringy-haired, twenty-five,

wanted to talk about the war; the students were indifferent. They crowded into his outer office, thirty of them; the secretaries stood aside, amused, as the teacher opened the conversation with a long preface on the role of the House, most of it inaccurate. Then she asked LaRuth about the war. What was the congressional role in the war?

"Not enough," LaRuth replied, and went on in some detail, addressing the students.

"Why not a congressional resolution demanding an end to this terrible immoral war?" the teacher demanded. "Congressman, why can't the House of Representatives take matters into its own hands?"

"Because"—LaRuth was icy, at once angry, tired, and bored—"because a majority of the members of this House do not want to lose Asia to the Communists. Irrelevant, perhaps. You may think it is a bad argument. I think it is a bad argument. But it is the way the members feel."

"But why can't that be *tested*? In votes."

The students came reluctantly awake, and were listening with little flickers of interest. The teacher was obviously a favorite, their mod pedagogue. LaRuth was watching a girl in the back of the room. She resembled the girls he'd known at home, short-haired, light summer dress, full-bodied; it was a body that would soon go heavy. He abruptly steered the conversation to his school bill, winding into it, giving them a stump speech, some flavor of home. He felt the students with him for a minute or two, then they drifted away. In five minutes they were somewhere else altogether. He said good-bye to them then, and shook their hands on the way out. The short-haired girl lingered a minute; she was the last one to go.

"It would be good if you could do something about the war," she said.

"Well, I've explained."

"My brother was killed there."

LaRuth closed his eyes for a second, and stood without speaking.

"Any gesture at all," she said.

"Gestures." He shook his head sadly. "They never do any good."

"Well," she said. "Thank you for your time." LaRuth thought her very grown-up, a well-spoken girl. She stood in the doorway, very pretty. The others had moved off down the hall; he could hear the teacher's high whine.

"How old was he?"

"Nineteen," she said. "Would've been twenty next birthday."

"Where?"

"They said it was an airplane."

"I'm so sorry."

"You wrote us a letter, don't you remember?"

"I don't know your name," LaRuth said gently.

"Ecker," she said. "My brother's name was Howard."

"I remember," he said. "It was . . . some time ago."

"Late last year," she said, looking at him.

"Yes, that would be just about it. I'm very sorry."

"So am I," she said, smiling brightly. Then she walked off to join the rest of her class. LaRuth stood in the doorway a moment, feeling the eyes of his secretary on his back. It had happened before; the South seemed to bear the brunt of the war. He'd written more than two hundred letters, to the families of poor boys, black and white. The deaths were disproportionate, poor to rich, black to white, South to North. Oh well, he thought. Oh hell. He walked back into his office and called Winston and told him he'd go along. In a limited way. For a limited period.

Later:

"It's rolling," Winston said.

"Have you talked to Wein?"

"I've talked to Wein."

"And what did Wein say?"

"Wein agrees to the revisions."

"Complaining?"

"The contrary. Wein sees himself as the spearhead of a great national movement. He sees scientists moving into political positions, cockpits of influence. His conscience is as clear as rainwater. He is very damp."

LaRuth laughed; it was a private joke.

"Wein is damp in Cambridge, then."

"I think that is a fair statement, Uncle Lou."

"How wonderful for him."

"He was pleased that you are with us. He said he misjudged you. He offers apologies. He fears he was a speck . . . harsh."

"Bully for Wein."

"I told everyone that you would be on board. I knew that when the chips were down you would not fail. I knew that you would examine your conscience and your heart and determine where the truth lay. I knew you would not be cynical or pessimistic. I know you want to see your old friend in the Senate."

They were laughing together. Winston was in one of his dry, mordant moods. He was very salty. He rattled off a dozen names, and cited the sources of each member's conscience: money and influence. "But to be fair—always be fair, Liberal Lou—there are a dozen more who are doing it because they want to do it. They think it's *right.*"

"*Faute de mieux.*"

"I am not schooled in the French language, Louis. You are always flinging French at me."

"It means, 'in the absence of anything better.' "

Winston grinned, then shrugged. LaRuth was depressed, the shadow lengthened, became darker.

"I've set up a press conference, a half dozen of us. All moderate men. Men of science, men of government. I'll be out front, doing all the talking. OK?"

"Sure." LaRuth was thinking about his school bill.

"It's going to be jim-dandy."

"Swell. But I want to see the statement beforehand, music man."

Winston smiled broadly, and spread his hands wide. Your friendly neighborhood legislator, concealing nothing; merely your average, open, honest fellow trying to do the right thing, trying to do his level best. "But of course," Winston said.

Some politicians have it; most don't. Winston has it, a fabulous sense of timing. Everything in politics is timing. For a fortnight, the resolution dominates congressional reportage. "An idea whose time has come," coinciding with a coup in Latin America and a surge of fighting in Indochina. The leadership is agitated, but forced to adopt a conciliatory line; the doves are in war paint. Winston appears regularly on the television evening news. There are hearings before the Foreign Affairs Committee, and these produce pictures and newsprint. Winston, a sober legislator, intones *feet to the fire.* There are flattering articles in the newsmagazines, and editorial support from the major newspapers, including the most influential paper in Winston's state. He and LaRuth are to appear on the cover of *Life,* but the cover is scrapped at the last minute. Amazing to LaRuth, the mail from his district runs about even. An old woman, a woman his mother has known for years, writes to tell him that he should run for President. Incredible, really: the Junior Chamber of Commerce composes a certificate of appreciation, commending his enterprise and spirit, "an example of the indestructible moral fiber of America." When the networks and the newspapers cannot find Winston, they fasten on LaRuth. He becomes something of a celebrity, and wary as a man entering darkness from daylight. He tailors his remarks in such a way as to force questions about his school bill. He finds his words have effect, although this is measurable in no definite way. His older colleagues are amused; they needle him gently about his new blue shirts.

He projects well on television, his appearance is striking, the black suits, the beard. So low-voiced, modest, diffident; no hysteria or hyperbole (an intuitive reporter would grasp that he has contempt for "the Winston Resolution," but intuition is in short supply). When an interviewer mentions his reticent manner, LaRuth smiles and says that he is not modest or diffident, he is pessimistic. But his mother is ecstatic. His secretary looks on him with new respect. Annette thinks he is one in a million.

No harm done. The resolution is redrafted into harmless form and is permitted to languish. The language incomprehensible, at the end it becomes an umbrella under which anyone could huddle. Wein is disillusioned, the media looks elsewhere for its news, and LaRuth returns to the House Education and Labor Committee. The work is backed up; the school bill has lost its momentum. One month of work lost, and now LaRuth is forced to redouble his energies. He speaks often of challenge and commitment. At length the bill is cleared from committee, and forwarded to the floor of the House, where it is passed; many members vote aye as a favor, either to LaRuth or to the chairman. The chairman is quite good about it, burying his reservations, grumbling a little, but going along. The bill has been, in the climactic phrase of the newspapers, watered down. The three years are now five. The billion is reduced to five hundred million. Amendments are written, and they are mostly restrictive. But the bill is better than nothing. The President signs it in formal ceremony, LaRuth at his elbow. The thing is now law.

The congressman, contemplating all of it, is both angry and sad. He has been a legislator too long to draw obvious morals, even if they were there to be drawn. He thinks that everything in his life is meant to end in irony and contradiction. LaRuth, at forty, has no secret answers. Nor any illusions. The House of Representatives is no simple place, neither innocent nor straightforward. Appearances there are as appearances elsewhere: deceptive. One is entitled to remain fastidious as to detail, realistic in approach.

Congratulations followed. In his hour of maximum triumph, the author of a law, LaRuth resolved to stay inside the belly of the whale, to become neither distracted nor moved. Of the world outside, he was weary and finally unconvinced. He knew who he

was. He'd stick with what he had, and take comfort from a favorite line, a passage toward the end of *Madame Bovary*. It was a
description of a minor character, and the line had stuck with
him, lodged in the back of his head. Seductive and attractive, in
a pessimistic way. *He grew thin, his figure became taller, his face
took on a saddened look that made it nearly interesting.*

THE NEGOTIATORS

Harvey Jacobs

17 May

Finally after months of haggling we have chosen a mutually
agreeable site. So I sit here in a grand arched room with waves of
light and shadow washing this beach in morning tide.

It is a changeable season, *spring in Paris*. Last night, before
sleep, I thought of other seasons in this female city. I am not
young anymore nor old. I have delicious memories but the memories still stir possibility. There is more urgency now to gather
both rosebuds and thorns. I tend to snatch at life like a greedy
grabber. But I grab nevertheless and there is sometimes pleasure.

Besides, I am full of honors now. No matter when my death
should come, it would be anticlimactic. There is a peace in
knowledge of that. A triumph. If I am like a nervous squirrel
smelling the ice under soft spring weather, still I have a bushy
dignity. It was wise of my nation to choose me to negotiate the
peace. My mirror image shows a man of solid sense and flickering
warmth. A man who has married, had children and grandchildren. A man who knows joy and sorrow with nothing to gain—
not really—from the war's end or continuation. I was a sensible
choice and glad to serve. Li Chu is young, tense and fidgety. His
nation is intent on selling an image of youth and tomorrows.
They are trying to disprove the bromide of ancestor worship that
haunts them and fills them with guilt. Poor Li Chu must fight a
tendency to bow to me for my years alone. It is hard for him.

And the place they agreed to! This room in Paris. It was a
victory for our intelligence if it was anything but a happy accident. The room with its stained windows and high ceilings and
thick walls, with its changing light and even the sounds of the
city, makes Li Chu squirm. He probably grew up in a hut. He
feels the weight of our history here. He is squashed under the

rump of sitting centuries, remembering most probably that it was
his people who invented firecrackers and gunpowder. There can't
be too much comfort in that. Nor can he take comfort in memories of draped rooms smelling of opium and incense where ancient slit-eyed buddhas sat talking of philosophy. That is not his
vision of civilization. No, he must rely on anger. Anger for inner
nourishment and controlled rage for public consumption. He has
a hard job. A muscle in his cheek twitches. It shakes his face. He
worries that it will reveal his mind. I have him.

Today I carry pictures of atrocities committed against women
and children in a small northern village. He carries photos of a
burned hospital and tape recordings of a captured pilot praying
for forgiveness. They balance out.

As for the war, it goes on.

Fifty of ours were killed today and a hundred twelve of theirs.
We lost a helicopter. They lost a suspension bridge.

We are ready to begin.

12 June
I ate snails. I have a stomach upset.

Li Chu is saying: "The tragic attack on Vin Von Tu is a clear
example of imperialist aggression feeding on its own entrails."
His face is grey and somber. He manifests fury as well as any
professional actor. Each morning he opens with an invective and
his face turns grey, which is no small task for an Oriental. As for
the attack on Vin Von Tu, it was not tragic but comic. Not comic
in a music-hall sense. Not at all. Comic in the cosmic sense with
the mask of laughter leaning over the world and dripping saliva.
Our planes and mortars attacked a village in error. The village
was leveled. Hundreds died. Of the hundreds no more than ten
percent were of the enemy. Error is always comic.

Li Chu continues: "Or was the accident an accident indeed?
We have reports that clearly show Vin Von Tu was about to
openly declare secession from the so-called central regime. Is it
inconceivable that the aggressor devils unleashed their fury in
order to avoid political embarrassment?"

In Li Chu's lexicon there is no room for accident either in the
death of a president or the eradication of an innocent village. He
must believe in the order of experience, of the interconnection of
events. His faith is religious and regressive. I think of a world
without accident and recoil. He trembles at the thought of a
world moved by random chance.

I bring up a bubble of gas and cover my mouth. The snails,
the snails. I nod a kind of apology. Li Chu acknowledges with a

nod of his own. Is it the tendency toward ancestor worship or is stomach gas considered apolitical? Perhaps that belch was a breakthrough. If so, it would mark the first.

I answer: "The attack on Vin Von Tu was indeed tragic and my government has expressed its regrets. It was an accident of war, not the first and unfortunately not the last. But let us remember that this war was caused by an invasion of alien troops across the sovereign borders of a neighboring state. The accident caused the tragedy and agony of Vin Von Tu, but it was the war—your war—that caused that accident."

I clear my throat. There is a vile taste in my mouth. I continue: "It is strange to hear the Distinguished Representative speak of 'aggressor devils' and 'unleashed fury.' I want to show the Distinguished Representative, and the world, five minutes of film taken by combat photographers at Ku Lok Den after Mr. Chu's peace-loving associates paid a visit to that village."

The film is projected. It is like all atrocity films, only this time, for this war, it is in color. The color makes a difference. The horror is more vivid. The private parts scattered around and the shattered heads of children and the open eyes and mouths of the dead and near dead take on dimension in full color. If I was nauseous before, I am more nauseous now. Even Li Chu is affected. He wipes his face in the semidark.

As for the war, it goes on.

Next week they will have a film to show. It will be less technically perfect but no less vivid. No snails in garlic sauce next week.

20 July
These names are impossible. Hok Suk Hill fell to our side this afternoon. I am told that the hill is strategic and precious ground. It dominates an infiltration route. I will be able to tell the effect of this victory, if any, by the twitch in Li Chu's cheek tomorrow.

Hok Suk Hill. The names, the names. What a series of names we have had to digest since World War II. Names of pimples on the world globe.

It is steaming hot today. Jungle weather. The city is dripping. If the evening is cooler I am going to dine in the country. And I am going myself. I must have some time alone. A simple meal and some privacy. The prospect is splendid.

I have informed the Secret Service. They will track me anyhow. I accept the fact that they know everything and I do not fight them anymore.

I accept them the way I accept the spaces between my toes.
Everyone has his job to do.
As for the war, it goes on.

21 July
More riots at home last night and of course Li Chu is making the
most of it. He is talking about the brutality of power. What else
can power be when it asserts itself? He is full of clichés today.
And he wears a new blue suit with a striped red tie. It gives him
confidence. His voice is firm. No doubt, if he survives, he has a
career ahead of him.

He is talking now about the protesters who claim the war is
immoral. He claims they are gaining support. He is correct. He
knows, I assume, that it is easier for people to decide that a war is
immoral than to admit that we are not winning simply and
cleanly, or even with filthy plodding. We are not winning and so
the war is immoral. Losing an immoral war connotes heavenly
intervention. It is a spiritual attitude. As if the nation were
being spanked by Providence for wrongdoing. For the mass it is a
comforting cave. Is any war moral? Are some wars more moral
than others? It seems so, yet the idea is idiotic.

Li Chu is not being very philosophical. He drones on about
police and marchers. What else can he do? The man—or boy—is
not exactly an original thinker. He is a lineman, a tackle or
guard. But he is good-looking and convincing. The suit and tie
are a vast improvement.

When he is finished with his lecture on morality and napalm I
will read from The *Times* report of an assault by three hundred
drugged soldiers on a remote outpost in the West. "Drug Crazed
Hordes." Where did I read that eighty percent of all troops in
that seminal sewer take marijuana or dope?

The same issue of The *Times* that carried the story of the
zombie attack had a story of the marijuana weed growing wild in
New Jersey. Thousands of acres in the Jersey swamps spawned,
the article said, from discarded sweepings from canary cages. It
seems the bird-food companies mixed the seeds with other grains
so that the males would be turned on. And the droppings and
sweepings which went to garbage took heart, germinated and
blossomed in the Jersey swamps. If Li Chu was really smart, he
would be talking of drugged canaries in millions of cages in our
land, not of morality. That is a tremendous story. Addict canaries. That kind of story can help bring an empire down. A
captured officer told us that his men were force-fed the drugs

before their charge. Seventy died. A hundred were wounded. Was it some kind of experiment or is the whole incident more mist from the sweaty foliage? Li Chu's face betrays nothing of last night. He is *inscrutable* all right. Even his cheek is still.

God, it is hot in this room for all the air conditioning. And Li Chu goes on. Last night it was hard enough to get him to grunt as he shoved food into his face. He juts his jaw forward when he talks, a most annoying habit. He eats like that, too, with peasant manners. Buttercups. As a child I played a game. You tickled under the chin and said you were looking for buttercups. It is tempting to hide a feather in my sleeve—a lush peacock feather smelling of overabundance and capitalist ego—and tickle Li Chu along his jugular vein. Coochie coo. He would keep talking.

Our meeting at the l'Horloge d'Or was the purest chance. L'Horloge was a restaurant I went to when I was a student here. No. It was during my forget-Elizabeth-Prinkle excursion. And Li Chu found the l'Horloge d'Or as a babyfat diplomat on his first assignment.

Oddly, we both came alone, that is, with the illusion of "alone" since we are constantly observed, recorded, photographed, and dossiered. I saw him sitting across the room coping with a craw-fish. And the devil ordered a bottle of wine. They like their pleasures all right and there is hope for the world in that.

If Li Chu saw me he made no sign. I offered the first gesture. I sent the waiter to his table with an invitation to join me for coffee. He weighed that carefully. Hidden eyes were on both of us. But he must have reasoned that, since the gesture was mine, he could comply. He came.

It was strange eating with him, watching him control his in-take of chocolate mousse. The dessert he ordered surprised me. Eating it one could imagine him counting beats the way a new dancer counts to himself on the floor. Then he would spoon the sweet mousse and gulp it as if it were an oyster. I was amused. There is a distinct charm to the boy.

And I had never seen Li Chu take anything in. He was always spouting garbage or simply not listening. Always pouring out. But he took in the mousse like a magnet.

We talked about nothing. The food. The weather. I gambled and mentioned that I missed my family. Would a personal flesh-reference elicit any response? It did. Li Chu said he had an infant daughter with a name that sounded like one of those villages. That was all the chatter. Yet I left with a feeling that we would meet again.

Li Chu is done. I must gather my papers on the Drug Crazed Hordes.

As for the war, it goes on.

28 July

I have accused them of escalation. A rocket attack devastated a passive hamlet outside the capital. My proof was excellently presented. Li Chu is ranting. He is claiming that the innocents were not innocent after all but secret agents, every one. I suggested that perhaps the inhabitants were really plastic robots manufactured as decoys for his vicious killers. Color came to his flat face.

Frankly the vehemence of Li Chu's attack annoyed me considerably. I recognize that what happens between us after hours has no place in the meetings (to say the least) but there must be some element of carry-over, even if it is on the most subtle human level. Can it be that he is overcompensating? Maybe I was not wrong or egotistic in recognizing that Anna Wang favored me. And what if she did? She is only a whore.

For all Li Chu's imposing credentials and racial identity it is fairly obvious that to a girl like her I must reek of dignity and time.

With me she knows beyond a doubt that she is with a man who has found a place in the history books. More. I represent the most potent country on the face of the planet. Perhaps in the universe. And the richest. Li Chu, whatever he is, is familiar ground to her. She is professionally suspicious of his youth and even his tenuous claim to power. Anna Wang has been around. She knows the game of cat and mouse. She knows in her wet parts that with the press of a button all the Li Chu's in the world would vanish.

More, I am a good lover. My body is not trained in karate but it is wise to the fingertips. I played Anna Wang like a cello. Li Chu mounted her like he would mount a problem. He loves like an engineer raping a bridge over a river. He fornicates like he eats chocolate mousse. Anna Wang was his idea in the first place.

We have met now for eight consecutive evenings. When our messengers crossed paths that second night it provided both of us with a humorous surprise. We agreed to dinner in a room selected by Li Chu. There too was an implicit recognition of relative power.

I was paternal with him. We ate some abysmal oriental concoction. Fish and more fish. But fish that must live in the bottoms of cesspools. What do they use for bait to catch creatures like those?

I ate tails and eyeballs and drank what must have been shark sweat all in the cause of cordiality. And we took off our jackets and talked. Of what, I can't remember. One thing we agreed upon. We would file no official reports or say a word to our bodyguards. That way, they would assume we were acting on orders so secret and profound the chances were they would file no report. And if they did, the readers would make the same assumption. Who among those idiots would imagine that we were simply attempting to form a friendship? Who among them remembers the days when diplomacy ended at dusk and the rising of the moon was the cue for a round of civilized pleasures? I hand it to Li Chu for suspecting the existence of a baroque past he never learned about in the comic books they fed him. Discovery of the past is, in the best people, the result of intuition.

The second night we met in my territory. Again it was a fine evening with talk of this and that and a game of checkers. On the third night we chose a third room. French food this time, and Li Chu brought a drug with him that left us in a frothy fog of amicability. We laughed together.

It was the sixth night that Anna Wang appeared. It was my birthday. Li Chu brought her to me as a gift. Or so he claimed.

She is a beautiful girl of mixed blood. She can be no more than twenty-three, but she moves like a candle flame in a church. She is a church and contains a ton of natural knowledge. She wore a dress of tan leather over some kind of black body stocking. Her hair gushed down like rain. She had strings of beads and bells around her neck and a perfume that must have contained some narcotic.

She ate with us and danced for us. Not to twangy Eastern music. It was The Beatles, I think. One of those groups. Then she stripped naked. Li Chu stripped too and they sat squatting, facing each other. He said it was a yogi position, precoital. He said if you sit that way you drift into each other. I reminded him that she was my present and he laughed and said a present is best when shared and a traveled road is more pleasing. I joined them, feeling ridiculous. I confess that I am self-conscious about every grey hair on my body. And I know I have a paunch.

But Anna Wang made me feel very much at home. She let me take her first. And, later, again. First and last. That first time I detected a pout around Li Chu's bluish chubby mouth, but I discounted it. The way he is carrying on today makes it clear that he is jealous. That does not make me feel exactly bad, a few days into my sixtieth year. He should be jealous. Last night Anna Wang would not let him do more than stroke her bony rear.

Under the circumstances, accusing them of *escalation* is a special slap in the jowls. Li Chu is practically howling. Tonight I will remind him that he could have given me a tiepin for my birthday.

As for the war, it goes on. A thousand died yesterday. Many more of theirs than ours.

19 August

Neither of us has heard a word from security. They must be befuddled. Getting rid of Anna Wang was a smart decision. And it was mutual. Cynthia Krane, the English girl, and Rachel Eshkenazi, the Jewish student, are not sea girls. They are as empty-headed as the tin man. With marvelous soft bodies and pits as moist as mouths.

There is no more conflict over women. In fact, the other night we did not touch them at all. We played Go. It is a compelling and demanding game. There has been a welcome break in the meetings. We reached an impasse after one of our aircraft accidentally strafed beyond the bombing line. They claimed immediately that it was purposeful and malicious. I had plenty of counter evidence, and even produced the actual pilot to testify. He was superb, a child of nineteen with a blond crew cut and freckles. But the talks were suspended indefinitely.

Li Chu and I are planning a holiday on the Riviera. It will be good to smell the salt again and hear the gulls. I can taste the prawns. Both of us are pale as phantoms from all the indoor living and lack of exercise. We are eager to leave Paris.

As for the war, it goes on.

30 September

Li Chu's tan is fading. He is coming back to his yellowish hue. I don't like it. Is that prejudice? Learned or inborn? The color doesn't bother me inordinately. But it is annoying. It is like knowing a person and liking them but not their breath. Does he feel that way about my epidermis? I will ask him someday. My tan is fading too.

Li Chu is haranguing about a plane hijacked by a nation friendly to his own. There are the usual moronic run-on sentences about violation of sovereign air space. In the age of satellites they warble over a reconnaissance plane, unarmed and obsolete as a Reuters pigeon. I have concluded my statement about piracy on the seas and in the heavens. They did capture the plane intact, which makes things a bit difficult. These splinters of news stick in the tail of history. Who cares? Nobody. Who yowls? Everybody.

The decision to give up our servant should make things better. Since we moved in together, Li Chu and I both have been behaving like college roommates nervous about the dormitory supervisor. The servant was safe enough. I'll vouch for that. But we are both paranoid and with some justification. It will be better alone. And doing the chores will help remind us of our humanity.

This is lonely work. To represent is to symbolize and to symbolize is to be depersonalized. Cleaning ashtrays and sweeping floors and cooking our own meals will be a reality check. I look forward to it and to the privacy.

A coup in Li Chu's government has given us some difficulty, but things are quieting. There was rumor of a coalition offer but that appears farfetched. Neither side is certain of its goals. Coalition of who representing what? Our concern was premature. As Li Chu says, it is best not to read even the dispatches, much less the newspapers. There have been student riots again in the city. The riots create a wind, take some of the mustiness out of the air. We welcome them.

As for the war, it goes on.

5 January
I with my Christmas cards and New Year greetings and Li Chu with his holiday of the Moon or somesuch. The apartment is jammed with papers and gifts. The season was exhausting and we saw little of each other. He was called home for a week. Nothing was said about our living arrangement, which was a relief.

The President visited here and we had amicable talks. There has been a stalemate on the battle line. And a holiday truce. We had fears that they would launch an offensive as they did last year, but nothing came. Some infiltration of supplies and men but that is minuscule. Thank God there was no move to obliterate the talks. Before the holiday there was some indication of a softening in their position. They abandoned a base to the southwest. We gave up a missile-launching position on an island northeast of the base. Northeast or southwest. To be specific, we gave up Po Li Dan and they evacuated Ry Sut Nim. Happy holidays!

Last night was the first night Li Chu and I had a chance to talk. We were both feeling mellow. A quart of Hine cognac helped some. I said that the truth about our century was ironic. We have the technology to eliminate the basic causes of conflict. With atoms and computers and God knows what, the earth could provide a bounty beyond imagination. It is my theory that, in our time, the key is not violence but the repression of violence.

I believe we are about to repress violence the way cannibalism and incest were repressed in the race. Our wars are anticlimactic. They are a mockery of real need. They are the dying gasp of violence. I believe the cannibals must have gone on an organ-grinding binge before the last official swallow was gulped, give or take New Guinea.

It is hard to give up war and the reasons for war. Mankind is left to face his pulsating holes without any excuse. I told Li Chu I pitied all races the end of their favorite toy. I said I did not know if the finish of violence was good or bad. And I don't. I told him to think about how many mamas and sisters and cousins and aunts must have been stuffed in the midnight of incest.

These wars for liberation are wars of masturbation. We are avoiding the horrible truth that war is antique. Li Chu listened in the dark.

Then the imp jabbed me with a nail clipper he brought to bed with him. That boy has developed a first-rate sense of humor. When we first met he would have broken his cheeks to smile.

As for the war, it goes on. At least we have heard no different. Neither of us so much as turned on a radio today.

11 March
"It was the action of pigs. Pig action."

"I must state that if the Distinguished Representative desires to roll in the mud with his language, then there is no point in continuing this meeting."

"The invasion of the Delta shows the world how much you want peace. Butchers! You are spilling the blood of children and women to gratify your growing thirst."

"It is always the one whose fangs sink first into the neck of freedom who protests that there are vampires walking in the darkness."

As for the war, it goes on.

16 May
We cannot believe that it is a *year*.

And tonight, celebrating in our apartment, Li Chu is beside himself. I feel a joy that I cannot ever remember feeling before.

The monsoon season has come. The fields are muck. No man

can move without sinking into slime. The mechanized battalions are paralyzed. The planes are grounded by fierce winds. Our weather satellites offer the prediction that since the deluge came late this year, it may last well into June. After that there will be rebuilding of natural damage before the destruction can resume.

As for the war, it goes on. Yes. And new weapons are being developed. Our people at home and in the field have shown a fresh resolve. Theirs are drenched in a cause.

No end is in sight. They reoccupied Ry Sut Nim and our missiles are back in Po Li Dan. The summer is assured.

Drunk and happy, Li Chu and I whirl around the room. We have made our own merry-go-round. He holds my life and I hold his. We spin like the world and we are singing.

THE DAY WE NAMED OUR CHILD WE HAD FISH FOR DINNER

Michael Rossman

"What shall I do with the filet?" asked Karen from the kitchen. "There are bones in it."

"Cook it," I said.

"I don't like it with bones."

"They come out easier after it's cooked. That's the way fish are."

"Oh, never mind." Clatter of pans, water running. Indistinctly: "Screw you, anyway."

"What was that?"

"I said, never mind."

"And what else? What after that?"

Clatter of pans, running water. I pulled myself up again, weary, and went into the kitchen. She was standing over the stove, stirring instant mashed potatoes. I couldn't read her back. I held her. "I think we're tearing ourselves apart because the world is coming apart."

"I think you're right," she said.

"Water the plants," I told her, as I went back into the front room, grimly ignoring the radio, the phone. "That's the thing to remember now, remember to water the plants."

It was the fourth night of Cambodia. I was watching the ferns when our brother Lonnie from San Diego came in. "Carol called to find out when you're coming back," I reported. "She says they're working for a school-wide strike on Thursday. The English Department already voted to go out. Farber brought them round, and the paper's agreed to support it."

"All up and down Telegraph they're talking about Kent State," he said, his face still flushed from walking, intense through his spectacles. "There's little knots of freaks just talking, all along the street. It's true, four were killed, the National Guard shot them down in the parking lots. I can't believe it."

We want to run a training program this summer, for public school teachers in the San Diego area: learn them a little political smarts to protect the learning they're learning. But Carol can't make the planning meeting, too busy with a crisis in the Woman Studies Program she's organizing in the college there. And she's hard to get hold of now: with the Minutemen at their door, they don't go back to the house much, and are learning to travel armed. Lonnie and I fumble to fix time for another meeting. Nothing will come into focus. He drifts out the door. I say, "Wait." We embrace.

Later Tom calls, from over in the next house, to tell me that Reagan has just ordered all the state colleges and universities closed through Sunday at least. Another first for California, the Golden State.

Three years before Cambodia I visited Kent, Ohio. Spring 1967. The media were just discovering the Haight and the Hippy. I was on my first round of visiting campuses, just starting to sort things out, to adjust my perspective from Berkeley-provincial to a national scope, and learn what work I could do in our ghetto. For the moment, I was writing a story on what the war was doing to what we then called the Student Movement, and I wanted some unknown dreary large public campus to play off against Antioch and Oberlin. So I chose Kent State, found a contact, and spent a couple of days there.

I mostly remember the flat apathy of the faces I met while on campus, these students of lower-class blood slack-weary from the mineral-drained hills of upland Ohio, many of them serving time for the upward mobility of the teaching credential. The buxom girls chattering in the morning Pancake House, as I sat over fourth coffee, road-grimed, hugging my sleeping bag.

Flat, that campus, flat. Some months earlier a first hiccup of antiwar protest had turned out a hundred for a lonely march. Now I found all told maybe a dozen committed to keeping active, trying to find a way to move it on. Isolated, embattled, embittered, taking refuge in an overtight group whose talk was laced with hurtful humor and flashes of longing.

They took me home for the night, the house was old and they had made their warm mark on its surfaces; they lived in what would become a commune, and then a family. Over late coffee we talked about organizing, about guerrilla theater, about holding together for warmth. Hang on, brothers and sisters, I said to them, some Spring is coming. And I left them the large *Yellow Submarine* poster I designed for Mario's birthday—an anarchist program for a disruptive festival of joy, "a generally loving retaliation against absurd attack." The poster commemorated the 1966 Second Strike at Berkeley—for us in the West, the first event in which freaks and politicos joined in public ritual, in song and an elaborate masque. We discussed community programs, wild with the energy of coming together, and broke into spontaneous joy, singing chorus after chorus of "Yellow Submarine"—imagining all our friends on board, the blue sky, the life-green sea.

Then next October, before I left to begin my second round of traveling campus work, we put on our feathers at dawn and marched 7,000 strong down into Oakland to block the doors of the Induction Center. After we got the shit clubbed out of 200 people, we tied up the downtown for the rest of the week, dodging the heat and chanting, "We are the people!" in the intersections.

So long ago. *Saturday in Kent they trashed the town in protest, breaking 56 windows.* I was in Rock Island, Illinois, with my brother Russell from our theater troupe, talking about the death of a culture and teaching college kids how to begin to play again, to live in their bodies. *Sunday in Kent they burned down the Army ROTC building.* I was home in Berkeley, in the house we call Dragon's Eye. Sixteen of our family were learning to play a holy gambling game together, device for pooling psychic force, handed down from the Indians through Stewart Brand of the Pranksters. *Today in Kent on the fourth of Cambodia 2,000 turned out, and they shot 4 dead in the parking lots.* O let us laugh and canter. O I will play the Fool, grant me my mad anger, I still believe that art will see us through.

October evening falling in 1964. Berkeley. I was standing in Sproul Plaza beside the police car that held Jack Weinberg captive, I was changing in the crucible that formed the Free Speech Movement, the first campus explosion. It was the thirtieth hour since a thousand had captured the car and Mario stepped on top to begin the first open public dialogue I had heard in America. Behind Sproul Hall 600 cops were preparing, around us the Greeks were chanting drunkenly, "We want blood! We want blood!" We were sharing out green apples and bread, waiting for them to wade in clubbing, and singing "We are not afraid" in voices shaking with fear, betrayed into life by our longing for the pure radiations of community which we first there kindled among us, bright as imagination.

And I had a heavy flash, and said it to some friend: *"Five years from now they'll be killing kids on campuses, all over America."* They began with the blacks, with the Orangeburg Three massacred in '68, and they killed the first white brother, James Rector, at People's Park in Berkeley nine months later. And now Kent State: only the first in this, the fifth Spring.

(Rewriting now on the sixth of Cambodia, the plastic "underground" radio turns real as it tells me how the girl's leg broke as they beat her and threw her off the wall, an hour ago up on campus, and how 2,000 National Guardsmen have been ordered into Urbana, Illinois. I've spent ten separate weeks in Urbana, we have family there. Vic centers it, he works in wood and is making a cradle for the baby. Last month I saw him. He was organizing a craft-food-garage cooperative. The week before he had charged the pigs for the first time to help rescue a brother, was still shaken.)

But I had that flash and said that thing, I truly did, and have five years of poems to prove it, canceled stubs on the checking account of my sorrow, a long coming to terms. Sure, I'm a prophet, my name is Michael, I've shared total consciousness and seen the magicians summon the Powers. Prophets are common in Berkeley, and I've met quite a few on the road, mixed with the saints who now walk among us. What else do you expect to appear when our energy comes somewhat truly to focus?

It is time to own up to what we are doing. Everyone knows or suspects a snatch of the holy language of Energy, via acid, confrontation, or contact. The wavelengths of our common transformations flow strongly through Berkeley: for twelve years now, what happens here and across the Bay happens a year or two later in concentric circles spreading out across the young of America. I've lived here all that time. Most leave. If you stay, you close off or go mad. Or you stay open, and are transformed into an active conduit for the common sea of our Energy: lines of its organizing come to flow through you. I think I am learning to feel them in my body. It is frightening, it is always frightening not to have a language in which to wrap the nakedness of your experience. Cold wind of the new, hanging on the tip of the rushing wave.

For three years, linked into a growing net of comrades in work, I wandered from Berkeley through our involuntary ghetto. Four hundred days on the road, 150,000 miles. I visited seventy campuses, *worked* on forty, training and organizing, trying to follow the Tao of transformation in furthering the change that is happening through us. Call me an action sociologist, a specialist in learning and student of change; and color me proud to be supported mostly by my own people, freaks and radicals, plus some rip-offs from "adult" institutions and the media. I hustled to be free to put my energy where I draw my warmth, and luck was kind. And my trip is one among many. Our own and our best are staying with us now, instead of being bought off by the stale rewards of a dying System, and our change accelerates the more.

And I know where it's going, for a little way at least. For Berkeley is truly a barometer. Every college in the country is undergoing an evolution in the culture and politics of its captive transient population; and each evolution is essentially like Berkeley's. I have watched it happening on every kind of campus, from upper-class Catholic girls' schools to working-class junior colleges. Activism begins slow, diversifies to departmental organizing, antidraft work, and guerrilla theater; the dance of confrontation proceeds in growing ranks, the administration grows slicker but finally blows its cool; dope culture spreads, the girls chuck their bras—wow, you wouldn't believe the wealth of data.

And then beyond the campus the *voluntary* ghetto forms. Freak community sinks roots and begins to generate communes, families, head shops and food co-ops, freak media, friendly dog packs and dog shit, links with the farm communes—there are ten within fifteen miles of Rock Island, micro-sample of America. O, it is happening everywhere just like in Berkeley, only faster now: long-haired kids on the street, merchants' complaints, heavy dope busts, teachers fired, kids suspended, leash laws, narcs and agents and street sweeps and riot practice for the neighboring precincts, and dynamite at the farmhouse.

Here now in Berkeley it is the fourth night of Cambodia. Kent State is catching up fast. We shall have to go some to keep ahead. But like the University we have broad strength in our Departments, their lintels display the Tao of Life and Death. The Free Bakery has opened, capacity 2,000 loaves a day, put together by a family of forty living mostly on welfare: people drop by to pick up bread or learn how to bake, and linger. The city government is trying to get $175,000 for two helicopters to maintain a full-time patrol over the city; the City Council has decided not to make its meetings public, because of disruption; we will shoot their birds down, I am sure. A thousand tenants are out on rent strike; now the evictions begin. Governor Reagan is calling for a bloodbath. Gay Liberation flames buoyant in the front lines of demonstrations. Our medics are special targets, speed and smack are spreading like crazy. Six hundred Berkeley families are linked into the Great Food Conspiracy, buying cooperative spinach and cheese. The campus has the third-largest police force in the whole county, the leaves are beginning to wilt from the teargas. The people who hand-deliver the high-graphic newsletter *Kaliflower* to 150 communes in Berkeley and S.F., cycling goods and needs and lore and advice, come by and leave us a rap on planting and compost. My kid brother by blood was busted on campus last week, charged with assaulting a police officer with a deadly weapon, i.e., chucking a rock at a cop, $5,000 bail. He didn't do it, no matter: the Grand Jury's seeking indictments. The leaflet from the Berkeley Labor Gift Plan says, "*Together*, brothers and sisters, we can build a new community of labor and of love." Each time we go into the streets they test some new piece of technology upon us, last week it was cars spewing pepperfog from their exhausts. The leaflet from the Leopold Family begs the community not to rip off records from the people's own store. On the radio a brother is reporting from Kent, he says he had to drive forty miles to get out from under the phone blankout the government has clamped over the area. Berkeley was an exemplary city, you know. She had a progressive form of government and an overtly liberal party in power for years. She dazzled the nation with thoughtful, advanced programs of curricular enrichment and racial integration. Active support for the schools was her proudest civic tradition. O, Berkeley was always noted for how she cared for her children.

Cold wind coming. Sky turning black, the missiles sulk in their cages, the green net of the ocean grows dangerous thin, the terrorism of bombs begins, the Minutemen multiply bunkers, the economy chokes and staggers, the blacks grow yet more desperate, the War is coming home. I figure I'm likely to die in this decade, perhaps in this city I love, down the street beyond the neighborhood garden, in some warm summer twilight when people sit on their porches and the joy of live music drifts out from their windows. That's a cold political judgment, without much to do with what's also true: that since I woke at fifteen I've never been able to imagine past about thirty-five, it's been only a blank in my mind, always the same through the years, down to now, when I'm thirty. Do you mind if I finger my intimate fragments in front of you, awkwardly? I can't fit them together. But what else is a man to do in this mad time, pretend that everything's only at its usual standard of incoherence? For I have also been One with the great two-headed snake of the Universe, and I have seen us begin to recover our bodies and share our will, seen us learn that realities are collective conspiracies. Now in the families forming and linking we are weaving a blank social canvas for the play of our imagination. I have seen the first sketches of group will, love, and art, and a whole life, the first organized forms of human energy liberated one more degree. They transfix me with awe. I was never taught to dream so boldly, I had to learn for myself. I was not alone. For all our failures and unfinished business, what we are pulling together is bright and well begun. If we are let live through this decade and the next, we will be strong, strong, our women will be powerful and our men beautiful.

So all of this is running through my mind on the fourth night of Cambodia, I'd just got back the night before from three months of hustling my ass around the country to pile up bread for the baby and the coming recession, in the process cutting through maybe sixty family groups in twenty cities, cross-fertilizing news and goods and paper and trinkets, a bee in the meadow of change. I came back stoned and mellow at how fast and strong it is coming together among us, even within the strain of the War, and bearing the love of a dozen fine women and men for Karen. All day now through the cottage people have been flooding with these atrocity tales, I wallow in the gloomy pleasures of verification. Diagnosis: Fascism, soft form turning hard, terminal cultural cancer. The radio tells me 258 campuses are out on strike, and then sings to me: *"Rejoice, rejoice, you have no choice."* I take another toke, last of the good stuff: been running too fast to score, and summer's customary drought is almost upon us. The typewriter beckons. Torn between life and death I calm my chattering schizophrenic, refuse, and turn to the guitar, god damn! the sweet guitar who embraces all of me in her stroking vibrations when I touch her well. *O, how I need to go to the sea!*
Music is magical, music is my balm, music suspends me and aligns the frame of my spirit. O, shit, I wish I could sing to you, I am no longer ashamed, it is time to come out with it all, nothing less will do, the child will be born. I hate these pages, hate these mechanical fingers. Sometimes I pop for a moment above the surface of sanity and grab for the floating flute or guitar, manage to clear the Breath of my energy for a time from the choking hurrying flow of vital and desperate information, rapping words healing words data words analysis words magic words maggots

and birds on the acid wallpaper of my mind. And I water the plants, the ferns in particular. When I am broken jagged like tonight I think it is because I mostly cannot cry, and that I travel the crystal rapids of melody for this reason too, singing because I cannot weep. When I'm together I see it as a way of keeping in touch with the slower rhythms. Either way the ferns are grateful, and they sing to me with their green misty love, and the spiders arch their webs in the corners of the window frames.

And I sing to them back, and to the dog my familiar, and to the pregnant animal Karen crouched unseen in her den—to them all, but softly to myself—a song I have made for her from a

(2)

Some say the city, a farm would be pretty,
the mountains refuse to be blue.*
Come, with me wander, while they seek us yonder:
what else could you choose to do?

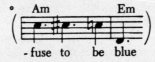

(3)

But pray for the baby whose birthday is Maybe,
and meet me at two in the moon.
Keep warm if you're able and fight for the cradle,
we can't hide, let's ride this one through.

Keep warm if you're able and fight for the cradle,
we can't hide, let's ride this one through.

fragment another singer left in my mind. Karen comes in from
the kitchen, plate and bowl of dinner in her hand, sets it down,
retreats from the shaken animal in his den. While the rock cod
cools, I sing the song again, for the first time loudly.

"Now damn," I think, with bitter satisfaction, "ain't that a
song to inspire pity and awe and all! Not bad for a first lullaby,
opus 7. I sure would like to spend a long stretch of years writing
some songs. I'd be grateful if they just kept on coming three or
four a year, now that I know they're coming." And I rack the
guitar, pick up the plate, and wander into the bedroom to eat
with Karen.

In the next room my love is curled weeping on the black
leather chair, the dog is anxiously kissing her, careful of her
belly. I hold the song of her sobbing. "Ah, little princess," I say,
"you didn't know what it would cost to be my muse." Through
my head spin Cambodia, Babylon, that five-year-old flash by the
cop-car, growing up during the McCarthy years with the FBI at
the door, the times we have been in the street together, our trips,
our campus travels. "But there's spin-off, you know," I say.
"We're maybe better prepared spiritually for what's coming than
most, advantage of foresight and practice, pay of the bruises.
We've been making our peace for a while." No ultimate blame:
culture changing too fast for its able. But the child will be born,
though they tie the mother's legs.

"Yes," she says, "but I didn't know it would be this sudden."
And then: "But if the gods are stingy with time, at least they've
been generous in other ways."

On my lap. I see. Wavering. The plastic plate with pink decal
flowers from the Goodwill. Fresh fish filet our cousin family
brought us from up the Sonoma coast. Cheese sauce, recently
mastered, with chopped green onions. Dehydrated mashed potatoes. In the stoneware bowls my sister Deborah made and laid on

us for our anniversary—before she went down South again to the
Army-base coffee shop she helped start, to watch her successors
get six years and then go off to help organize another—in my
dear blood sister's bowls is fresh spinach salad, well-flavored, we
are learning to tend our bodies. Anticipation of apple juice in
the refrigerator. This is how it is, you see, I am sitting here
eating this food, and Bull is watching us very intently while the
puppy from next door chews on his dinner, and my feet are up
cuddled around the ball of her belly, watermelon-hard in its last
weeks. I sing to her, we share the cooking, the dog eats when we
do, mostly. She is bearing our child, on the bed under the light
and the ferns is the government pamphlet on how to raise a child
during the first year, it's not bad.

And she says, "What do you think of Lorca?"

"I think I can dig it, for a boy," I say slowly, "I been thinking
about it, and I can."

"I'm glad," she says softly, the blush of shy triumphant pleasure crowning round her eyes. "Your mother and I were having
lunch, and we started to think of the names of Spanish poets.
'García Rossman,' she said, 'no, that's impossible.' 'Federico . . .' I
said. And then we just looked at each other, and we *knew*. And it
has a nice sound."

I sink into the thought and mirror of her love, reach for the
resonances, roots in the soil, and start to cry. Is it for the first
time or the tenth, on this fourth night of Cambodia? Lorca was
my first song teacher, the man who opened the keys of Metaphor
to me: for ten years I relived his poems into my American language. "I have lost myself many times in the the sea," he sang,
"with my ear full of freshly cut flowers, with my tongue full of
love and of agony. Many times I have lost myself in the sea, as I
lose myself in the heart of certain children. . . ." Hold on, dear
heart, jagged at this four A.M., now is not the time to tear. From
Federico's arms I passed through those of grandfather Neruda,
and then into Vallejo's volcano, which finished for me what acid
began and gave me open form to integrate my fragments.

But Lorca began me, long before I learned how death found
him in a Fascist trench, how he went to sleep forever in the
autumn night of the gypsies, beyond the lemon moon. Mercurial
brightest spirit of the second Golden Age of his tongue's power,
murdered in Granada by Franco's highwaymen, in the first summer of the Civil War. All the poets, all, all the singers were on
one side in that great division, perhaps as never before since old
Athens. And the schools and the hospitals of the brief flowering
of Republican Spain went down under German planes and Ital-

ian artillery, the dogs of Church and Greed. And all the poets
perished or fled.

Torn, my father watched the Fascists rehearse, with their scien-
tific grace; stayed to organize at home with his trade of words
and a red perspective. I was born six months after the fall of
Madrid, while he was editing the Mine, Mill and Smelter Workers' Union paper in Denver. Pablo Neruda was in exile from the
Fascists in Chile. Cesár Vallejo was dead of hunger and heart-
break for Spain. Lorca's grave was never found, in a hundred
lands and Franco's jails the poets of his race who survived sang
him their tenderest elegies. Lincoln Steffens began a new family
and life at sixty, his *Autobiography* instructed my father. When
he died the last lines in his typewriter read, "the Spanish Civil
War is the opening battle in mankind's struggle against Fascism."
Steffens' son Peter taught my sister Deborah before she went
South, I have touched his children. Even the high-school babysit-
ters I hitched home from the airport with know what's coming
down.

A week before Cambodia I was at a conference in Boston,
thrown by some church folk and book people, on "the religious
dimension of the Movement." Indeed. It was quite a happening,
believe me: a bunch of us freaks from the families got together
behind some mellow mescaline and opened up some free space,
some Chaos. Then someone asked about Ritual, and little incredible Raymond Mungo opened up in a musing country style,
speaking the sainted baby babble.

"Well, we get up in the morning," he says, "and we look at the
light and we eat, we eat together. And we go to sleep when it gets
dark, sometimes alone and sometimes together, for there is no
light. But sometimes at night we watch the moon. During the
day we plant. We chop wood. We use the wood for fire. We eat
when the sun goes down. From April to October there is very
much food. We have to find ways to give it away. We have to,
there is very much. There is the summer solstice, and then there
is the autumn solstice, and so on. In spring the solstice was very
cold, very cold. We chopped some wood and put it in a box. I
made a mantra: *Equinox/sticks in box/ soon it will be warm/big
dog.* And a big dog came, and it grew warm. And sometimes we
go out when there is no moon and run around in the grass. And
then we come back to the houses we build. Last week one of our
houses burned down, it was very warm. We lost four brothers
and sisters. I think we're going to learn to build better chimneys."

O, I met a little saint in Boston, he organizes energy, used to be founding Czar of Liberation News Service, then he figured out the cities were dying, now in his Vermont town of 800, over a quarter live in communes, and he studies the government pamphlet to learn to build better chimneys. We're met on the fifteenth floor, overlooking the river of death called the Charles, the plastic pastries and draperies are poisoning our bodies, our minds, we've come to talk about rituals for living with fire. Mitch Goodman loves us and he's frantic with terror, sees the black sky looming, MIRV's lurking, etc., etc., he's positively yelling at Raymond, half his age and weight, scarecrow child in oversized coveralls: *"but what about Fascism?"* And somehow we can't quite get it through to him there that Raymond is not simply talking about farms, pigs, dinner, etc., but about the house burning down and learning to make better chimneys and going on in season, and about Lorca and Vallejo and my brother and my sister and two of each dead in Kent and my lover lazy with child, whose belly my baboon feet grip as if I stand on the round of the world, spinning through all time.

I was translating a poem of Lorca's when I got the call that my grandfather was suddenly dead. The poem follows a brief skit for puppet theater, in which the gypsy whose name is *Anything* is captured on the bridge of all the rivers while building a tower of candlelight, and is brought before the Lieutenant-Colonel of the Spanish Civil Guard to be interrogated.

He, Harry, my mother's father, was a Bolshevik. He organized a strike in the machine shop, was jailed, loved his tutor, she died of consumption, he fled here in 1906 to dodge the interrogations of the Czar, clerked and warehoused to send Mother through college. He wanted her to learn. I have his blue eyes. He taught me to carve, and cried with memory when I told him in '60, during that spring of Chessman and HUAC, how they beat us and hosed us down the steps of City Hall in San Francisco. "That was how it started, you know . . ." he said. And three years later the phone call came and was, and I put down the receiver and thought for a moment, and said somewhere inwardly and quite distinctly, I will file this for future reference, I will weep for you some day, Grandfather. And I turned back to finish reworking the poem, for there was nothing to do but go on, I knew it would take years to comprehend that grief.

Sitting in my rocker, plate on my lap, our eyes intertwining and my feet on the future, the ferns turn to oleander and the cottage to a patio, and the song of the beaten gypsy rises up in the well of his absence.

> *Twenty-four slaps,*
> *twenty-five slaps,*
> *then at night my mother*
> *will wrap me in silver paper.*
>
> *Civil Guard of the roads,*
> *give me a sip of water.*
> *Water with fishes and boats.*
> *Water, water, water.*
>
> *Aii, boss of the Guard,*
> *standing upstairs in your parlor!*
> *There'll be no silk handkerchieves*
> *to clean my face!*

And the tears rip through me Grandfather deep, and out everything open and open and echo in hers, and we touch and cling and are shaken. And the dog, our first child and familiar, pushes up anxious between us and offers her his nose and me his nads, which we take to complete the circle of energy, love, and time around the child to be born in Cambodia.

"Yes," I say, "Lorca, if it's a boy."

"Maybe even a girl," she says, "it has a nice sound."

"Maybe a girl," I say, "yes."

And she says I'm glad with her eyes.

And the radio sings, *"Rejoice, rejoice, you have no choice,"* and the acid magic of those moments, of that state we once called existential, goes on and on forever, and I go off to set down the brief notes of these thoughts, like the rib-thin eaten skeleton of the dinner fish, to flesh back out later. And then we take off for the City, to try to be with our people, our theater troupe in rehearsal coming suddenly real. For it is clearly a time for coming together with those we are dear with, and we must take care that the Wedding go on within the War.

ON THE PERIMETER

Robert Chatain

Zone

The tattered jungle beyond the barbed wire had been declared a free-fire zone in late June. Looking forward to spending at least five of my remaining ten weeks of war in permanent duty on the bunker line (the unofficial transfer was complete; even my "Visit Gay, Historic Vietnam" poster had been torn from the AG barracks wall and sent along with me to the ordnance company's security platoon, so determined was Colonel Hamilton to purge from his new command any taint of the pacifist subversion he had uncovered), I decided to free-fire.

I had access, over the weeks, to M-14's, M-16's, machine guns, grenade launchers, and an occasional pistol. The M-14 had been my weapon in basic training; I was a good shot. With it I could cut down plant stalks at ten meters, hit beer cans and bottles at thirty; I drew beads on man-sized stumps and bushes as far away as I could see them and was sure some of my shots found their targets. I could also kill birds.

The M-16 I found disappointing. Its horizontal drift gave me trouble. Its ugly black stock was not long enough for my reach. The pistol grip fell awkwardly into my palm. Its sight was blunt. Obviously the weapon had not been designed for target practice. Remembering an old account of Marines dead on the slopes of Hill 881 with their M-16's broken down beside them, I wondered what it had been designed for.

The M-60 machine gun was a thrill. Fire at a patch of bare earth produced satisfying explosions of dirt, leaves, garbage, and anything else lying in the radius of my bullets. With a short burst one evening I tore a metal water can to shreds. The next night I opened up on the struts and wires of the old crippled powerline support tower I had begun to think of almost as a friend. Most of the rounds went through into empty air.

The powerlines were also a good place to aim the M-79 grenade launcher. If I connected, the grenades exploded high above the ground and fragmentation pellets clattered on the worn steel.

I discovered that pistols demanded more practice than I could manage without attracting attention. Free-fire was permitted, but some discretion was expected. Exorbitant waste of ammunition was discouraged. At the infrequent moments when a pistol found itself in my hand I shot at the rats foraging openly in the barbed wire for scraps of food. I never hit them.

I did this free-firing at dusk, after the trucks had gone back across no-man's-land through the interior perimeter gate into the ammunition depot; if the sergeant on my section of the perimeter called, I could explain that I was testing my bunker's arsenal. Firing after dark always drew such panic from the neighboring bunkers that I soon gave it up. Firing at dawn—I never fired at dawn. Dawn did not seem like the right time to fire.

Once I would have been ashamed to find myself willingly associating with these weapons. But I was alone. The guns were clean, well-made, efficient, impersonal. And I suppose that the problem of my former negative feelings toward weaponry had been solved. Guns were of some use, I admitted. In the proper circumstances I think I could have shot Colonel Hamilton without batting an eye.

Formicary

Lying one mild afternoon on a soft wool blanket spread beneath tall birch and thick cedar, my wife-to-be had outlined her ant theories. Ants, she said, are capitalists. They're disgustingly greedy. And they're middle-class. They work twenty-four hours a day hoarding food and adding superfluous tunnels to their antholes. Did I know that some ants tend gardens? That some ants herd cows? That some keep slaves? And, of course, ants make war. Armies march into each other's territories and attack instinctively. Individual battles might last for hours. (Finishing my circuit of the bunker without finding what I'd been looking for, I returned up the hill of sandbags and slid into the half-buried enclosure. It was already too dark. I would continue the search in the morning.) Are they brave? I asked. No, she said, they're not brave, an ant might think he's brave but actually he's just doing what all the other ants are doing. If an ant were really brave,

he'd refuse to fight. (At dawn and again at dusk the cracks between the sandbags were alive with large black ants. I noticed
no particular pattern to their movements. Each night I spent a
few minutes covering the surface of the hill looking for the main
entrance to their nest.) They'd throw him in jail, I argued. It
doesn't matter, she said, he would know he was a moral ant. He'd
be setting an example for the other ants. But, I said, suppose he
doesn't care much about the other ants? He's still better off in
jail, she said, he won't get killed. But if he doesn't want to get
pushed around? Ants always get pushed around, she answered.
Then, I said, he plays it by ear. We laughed. And ants don't hear
very well, I added. (Later we made love on the floor of the forest,
sunlight through the trees camouflaging our bare skin with
irregular blotches of light and darkness; I stretched this recollec-
tion out to fill my mind for an entire watch, even forgetting the
discomfort of sitting upon stacked ammunition crates.)

Discourse

They liked to divide the members of the security platoon
evenly along the length of the perimeter, no two "veterans" in
any one bunker, and fill out the remaining positions with ordinary clerks on detail from the various units of Long Binh. Occasionally the roster put me with people from my old company,
but usually I spent the night with strangers. In the intimacy of
the bunker they could not keep their mouths shut. I had to
listen, smoldering, to hours of rumor, complaint, prejudice, and
platitude. By the time dawn carried them back to their safe
barracks I would know whether they had been drafted or had
volunteered for the draft or enlisted or been tricked into enlist-
ing or railroaded by their local boards, their families, or the
courts; I would have found out where they had received training,
how they had come to Vietnam, what they thought they had
discovered about themselves, God, and their country, and when
they would get out; I would have heard some of their most
interesting Army experiences; I would have been told their opin-
ions on the manners and morals of the peoples of Europe, Asia,
and the other places their uniforms had taken them, and I would
have learned their attitudes toward the war, toward international communism, toward the peace movement, and finally
toward the chance that they might be killed during the night, a
possibility that I sometimes came to anticipate with pleasure long
before they had finished talking.

Maze

A rat's sleek head caught in the red beam of the flashlight triggered somber, fretful ruminations. How deep do they burrow? How many live in this hill with me? How do they know to avoid the pale yellow sticks of rat poison scattered in the corners of the bunker and outside under the clean starlight? Intelligent rats, well-fed on candy bars and C-ration tins, uninterested in poison. Their squeaks as they prowled around the base of my high perch on the stacked ammunition boxes. Their scuttling down below my dangling feet with cockroaches and scorpions. Don't reach down there, not for ammunition, not for anything. If you drop something, leave it until morning. Thousands in this mound of earth. Holes in the floorboards, holes in the walls, holes in the heavy timbers overhead. The sandbag slope alive with rats scurrying in the moonlight. Nocturnal. Remaining in tunnels during the day. Long tunnels, winding back upon themselves, coiling for miles. VC moving south in such tunnels, some captured with stories of traveling two hundred miles underground. Black-clad VC no older than fifteen sitting with their backs to dirt tunnel walls, singing. Underground hospitals. Operations underground, emergency lights flickering. Underground at Dien Bien Phu the wounded finding their wounds infested with maggots. The maggots beneficial, eating rotten tissue, leaving healthy. Time passing slowly. The wounded lying in darkness tended by blind worms.

I shifted my position. The rat vanished into its cavity.

Test

Just before midnight the sound of a jeep on the perimeter road pulled me to the back of the bunker. Without hesitation I challenged the man who emerged; I was an old hand at the game. He identified himself as a corporal on official business. I let him climb the catwalk. He dropped into the bunker next to me and told me to relax. I relaxed. The corporal struck a match and studied his watch. I loaned him my flashlight. I saw that he carried a clipboard and a folded piece of paper. At what must have been precisely midnight, he ceremoniously handed me the paper. I asked him what the hell it was. "Black handicap message," he announced.

"What the hell is that?"

He seemed surprised. "A black handicap message," he repeated.

I looked at the piece of paper, unfolding it, and read only a small group of neatly typed numbers.

"It's a test," he said. "Don't you know what to do?"

Obviously I did not know what to do.

The corporal shook his head and sighed. "You guys are all supposed to know what to do with one of these. That's the way it goes, you don't know what you're doing, they don't know what they're doing, and I sure don't know what I'm doing."

"So what's it all about?" I asked.

"All right," he said, "you call your command bunker and tell the sergeant you've got a black handicap message. You read off the numbers. The sergeant copies them down and passes them on."

"Should I do it now?"

"Yeah, you should do it now."

I cranked the field phone, reached the sergeant in Bunker 12, gave him my information, and hung up. The corporal retrieved his piece of paper and turned to go.

"Hold it," I said. "What the hell is going on?"

He explained. A black handicap message tested the efficiency of communications along the chain of command. Originating in my humble bunker, those numbers would be passed from one headquarters to the next until they arrived at the Pentagon itself. Crucial to the test was not only correct transmission of the number series, but also the amount of time required to pass information through command channels. "Are you bullshitting me?" I asked.

"Would anyone come way out here in the middle of the night to bullshit you?" The corporal hoisted himself up out of the bunker and descended the catwalk to his jeep.

"Hey, how long does it usually take?" I asked.

"I don't know. A couple of hours. Who gives a shit?" He wheeled his jeep around on the narrow road and raced back along the perimeter into the night, anxious for the safety of the depot.

Miami

The passing of the broom from one bunker to the next was a time-honored ritual that had survived the earlier attacks on the ammunition depot, the physical deterioration of the bunkers during the months since their construction, even the coming of the monsoon and subsequent reduction in the amount of dust to be swept from the bunks and floorboards. No one remembered when the last inspection of the bunker line had been made, but still the broom passed every night. It was a good chance to catch up on the news.

"You hear about Fine?"

"No."

"Got orders for the Congo. Diplomatic mission. Far out."

"Hm."

"You haven't heard about the new offensive in September?"

"No."

"Supposed to be a big offensive in September, big as Tet."

"Hm."

"You hear about all the fucking money they dug up near Qui Nhon?"

"No."

"A hundred and fifty grand, all in fifty-dollar bills. The Treasury Department says there isn't supposed to be any fifty-dollar bills over here. We're paying for both fucking sides of this war."

"Hm."

"You hear about the Republicans?"

"No."

"Nominated Richard Nixon."

"Hm."

Perfume

We lit up any time after midnight. No one traveled the perimeter road after midnight.

"Ah-ha!"

Voice and boots on the catwalk startled us.

"What is that delightful odor? Could it be—? Yes, I think it is!" A stranger climbed unhindered into our bunker. I was too stunned even to try to challenge him. But there was nothing to fear. He was a PFC from that night's reaction force, out alone for a hike and a smoke.

"We've got an IG. The fools are awake cleaning the barracks. I snuck out."

We got acquainted.

"Let me lay some of this on you people."

I inhaled.

The stranger went his way.

One of the two guards spending the night with me slept; in slow motion, the other climbed onto the upper bunk. "Jesus, what a buzz I've got. Wow, I can't stand up, I've got to sit down. Wow, I think I might get sick."

I draped my arm over the machine gun and bored into the luminous jungle with my eyes.

Release

One of those nights of brilliant stars motionless above the earth whose grinding stones you can feel move beneath your feet. Even through thick-soled military shoes. The ground turning, tumbling around an axis fixed now nearly on the horizon, but not quite right, the wrongness more apparent at this latitude than farther north where the pole star hangs high in the air and a cold wind keeps your head clear. Eyes closed, you can hear the stones wrenching themselves slowly through each new alignment. The spindle has slipped from its proper place. The gears are binding.

I spent many watches completely outside the bunker, sitting on the roof or stretched full-length on the front of the sandbag hill gazing benignly into hostile territory. Sometimes I stood on the catwalk identifying stars and counting artillery bursts in the hills to the east. When it rained I crouched under the bunker eaves and caught the smells raised by moisture in the jungle and carried by the wind across clearings and through barbed wire. I did some undisciplined and inconclusive thinking. I daydreamed.

But the nights seemed to invite some physical participation, so from time to time I unbuttoned my fatigues and masturbated, stirring great clouds of sediment in my mind. From one of them I extracted this notion that the earth's axis had slid out of alignment and was wandering through the heavens. Under such celestial circumstances there could be no idea of progress, no notion of human accountability for human actions. Only the apocalypse could restore order. On subsequent nights I entertained further revelations of cosmic significance, all of which were cut short by the crisp sound of my sperm landing on the weathered canvas of the sandbags.

Duty

"Hello?"
"Hello?"
"Hello?"

"Who called?"

"Bunker 18?"

"Right here."

"This is Bunker 15."

"Who called?"

"Ah, men, this is Bunker 17, ah, we've been notified of suspected movement to our immediate front, ah, I'm instructed to announce that, ah, we're going on seventy-five percent alert, ah, this means two men will be awake at all times."

"This is Bunker 17, ah, everyone on the line acknowledge please."

"Bunker 15, roger."

"Bunker 16, we read you lima charlie."

"Bunker 20, roger."

"Bunker 18?"

"Bunker 18, right, seventy-five percent alert."

"Bunker 19?"

"Bunker 19? Bunker 17 calling Bunker 19, acknowledge please."

"All right, Bunker 19, answer your fucking phone."

"Bunker 18, will you shout over to Bunker 19 and wake those people up?"

"This is Bunker 18, sarge, 19 says they're on the line and can hear you okay, but you can't hear them."

"All right, 19, sorry. Stay on the line."

"Bunker 17?"

"This is Bunker 17."

"Bunker 17, this is Bunker 15, about this seventy-five percent alert: two men awake, one asleep only makes sixty-six and two-thirds percent alert. To bring it up to a full seventy-five percent I'm going to have to wake up eight and a third percent of the last guy."

"Just do the best you can, Bunker 15."

"Hello?"

"Hello?"

"Who called?"

"Is this Bunker 17?"

"This is 17."

"Bunker 17? Come in, Bunker 17."

"This is Bunker 17, I read you lima charlie."

"Bunker 17?"

"What, for Christ's sake?"

"Hey, Bunker 17, this is Bunker 20, there's something in our wire."

"What is it?"

"Too dark to tell."

" 'Too dark to tell.' Shit, man."

"Who is that?"

"All right, 20, pop one, let's see what it is."

"Bunker 19, did you shoot off that second flare?"

"Keep observing, Bunker 18, I think it was a wild pig."

"You're a wild pig."

"Who is that? Let's keep this line clear, men!"

"Bunker 16?"

"Shut up. Go to hell."

"Bunker 17?"

"This is 17."

"Hey, Bunker 17, this is Bunker 20. All the crickets and frogs and shit have stopped making noise out in front of us. Bunker 17? Hey, Bunker 17? Bunker 17? What do we do? Come on, Bunker 17!"

Aubade

You notice first the stilling of the night breeze. It happens abruptly; one minute your skin is cooled by the vague slow movement of air which began at dusk, the next it is not. From the jungle come tiny sounds previously masked by the whisper of leaves and branches. Then they, too, vanish. Nothing moves. Nothing. You look to the east, where you know the hills lie unevenly on the horizon you cannot see. You try to pick them out, straining to catch the first instant that they appear, staring where you think they will be; suddenly they are there, higher or lower than you had expected, the world has solidified and divided into two shades of black. Dawn is a livid, slowly spreading bruise on the face of the darkness. Birds rustle and murmur. The horizon fans to the north and south. In back of you is a strange murk, confused by several indefinable colors. Clouds form, hard shapes near the hilltops, soft shadows overhead. The sky turns blue, pink, light orange, yellow, pale gold. The buzz of a locust is followed by the flap of large wings. Details emerge in the land below the crests of the hills, some trees show their skeletons, brown and green are added to the spectrum of the visible. To the left and right other bunkers are gloomy neolithic mounds topped by thick slab roofs the color of very old rust. Flying insects rise in swarms to begin work. Grass and bushes sigh. The sky is light now, lightest just over the hump of the hill slightly to the north of east. Blue becomes white; white flashes incandescent as the tip of the sun blinds you. You turn your head away. The air is not clear; columns of smoke line the sky. Haze and fog lie in the low places. The river to the southeast is buried in white floss. Black dots of helicopters float in single file through the air above the hills, bringing night patrols home to their bases. A slight wind brings an oily smell to your nose. You itch. From somewhere comes the sound of an engine. The sun climbs. You face a day glistening, reptilian, fresh from its shell.

Lobster

"Imagine my surprise (the medic narrated loudly as four of us sprawled in a deuce-and-a-half tearing at top speed through the depot to breakfast), man, six months in this sewer of an outfit, you can't get a transfer out of here, you can't get TDY, you can't even get your ass attached to the fucking dispensary, so the complaints start up, I write some, everybody writes some, we get those Congressmen on the horn and we expect things to happen, you know? We got a union. I'm not shittin' you guys, a union. We make demands. We go up through channels like it says, you know, but we make demands. So one of our demands is about the crap we eat. That's our demand, right? Better food? Right. So last night, we head over to the mess hall, it's a Saturday and we expect hamburgers, figuring no C-ration hamburgers this time because the roads have been clear for three fucking weeks and it's about time the old ground beef turns up again. So we head over, and you know what they're serving? Lobster tails! Lobster tails? What are they doing serving lobster tails? What's going on? Drawn butter, the whole works. Lobster tails! Far fucking out. I figured that right after dinner they were going to tell us to line up for the ground assault on Hanoi, but I eat anyway. Figured they were going to make us paint the mess hall. Something like that. But I eat, and it's good, you know?"

Armageddon

Long, very hot morning, bird cries at regular intervals from the trees. Nodding over my book. When it comes, the attack rolls through the bunker line effortlessly. Some of us escape by hiding in the foliage on the other side of the road. The depot is destroyed. Long Binh's thousands of clerks are mobilized and fight holding actions for their positions. A general offensive throughout Vietnam threatens to bring down the Saigon government. Fresh U.S. combat troops are airlifted in. Unrestricted bombing of the North is resumed. South Vietnamese units sweep into the Delta and encounter fierce resistance. North Vietnamese troops emerge from Cambodian sanctuaries and strike Saigon in force. U.S. ships blockade Haiphong harbor. Communist divisions operating in the Central Highlands lay siege to isolated U.S. fire bases. A joint force of American, South Vietnamese, Korean, and Australian units engage main-strength Communist elements at the DMZ. Chinese troops join in the defense of North Vietnam. Laos is invaded simultaneously by American and Chinese armored columns attempting end-runs of the battle line. Russia calls an emergency session of the United Nations Security Council. In major clashes on both sides of the DMZ neither army gains clear advantage. Protracted artillery duels begin. Mass uprisings throw Saigon into chaos and South Vietnamese government leaders are evacuated to ships of the Sixth Fleet. A provisional government is established by neutralist and pro-Communist political leaders. High-level private negotiations begin at Geneva. Chinese and American troops withdraw from their entrenched positions along the DMZ. Formal peace talks are convened. Cease-fire is declared.

Czechoslovakia

The well-informed were discussing current events over the field phone. I listened, but stayed out of it.

"If they've taken Dubček to Moscow he's probably dead by now."

"I just didn't believe they'd actually go through with it."

"The radio stations knew about it in advance and set up secret spots to broadcast from. They kept everybody cool."

"You've got to hand it to kids who throw stones at tanks."

"Well, there are good guys and bad guys in the Kremlin just as there are good guys and bad guys in Washington. The bad guys won."

A new voice cut in. "We should bomb the shit out of them."

"One war at a time, huh?"

Product

The C-rations had been packed a long time ago, everybody knew, but nobody knew just when, perhaps as far back as World War II. Most of the food tasted pretty good, considering. Inside the unmarked gray cardboard cartons there were tins of "main dish," various small tins (cheese and crackers in one, fruit dessert in another, etc.), and cellophane bags containing fork, napkin, salt, pepper, sugar, dehydrated cream, and ten cigarettes. Of the main dish selections, some were choice (tuna, ham), some not so choice (veal, hamburgers), some inedible (bacon and eggs). All of the tins were olive green; contents were printed in black according to a standard form, noun first, adjectives trailing with their commas. Brand name appeared only as a means of identifying the packer. I visualized dozens of cartoon factories turning out these uniform dark green tins and gray cardboard boxes, selfless owners and managers eschewing profitable competition to serve their country, patriotic stockholders approving, grim-faced workers unaware of any change.

In the bunkers we encountered one major problem with C-rations: the familiar ingenious government-issue P-38 can opener was not included in every C-ration box. In fact, finding a P-38 in your box was a little like finding a prize in a package of breakfast cereal. It was something to cherish, because those C-ration cans were *hard*. They conformed to *government specifications*. They were *tin cans*, not aluminum cans or vinyl-covered cardboard cans. With a good pair of pliers and a lot of time you could worry one open; artful wielding of a bayonet produced primitive but satisfactory results; blunt instruments cracked the cans but wasted most of their contents; shooting them, although entertaining, was not a good idea nourishmentwise; various other schemes occurred to me at various times, but a P-38 was the only guaranteed method of success. Without one, you might go hungry. I knew several men who carried them around their necks where they hung their dog-tags. One man wore a P-38 on the same chain with his crucifix.

Guidance

Miller came out on what was probably to be his last twenty-four-hour guard duty, managed to find out which bunker I was in and walked down early in the afternoon to say hello. He looked happy. "How many days?" I asked him.

"I won't tell you. You'll just get depressed."

Instead, Miller talked about the changes that had taken place since Colonel Hamilton had assumed command of the office.

"The man's insane. First thing, he decides he's got to have his own private partitions, and we do the plywood and mahogany stain thing again. He scrounges another air conditioner. He hires a new secretary."

"Suzanne's gone?"

"Downstairs. This new one is a real pig. Hamilton says he wants someone to serve his guests coffee."

"Good grief."

"Then he sets up new, streamlined organizational machinery, and I've got to type such gems as this."

I took the disposition form he handed me and read, "SUBJECT: Requests for Command Guidance. TO: All AG Officers. 1. It may be necessary on occasion for you to request command guidance from the Adjutant General concerning various problems which occur. 2. Effective immediately, no problem will be presented to the Adjutant General without the accompaniment of a proposed solution, regardless of the manner of presentation, i. e., written or oral. R. A. Hamilton, LTC, AGC, Adjutant General."

"Classic," I said.

"I brought it out to make you feel better. We're all going crazy. There's a new lieutenant now, he's floundering trying to figure out your filing system, he can't get through to the units because he doesn't know any of the clerks, it takes him three drafts before the Chief of Staff will let his letters pass, and, on top of all that, Hamilton hits him with this."

I took another disposition form. "SUBJECT: Adjutant General Liaison to Information Office. TO: 1LT Robert D. Wexler. 1. You are hereby appointed to act as my liaison with the Information Officer for the purpose of insuring that all aspects of my section to include those elements under my operational control and under my staff supervision are properly recognized for their accomplishments through the use of hometown news releases and articles for various service papers. In this connection it is not necessary nor do I expect you to write articles, edit articles, or in any way act as an information specialist. All I expect you to do is to insure that the Information Officer is made aware of newsworthy items occurring in this section. 2. In connection with routine items such as arrivals, departures, awards, and promotions you are expected to make DA Form 1526 available to those individuals desiring such information to appear in hometown newspapers and to offer such assistance as may be requested. 3. In performing these duties you are authorized direct contact with the Information Officer, this command, any branch in this section, and the Commanders of all subordinate units or their authorized representatives. 4. You will clear any request for other than routine individual hometown news releases with me before presentation to the Information Officer. 5. This appointment is not intended to consume your entire working day, in fact it should not take more than five percent of your time. If it appears that you will become involved for a greater period of time, advise me, in writing, of the reasons therefor. R. A. Hamilton, LTC, AGC, Adjutant General."

I handed the copy back to him.

"He's got everybody pissed off. No crossword puzzles on duty, so Major McCarthy spends all day at the PX. No reading on duty, so we all sit around like bumps on a log waiting for mealtimes to roll around. And these mad DF's keep coming."

"I know McCarthy's no use, but can't Major Inhalt do anything?"

"Major Inhalt is threatening to become Lieutenant-Colonel Inhalt and be transferred to MACV at Tan Son Nhut."

"What about Sergeant Kroeber?"

"He's short."

"Short? You mean he didn't extend again?"

"No, he says the war's over now and the horseshit's getting started."

We talked for a little while longer, and then Pete climbed out of my bunker and scrambled down the hill. I watched his listless walk along the perimeter road, annoyed that I missed him.

Ragnarok

When it comes, the attack rolls through the bunker line effortlessly. Some of us escape by lying in our bunkers pretending to be dead. The depot is destroyed; Long Binh's thousands of clerks take to the woods. A general offensive throughout Vietnam panics the U.S. commanders and triggers full-scale bombing raids on Hanoi, Haiphong, the panhandle, and the Ho Chi Minh trail. We cross the DMZ and fight our way deep into North Vietnamese territory. Chinese troops enter the war and bring us to a standstill. Russian, Chinese, North Vietnamese, South Vietnamese, Laotian, and American aircraft battle in the skies. U.S. ships engage Russian and North Vietnamese craft at the approaches to Haiphong harbor. Our bombers strike at supply routes on both sides of the Chinese border. Fire storms destroy Saigon; the government falls. A provisional coalition government is formed. Plans are announced for the possible evacuation of all American troops from Indochina. The President of the United States is assassinated and right-wing pressure forces the new President to take strong military action in Southeast Asia. Our troops make amphibious landings along the North Vietnamese Red River Delta and strike directly for Hanoi. Chinese planes attack ships of the Sixth Fleet. Limited nuclear war begins. Landbased missiles are launched against enemy missile sites. China's government is destroyed. The United States suffers fifteen percent casualties. Russia suffers ten percent casualties. Ballistic missile submarines at sea are given orders to strike population centers. Everybody dies.

Ordnance

At four-forty-five, if I was in one of the bunkers on the eastern side of the depot, I pulled out my borrowed watch and began to count the minutes until the five o'clock fireworks display. I had watched this show often but was still not tired of it. During the day, trucks carried the outdated ammunition a quarter-mile from the depot and left it in a clearing I could just barely make out if my bunker was on high ground. Before the detonation a helicopter flew over the site. Then there were long moments of waiting; I could not trust my watch and never turned my eyes away from the spot. If I was still looking when the explosion came I saw the smooth hemisphere of fire, the shock wave bubble, the flattened trees and the wall of dust in silence until huge noise slammed into the bunker. Sometimes other, smaller explosions followed, but more often everything went up in one grand blast. HA-*BLAM*! Smoke poured into the sky afterward. What a great sight. And what a great noise! KA-*BOOM*! Terrific.

Chicago

First I heard that large demonstrations were planned, which was to be expected, and that the Mayor had announced he would keep order, which was also to be expected. Then I heard that twenty thousand troops would be on hand and that sixty black GI's had staged a sit-down strike at Fort Hood when ordered to go. From an amateur political analyst I understood that Gene had no chance, George had no chance, and if Hubert didn't take it on the first ballot, Teddy would get the nod. I was reminded that labor troubles in the city had affected transportation and communications. I discovered that the FBI had unearthed plans to dump LSD into the city's water supply. I read that the Unit Rule had been abolished, a "peace plank" had been proposed by a minority of the Platform Committee, and Georgia's Lester Maddox group had not been seated pending the outcome of a challenge by a rival delegation. A sergeant told me about a lot of violence in Lincoln Park. I found out that the peace plank had been respectably defeated. I was informed that city police had apparently gone crazy, injuring hundreds of people. A crowd had been pushed through the plate-glass window of the Hilton Hotel's Haymarket Lounge, someone reported. I saw a remarkable *Stars and Stripes* headline which read, "Police Storm Hotel, Beat McCarthy Aides." There was speculation that newsmen were being deliberately assaulted. I learned that Hubert Humphrey had received the Democratic nomination. I was told of a silent candlelight parade by delegates from the Amphitheater to the Loop.

Riot

The MP was unsympathetic. "We'll let them live in their own filth as long as they want."

"You mean they're still loose?"

"Loose? Hell, no. They got one part of the compound, is all. They're not going anywhere."

"Did some escape?"

He shrugged. "Hard to tell, with all the records gone. May be a couple of weeks before they get a good head count."

"I wonder if a guy named Forbes was in the stockade."

"No idea."

"Larry Forbes. He was in for pot. I understood that they were going to move all the narcotics guys to Okinawa."

"I don't know. I don't think so." He lit a cigarette and glanced at the rain heading toward us.

"Was a guy named Haines Cook still there?"

"What, do you know everybody in LBJ?"

I chuckled nervously.

"The whole deal was chicken-shit," the MP said.

"But somebody got killed, didn't he?"

"Yeah. Big deal. One out of seven hundred."

"Out of how many?"

"About seven hundred, more or less. Give or take a few."

"In that one spot? I've seen it; it's only two blocks long!"

"It's a lot smaller than that now, and most of what's left is charcoal."

A few drops of rain fell.

"I've got to take off, I'm going to get wet," the MP said.

"Did you guys use tear gas?"

"Shit yeah."

"Many people get hurt?"

"Mostly them."

"How come you went in?"

"Well, what are you going to do? Let a bunch of militants take the place over?"

Rain was falling harder. On the road the other men in the detail struggled to secure a tarpaulin over the trailer-load of old ammunition they had collected from the bunker. At my feet, my new shells gleamed in their fresh boxes.

"What's the status of things now?" I asked.

"Most everyone is sleeping outside; the fucking Afros are fenced off by themselves. When they feel like giving their right names, they can come out."

"I guess technically it was the worst stockade riot in Army history."

The MP sneered. "Technically."

Garbage

As I approached the magic thirty-day mark, that date when I could no longer be reassigned, transferred, lent out on temporary duty, or otherwise fucked with, the orderly room sent me an out-processing slip and told me to begin working on it. The next day an order arrived removing me from the guard roster and dumping me back into Headquarters Company as a nominal duty soldier, although I was expected to spend most of my time staying out of everybody's way. Reshevsky let me know that I was not supposed to report back to the AG Section. This was fine with me.

On the last night out I caught a ride from the bunker line directly back to the company area. Hart was driving; it seems that Colonel Hamilton had overheard one of his monologues on death and had reassigned him to the orderly room. I sat in the cab of the truck with him. His headlights didn't work and he wanted to make it back before the light failed; he asked me about a short cut along the perimeter road to the construction work at the new supply battalion warehouses. I had seen jeeps travel off in that direction, so we gave it a try. Hart must have missed the turn. We wound up in pitch darkness somewhere southeast of Long Binh looking for the 1st Aviation helipad. I spotted a glow on our left and we drove overland toward it. Hart bounced the truck through a series of shallow trenches and then we were in the midst of the Long Binh garbage dump. The stench was dizzying. Murky fires flickered and smoldered. Smoke blinded us. I climbed out on the running board and tried to tell Hart which way to turn. The engine stalled. Hart began to cry. I considered it, but collapsed instead into helpless laughter.

THE UNIVERSITY OF DEATH

J. G. Ballard

The Conceptual Death. A disturbing aspect of these seminars, which by now had become a daily inquisition into Talbot's growing distress and uncertainty, was the conscious complicity of the class in this long-anticipated breakdown. Dr. Nathan paused in the doorway of the lecture-theatre, debating whether to end this unique but unsavoury experiment. The students waited as Talbot stared at the photographs of himself arranged in sequence on the blackboard, his attention distracted by the elegant but severe figure of Catherine Austin watching from the empty seats beside the film projector. The simulated newsreels of auto crashes and Vietnam atrocities (an apt commentary on her own destructive sexuality) illustrated the scenario of World War III on which the students were ostensibly engaged. However, as Dr. Nathan realised, its real focus lay elsewhere. An unexpected figure now dominated the climax of the scenario. Using the identity of their own lecturer, the students had devised the first conceptual death.

Auto-erotic. As he rested in Catherine Austin's bedroom, Talbot listened to the helicopters flying along the motorway from the airport. Symbols in a machine apocalypse, they seeded the cores of unknown memories in the furniture of the apartment, the gestures of unspoken affections. He lowered his eyes from the window. Catherine Austin sat on the bed beside him. Her naked body was held forward like some bizarre exhibit, its anatomy a junction of sterile cleft and flaccid mons. He placed his palm against the mud-coloured areola of her left nipple. The concrete landscape of underpass and flyover mediated a more real presence, the geometry of a neural interval, the identity latent within his own musculature.

Obscene Mannequin. "Shall I lie down with you?" Ignoring her question, Talbot studied her broad hips, with their now empty

contours of touch and feeling. Already she had the texture of a
rubber mannequin, fitted with explicit vents, an obscene mas-
turbatory appliance. As he stood up he saw the diaphragm in her
handbag, useless cache-sexe. He listened to the helicopters. They
seemed to alight on some invisible landing zone in the margins of
his mind. On the garage roof stood the sculpture he had labori-
ously built during the past month: antennae of metal aerials
holding glass faces to the sun, the slides of diseased spinal levels
he had taken from the laboratory. All night he watched the sky,
listening to the time-music of the quasars.

Left Orbit and Temple. Below the window a thickset young
man, wearing the black military overcoat affected by the students, was loading a large display hoarding into a truck outside
the Neurology department, a photo-reproduction of Talbot's left
orbit and temple. He stared up at the sculpture on the roof. His
sallow, bearded face had pursued Talbot for the past weeks during the conception of the scenario. It was at Koester's instigation
that the class were now devising the optimum death of World
War III's first casualty, a wound profile more and more clearly
revealed as Talbot's. A marked physical hostility existed between
them, a compound of sexual rivalry over Catherine Austin and
homoerotic jealousy.

A Sophisticated Entertainment. Dr. Nathan gazed at the display
photographs of terminal syphilitics in the cinema foyer. Already
members of the public were leaving. Despite the scandal that
would ensue he had deliberately authorised this "Festival of
Atrocity Films," which Talbot had suggested as one of his last
coherent acts. Behind their display frames the images of Nader
and J.F.K., napalm and air-crash victims revealed the considerable ingenuity of the filmmakers. Yet the results were disappointing; whatever Talbot had hoped for had clearly not materialised.
The violence was little more than a sophisticated entertainment.
One day he would carry out a Marxist analysis of this lumpen-
intelligentsia. More properly, the programme should be called a
festival of home movies. He lit a gold-tipped cigarette, noticing
that a photograph of Talbot had been cleverly montaged over a
reproduction of Dali's "Hypercubic Christ." Even the film festival
had been devised as part of the scenario's calculated psychodrama.

A Shabby Voyeur. As she parked the car, Karen Novotny could
see the silver bowls of the three radio-telescopes above the trees.

The tall man in the shabby flying jacket walked towards the perimeter fence, bars of sunlight crossing his face. Why had she followed him here? She had picked him up in the empty hotel cinema after the conference on space medicine, then taken him back to her apartment. All week he had been watching the telescopes with the same fixity of expression, an optical rigor like that of a disappointed voyeur. Who was he?—some fugitive from time and space, clearly moving now into his own landscape. His room was filled with grotesque magazine photographs: the obsessive geometry of flyovers, like fragments of her own body; X-rays of unborn children; a series of genital deformations; a hundred close-ups of hands. She stepped from the car, the coil hanging in her womb like a steel foetus, a still-born star. She smoothed her white linen skirt as Talbot ran back from the fence, ripping the cassette from his camera. Between them had sprung up a relationship of intense sexuality.

The Image Maze. Talbot followed the helicopter pilot across the rain-washed concrete. For the first time, as he wandered along the embankment, one of the aircraft had landed. The slim figure of the pilot left no reflections in the silver pools. The exhibition hall was deserted. Beyond a tableau sculpture of a Saigon street-execution stood a maze constructed from photographic hoardings. The pilot stepped through a doorway cut into an image of Talbot's face. He looked up at the photograph of himself, snapped with a lapel camera during his last seminar. Over the exhausted eyes presided the invisible hierarchies of the quasars. Reading the maze, Talbot made his way among the corridors. Details of his hands and mouth sign-posted its significant junctions.

Spinal Levels. Sixties iconography: the nasal prepuce of L.B.J., crashed helicopters, the pudenda of Ralph Nader, Eichmann in drag, the climax of a New York happening: a dead child. In the patio at the centre of the maze a young woman in a flowered white dress sat behind a desk covered with catalogues. Her blanched skin exposed the hollow plane of her face. Like the pilot, Talbot recognised her as a student at his seminar. Her nervous smile revealed the wound that disfigured the inside of her mouth.

Towards the DMZ. Later, as he sat in the cabin of the helicopter, Talbot looked down at the motorway below them. The speeding cars wound through the clover-leaves. The concrete causeways

formed an immense cipher, the templates of an unseen posture.
The young woman in the white dress sat beside him. Her breasts
and shoulders recapitulated the forgotten contours of Karen
Novotny's body, the motion-sculpture of the highways. Afraid to
smile at him, she stared at his hands as if they held some invisible
weapon. The flowering tissue of her mouth reminded him of the
porous esplanades of Ernst's "Silence," the pumicelike beaches of
a dead sea. His committal into the authority of these two couriers
had at last freed him from his memories of Koester and Catherine Austin. The erosion of that waking landscape continued.
Meanwhile the quasars burned dimly from the dark peaks of the
universe, sections of his brain reborn in the island galaxies.

Mimetised Disasters. The helicopter banked abruptly, pulled
round in a gesture of impatience by the pilot. They plunged
towards the underpass, the huge fans of the Sikorski sliding
through the air like the wings of a falling archangel. A multiple
collision had occurred in the approach to the underpass. *After
the police had left they walked for an hour among the cars, staring
through the steam at the bodies propped against the fractured
windshields. Here he would find his alternate death, the mimetised disasters of Viet Nam and the Congo recapitulated in the
contours of these broken fenders and radiator assemblies.* As they
circled overhead the shells of the vehicles lay in the dusk like the
crushed wings of an aerial armada.

No U-Turn. "Above all, the notion of the conceptual auto
disaster has preoccupied Talbot during the final stages of his
breakdown," Dr. Nathan wrote. "But even more disturbing is
Talbot's deliberate self-involvement in the narrative of the
scenario. Far from the students making an exhibition of an
overwrought instructor, transforming him into a kind of Ur-Crist
of the communications landscape, Talbot has in fact exploited
them. This has altered the entire direction of the scenario, turning it from an exercise on the theme of 'The end of the world'
into a psychodrama of increasingly tragic perspectives."

The Persistence of Memory. An empty beach with its fused sand.
Here clock time is no longer valid. Even the embryo, symbol of
secret growth and possibility, is drained and limp. These images
are the residues of a remembered moment of time. For Talbot
the most disturbing elements are the rectilinear sections of the
beach and sea. The displacement of these two images through

time, and their marriage with his own continuum, has warped them into the rigid and unyielding structures of his own consciousness. Later, walking along the flyover, he realised that the rectilinear forms of his conscious reality were warped elements from some placid and harmonious future.

Arrival at the Zone. They sat in the unfading sunlight on the sloping concrete. The abandoned motorway ran off into the haze, silver firs growing through its sections. Shivering in the cold air, Talbot looked out over this landscape of broken flyovers and crushed underpasses. The pilot walked down the slope to a rusting grader surrounded by tyres and fuel drums. Beyond it a quonset tilted into a pool of mud. Talbot waited for the young woman to speak to him, but she stared at her hands, lips clenched against her teeth. Against the drab concrete the white fabric of her dress shone with an almost luminescent intensity. How long had they sat there?

The Plaza. Later, when his two couriers had moved away along the ridge of the embankment, Talbot began to explore the terrain. Covered by the same even light, the landscape of derelict roadways spread to the horizon. On the ridge the pilot squatted under the tail of the helicopter, the young woman behind him. Their impassive, unlit faces seemed an extension of the landscape. Talbot followed the concrete beach. Here and there sections of the banking had fallen, revealing the steel buttresses below. An orchard of miniature fruit trees grew from the sutures between the concrete slabs. Three hundred yards from the helicopter he entered a sunken plaza where two convergent highways moved below an underpass. The shells of long-abandoned automobiles lay below the arches. Talbot brought the young woman and guided her down the embankment. For several hours they waited on the concrete slope. The geometry of the plaza exercised a unique fascination upon Talbot's mind.

The Annunciation. Partly veiled by the afternoon clouds, the enormous image of a woman's hands moved across the sky. Talbot stood up, for a moment losing his balance on the sloping concrete. Raised as if to form an arch over an invisible child, the hands passed through the air over the plaza. They hung in the sunlight like immense doves. Talbot climbed the slope, following this spectre along the embankment. He had witnessed the annunciation of a unique event. Looking down at the plaza, he murmured without thinking: "Ralph Nader."

The Geometry of Her Face. In the perspectives of the plaza, the junctions of the underpass and embankment, Talbot at last recognised a modulus that could be multiplied into the landscape of his consciousness. The descending triangle of the plaza was repeated in the facial geometry of the young woman. The diagram of her bones formed a key to his own postures and musculature, and to the scenario that had preoccupied him at the Institute. He began to prepare for departure. The pilot and the young woman now deferred to him. The fans of the helicopter turned in the dark air, casting elongated ciphers on the dying concrete.

Transliterated Pudenda. Dr. Nathan showed his pass to the guard at the gatehouse. As they drove towards the testing area he was aware of Catherine Austin peering through the windshield, her sexuality keening now that Talbot was within range. Nathan glanced down at her broad thighs, calculating the jut and rake of her pubis. "Talbot's belief—and this is confirmed by the logic of the scenario—is that automobile crashes play very different roles from the ones we assign them. Apart from its ontological function, redefining the elements of space and time in terms of our most potent consumer durable, the car crash may be perceived unconsciously as a fertilising rather than a destructive event—a liberation of sexual energy—mediating the sexuality of those who have died with an intensity impossible in any other form: James Dean and Miss Mansfield, Camus and the late President. In the eucharist of the simulated auto disaster we see the transliterated pudenda of Ralph Nader, our nearest image of the blood and body of Christ." They stopped by the test course. A group of engineers watched a crushed Lincoln dragged away through the morning air. The hairless plastic mannequin of a woman sat propped on the grass, injury sites marked on her legs and thorax.

Journeys to an Interior. Waiting in Karen Novotny's apartment, Talbot made certain transits: (1) Spinal: "The Eye of Silence"— these porous rocktowers, with the luminosity of exposed organs, contained an immense planetary silence. Moving across the iodine water of these corroded lagoons, Talbot followed the solitary nymph through the causeways of rock, the palaces of his own flesh and bone. (2) Media: montage landscapes of war—webbing heaped in pits beside the Shanghai-Nanking railway; bar-girls' cabins built out of tyres and fuel drums; dead Japanese stacked like firewood in LCT's off Woosung pier. (3) Contour: the unique parameters of Karen's body—beckoning vents of mouth and vulva, the soft hypogeum of the anus. (4) Astral: segments of his postures mimetised in the processions of space. These transits contained an image of the renascent geometry assembling itself in the musculature of the young woman, in their postures during intercourse, in the angles between the walls of the apartment.

Stochastic Analysis. Karen Novotny paused over the wet stockings in the handbasin. As his fingers touched her armpits she stared down into the sculpture garden between the apartment blocks. The sallow-faced young man in the fascist overcoat who had followed her all week was sitting on the bench beside the Paolozzi. His paranoid eyes, with their fusion of passion and duplicity, had watched her like a rapist's across the cafe tables. Talbot's bruised hands were lifting her breasts, as if weighing their heavy curvatures against some more plausible alternative. The landscape of highways obsessed him, the rear mouldings of automobiles. All day he had been building his bizarre antenna on the roof of the apartment block, staring into the sky as if trying to force a corridor to the sun. Searching in his suitcase, she found clippings of his face taken from as yet unpublished news stories in *Oggi* and *Newsweek*. In the evening, while she bathed, waiting for him to enter the bathroom as she powdered her body, he crouched over the blueprints spread between the sofas in the lounge, calculating a stochastic analysis of the Pentagon car park.

Crash Magazine. Catherine Austin moved through the exhibits towards the dark-skinned young man in the black coat. He leaned against one of the cars, his face covered by the rainbows reflected from a frosted windshield. Who was Koester: a student in Talbot's class; Judas in this scenario; a rabbi serving a sinister novitiate? Why had he organised this exhibition of crashed cars? The truncated vehicles, with their ruptured radiator grilles, were arranged in lines down the show-room floor. His warped sexuality, of which she had been aware since his arrival at the first semester, had something of the same quality as these maimed vehicles. He had even produced a magazine devoted solely to car accidents: *Crash!* The dismembered bodies of Jayne Mansfield, Camus and Dean presided over its pages, epiphanies of violence and desire.

A Cosmetic Problem. The star of the show was J.F.K., victim of the first conceptual car crash. A damaged Lincoln had been given the place of honour, plastic models of the late President and his wife in the rear seat. An elaborate attempt had been made to represent cosmetically the expressed brain-tissue of the President.

As she touched the white acrylic smears across the trunk Koester swung himself aggressively out of the driver's seat. While he lit her cigarette she leaned against the fender of a white Pontiac, her thighs almost touching his. Koester took her arm with a nervous gesture. "Ah, Dr. Austin . . ." The flow of small talk modulated their sexual encounter. ". . . surely Christ's crucifixion could be regarded as the first traffic accident—certainly if we accept Jarry's happy piece of anti-clericalism . . ."

The 60-Minute Zoom. As they moved from apartment to apartment along the motorway, Karen Novotny was conscious of the continuing dissociation of the events around her. Talbot followed her about the apartment, drawing chalk outlines on the floor around her chair, around the cups and utensils on the breakfast table as she drank her coffee, and lastly around herself: (1) sitting, in the posture of Rodin's "Thinker," on the edge of the bidet, (2) watching from the balcony as she waited for Koester to catch up with them again, (3) making love to Talbot on the bed. He worked silently at the chalk outlines, now and then rearranging her limbs. The noise of the helicopters had become incessant. One morning she woke in complete silence to find that Talbot had gone.

A Question of Definition. The multiplying outlines covered the walls and floors, a frieze of hieratic poses and priapic dances— crash victims, a crucified man, children in intercourse. The outline of a helicopter covered the cinder surface of the tennis court below like the profile of an archangel. She returned after a fruitless search among the cafes to find the furniture removed from the apartment. Koester and his student gang were photographing the chalk outlines. Her own name had been written into the silhouette of herself in the bath. " '*Novotny, masturbating,*' " she read out aloud. "Are you writing me into your scenario, Mr. Koester?" she asked with an attempt at irony. His irritated eyes compared her figure with the outline in the bath. "*We* know where he is, Miss Novotny." She stared at the outline of her breasts on the black tiles of the shower stall, Talbot's hands traced around them. Hands multiplied around the rooms, soundlessly clapping, a welcoming host.

The Unidentified Female Orifice. These leg-stances preoccupied Talbot—Karen Novotny (1) stepping from the driving seat of the Pontiac, median surface of thighs exposed, (2) squatting on the bathroom floor, knees laterally displaced, fingers searching for the diaphragm lip, (3) in the a tergo posture, thighs pressing against Talbot, (4) collision: crushed right fibia against the instrument console, left patella impacted by the handbrake.

The Optimum Wound Profile. "One must bear in mind that rollover followed by a head-on collision produces complex occupant movements and injuries from unknown sources," Dr. Nathan explained to Captain Webster. He held up the montage photograph he had found in Koester's cubicle, the figure of a man with itemised wound areas. "However, here we have a wholly uncharacteristic emphasis on palm, ankle and abdominal injuries. Even allowing for the excessive crushing movements in a severe impact it is difficult to reconstruct the likely accident mode. In this case, taken from Koester's scenario of Talbot's death, the injuries seem to have been sustained in an optimised auto fatality, conceived by the driver as some kind of bizarre crucifixion. He would need to be mounted in the crash vehicle in an obscene position as if taking part in some grotesque act of intercourse—Christ crucified on the sodomised body of his own mother."

The Impact Zone. At dusk Talbot drove around the deserted circuit of the research laboratory test-track. Grass grew waist-high through the untended concrete, wheel-less cars rusting in the undergrowth along the verge. Overhead the helicopter moved across the trees, its fans churning up a storm of leaves and cigarette cartons. Talbot steered the car among the broken tyres and oil drums. Beside him the young woman leaned against his shoulder, her grey eyes surveying Talbot with an almost minatory calm. He turned onto a concrete track between the trees. The collision course ran forwards through the dim light, crushed cars shackled to steel gondolas above a catapult. Plastic mannequins spilled through the burst doors and panels. As they walked along the catapult rails Talbot was aware of the young woman pacing out the triangle of approach roads. Her face contained the geometry of the plaza. He worked until dawn, towing the wrecks into the posture of a motorcade.

Talbot: False Deaths. (1) The flesh impact: Karen Novotny's beckoning figure in the shower stall, open thighs and exposed pubis—traffic fatalities screamed in this soft collision. (2) The flyover below the apartment: the angles between the concrete buttresses contained for Talbot an immense anguish. (3) A crushed fender: in its broken geometry Talbot saw the dismembered body of Karen Novotny, the alternate death of Ralph Nader.

Unusual Poses. "You'll see why we're worried, Captain." Dr. Nathan beckoned Webster towards the photographs pinned to the walls of Talbot's office. "We can regard them in all cases as 'poses.' They show (1) the left orbit and zygomatic arch of President Kennedy magnified from Zapruder frame 230, (2) X-ray plates of the hands of Lee Harvey Oswald, (3) a sequence of corridor angles at the Broadmoor Hospital for the Criminally Insane, (4) Miss Karen Novotny, an intimate of Talbot's, in a series of unusual amatory positions. In fact, it is hard to tell whether the positions are those of Miss Novotny in intercourse or as an auto-crash fatality—to a large extent the difference is now meaningless." Captain Webster studied the exhibits. He fingered the shaving scar on his heavy jaw, envying Talbot the franchises of this young woman's body. "And together they make up a portrait of this American safety fellow—Nader?"

"In Death, Yes." Nathan nodded safely over his cigarette smoke. "In *death*, yes. That is, an alternate or 'false' death. These images of angles and postures constitute not so much a private gallery as a conceptual equation, a fusing device by which Talbot hopes to bring his scenario to a climax. The danger of an assassination attempt seems evident, one hypotenuse in this geometry of a murder. As to the figure of Nader—one must remember that Talbot is here distinguishing between the manifest content of reality and its latent content. Nader's true role is clearly very different from his apparent one, to be deciphered in terms of the postures we assume, our anxieties mimetised in the junction between wall and ceiling. In the post-Warhol era a single gesture such as uncrossing one's legs will have more significance than all the pages in 'War and Peace.' In 20th century terms the crucifixion, for example, would be re-enacted as a conceptual auto disaster."

Idiosyncrasies and Sin-crazed Idioms. As she leaned against the concrete parapet of the camera tower, Catherine Austin could feel Koester's hands moving around her shoulder straps. His rigid face was held six inches from her own, his mouth like the pecking orifice of some unpleasant machine. The planes of his cheekbones and temples intersected with the slabs of rain-washed cement, together forming a strange sexual modulus. A car moved along the perimeter of the test area. During the night the students had built an elaborate tableau on the impact site fifty feet below, a multi-vehicle auto crash. A dozen wrecked cars lay on their sides, broken fenders on the grass verges. Plastic mannequins had been embedded in the interlocked windshields and radiator grilles, wound areas marked on their broken bodies. Koester had named them: Jackie, Ralph, Abraham. Perhaps he saw the tableau as a rape? His hand hesitated on her left breast. He was watching the Novotny girl walking along the concrete aisle. She laughed, disengaging herself from Koester. Where were her own wound areas?

Speed Trials. Talbot opened the door of the Lincoln and took up his position in agent Greer's seat. Behind him the helicopter pilot and the young woman sat in the rear of the limousine. For the first time the young woman had begun to smile at Talbot, a soundless rictus of the mouth, deliberately exposing her wound as if showing him that her shyness had gone. Ignoring her now, Talbot looked out through the dawn light at the converging concrete aisles. Soon the climax of the scenario would come, J.F.K. would die again, his young wife raped by this conjunction of time and space. The enigmatic figure of Nader presided over the collision, its myths born from the crossovers of auto crashes and genitalia. He looked up from the wheel as the flares illuminated the impact zone. As the car surged forwards he realised that the two passengers had gone.

The Acceleration Couch. Half-zipping his trousers, Koester lay back against the torn upholstery, one hand still resting on the plump thigh of the sleeping young woman. The debris-filled compartment had not been the most comfortable site. This zombielike creature had strayed across the concrete runways like a fugitive from her own dreams, forever talking about Talbot as if unconsciously inviting Koester to betray him. Why was she wearing the Jackie Kennedy wig? He sat up, trying to open the rusty door. The students had christened the wreck "Dodge 38," furnishing the rear seat with empty beer bottles and contraceptive wallets. Abruptly the car jolted forwards, throwing him across the young woman. As she woke, pulling at her skirt, the sky whirled past the frosted windows. The clanking cable between the rails propelled them on a collision course with a speeding limousine below the camera tower.

Celebration. For Talbot the explosive collision of the two cars was a celebration of the unity of their soft geometries, the unique

creation of the pudenda of Ralph Nader. The dismembered
bodies of Karen Novotny and himself moved across the morning
landscape, recreated in a hundred crashing cars, in the perspectives of a thousand concrete embankments, in the sexual postures
of a million lovers.

Interlocked Bodies. Holding the bruise under his left nipple, Dr.
Nathan ran after Webster towards the burning wrecks. The cars
lay together at the centre of the collision corridor, the last steam
and smoke lifting from their cabins. Webster stepped over the
armless body of Karen Novotny hanging face down from the rear
window. The burning fuel had traced a delicate lacework of
expressed tissue across her naked thighs. Webster pulled open the
rear door of the Lincoln. "Where the hell is Talbot?" Holding
his throat with one hand, Dr. Nathan stared at the wig lying
among the beer bottles.

The Helicopters Are Burning. Talbot followed the young woman
between the burning helicopters. Their fuselages formed bonfires
across the dark fields. Her strong stride, with its itemised progress
across the foam-smeared concrete, carried within its rhythm a
calculated invitation to his own sexuality. Talbot stopped by the
burning wreck of a Sikorski. The body of Karen Novotny, with
its landscapes of touch and feeling, clung like a wraith to his
thighs and abdomen.

Fractured Smile. The hot sunlight lay across the suburban street.
From the radio of the car played a fading harmonic, the last
music of the quasars. Karen Novotny's fractured smile spread
across the windshield. Talbot looked up at his own face mediated
from the billboard beside the car park. Overhead the glass curtain walls of the apartment block presided over this first interval
of neural calm.

VIETNAM-SUPERFICTION

Alain Arias-Misson

(May 9–August 9) 1970

"Thus an essential property of language is that it provides the means for expressing indefinitely many thoughts and for reacting appropriately in an indefinite range of new situations. The grammar of a particular language, then, is to be supplemented by a universal grammar that accommodates the creative aspect of language use and expresses the deep-seated regularities which, being universal, are omitted from the grammar itself."

—ASPECTS OF THE THEORY OF SYNTAX, Chomsky.

"The things we have seen and read during these horrible years surpass belief. I have in front of me now an Associated Press photo from the *New York Times* . . . I cannot describe the pathos of this scene, or the expression on the face of the wounded child. . . ."

—AMERICAN POWER AND THE NEW MANDARINS, Chomsky.

July 6

I looked at their faces curiously. I feel a certain security, a freedom to speak, to interpret. I remember that luncheon with the journalists, almost two months ago. What is there between those faces, I wonder. I sense the comfort of the surroundings. The sofa, the textures. I know of course there is no more to describe here than outside. There are their titles: Secretary of State William P. Rogers, Ambassador Ellsworth Bunker, and South Vietnamese President Nguyen Van Thieu. There is nothing in their faces; nothing I can see. I feel I must watch myself carefully, watch the words I use. I know the reality of this language is in

Associated Press.

VIETNAM PARLEY—Secretary of State William P. Rogers, Ambassador Ellsworth Bunker and South Vietnamese President Nguyen Van Thieu talk in Saigon Saturday.

their names. I come a little closer to watch the expressions on their faces. There is a feeling of suspension in the room. I look at Secretary of State William P. Rogers; I realize there is nothing beyond naming him. I cannot see his eyes. Why is it, I wonder, that I feel at the same time a greater freedom and a lesser tension of the real. I am conscious of the blood and torn flesh involved in their talk. I wonder again what there is between them, I listen as they talk in low tones, I can hear no tension in their voices. I realize that the only relations are those which exist between their names, like pieces in a game. I am surprised by my readiness to interpret; I believe it is because of what lies in the background. I remember their screams and their eyes; they seem to be lost. I know there is nothing behind their names. They move here, and talk in Saigon Saturday, but I know it is the oscillation of their names. I would like to approach them, to touch one of them on the arm, to say something. I look more closely into the face of one of them, and I can make out nothing. I wonder if this language is wholly insubstantial. I think of the blood and pain I have seen

on their faces. There's a stillness in this meeting, the words I use
are too heavy, too loud. I realize this is the most silent scene I
have witnessed, my words occupy the foreground. I mean the
language has been drained from them, from their gestures, their
talk, into their names. Their faces are masks. I remember the
dying. I feel death in the air.

Associated Press.

**SILHOUETTE IN CAMBODIA—A Cambodian Army soldier crouches in the shadow of
a temple building at Krang Ponely, Cambodia, as his unit moves in on Viet Cong and
North Vietnamese troops who had occupied the Buddhist religious grounds. Several
temple buildings were set afire and destroyed during the battle which followed.**

July 7

I watch, crouching in the shadow; a Cambodian Army soldier
crouches in the shadow of a temple . . . his shape outlined against
the glare of the sun. What else is possible for me, I think. I
wonder for a moment who I am, what my role here is. I crouch in
the shadow of a temple building. My god, I think to myself, I am
absorbed, dominated by the language, and I only project my
shadow. I reconsider the phrase: a Cambodian Army soldier
crouches etc., and smile. I breathe the dusty air. I would like to

touch the wall beside me, I would like to say something to one of
my comrades; but I no longer have any use for this kind of refuge
from being there. To be here is enough, I think; I look about me,
taking in the various circumstances. What freedom do I have? I
have explored the confines of this context. I know the words
I have about me. I know what verbs, what actions I can take, I
know the nouns, the temple buildings, my body I suppose, why
should I elaborate on these? The temple building is here, the
dust, its stone walls. And my body, the intimate awareness, a
shadow outlined against the brilliant background; a Cambodian
Army soldier crouches . . . The words are soundless; I cannot
hear them today. We are limited in time also, nothing is ours.
Several temple buildings were set afire etc., I thought about the
sentence, and knew I was caught in the past.

"We looked down from a catwalk
through large openings, one for
each cell," Mr. Luce said. "There
were the tiger cages which were
not supposed to exist."

The prisoners, he said, gathered beneath the opening to shout
up at the foreigners. They seemed more defiant than the prisoners
in the regular camps, he said, and
he attributed this to their greater
desperation.

"The congressmen looked very
shocked—they seemed almost
speechless at first," Mr. Luce
said.

The Americans, in the presence
of Col. Ve, visited two buildings
containing the airless, hot, filthy
stone compartments. The first
building was for men: three to
four prisoners to a compartment
that seemed not quite five feet
wide and nine feet long, Mr. Luce
said.

"It was high enough for the
prisoners to stand up but none
of the men did," he said. "They
dragged themselves to the spot
where they could look up and
speak to us. They said they were
not able to stand up. Their legs
looked shriveled to a certain
extent. The men claimed they
were beaten, that they were very
hungry because they were only

given rice that had sand and pebbles in it."

The prisoners pleaded for water, he said, and cried out that they were sick and had no medicine.

Above each compartment, Mr. Luce said, was a bucket of white lime that Col. Ve said was used to whitewash the walls.

"But the prisoners told us that the lime was thrown down on them when they asked for food," Mr. Luce said. "The prisoners also said that when the lime was thrown on them they coughed and spat blood. Many said that they had the disease of the lungs [tuberculosis] and could not breathe when the lime was thrown on them."

July 8

I wondered where I was in this context. I knew my surroundings of course, but there was not enough room to exist in this context, "not supposed to exist." We had become used to living with barely the room to move, to breathe. We gathered beneath the opening to shout up at the foreigners. I looked up at the congressmen; I dug my nails into the grit of the walls. I was perfectly aware of our involvement, I mean the nature of our being there, there was very little left we could feel, or say. I took part in the actions of course, this was the extent of my freedom. I shouted with the others, I felt my face contorted with theirs. Would there ever be a possibility to communicate? We all knew what we were, in fact. We were not supposed to exist. We could see in their eyes who we were. I also dragged myself etc.; we spoke ourselves. We barely existed, we might no longer exist, this was the possibility to exist in the following words; we were not able to stand up; we were beaten; we were very hungry because we were only given rice that had sand and pebbles in it etc. I looked at the walls. I knew that I existed in this language, I recognized myself in these words: what we did, what we were, and what we said. I could not speak to my companions, this was a circle of language. In our cries and pleadings with the Americans, there might be, I felt, some possibility of communication. Otherwise, by now, our language had become sterile. There should be some reflection of what we were in what they said. I could not feel, or breathe deeply, just an unresting consciousness of the words, a need to communicate how we existed, to see ourselves reflected in words.

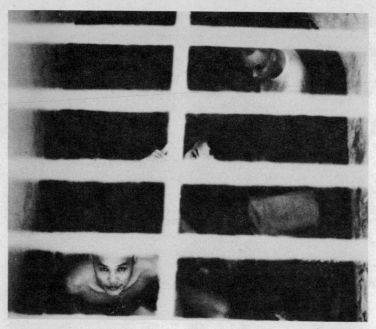

"TIGER CAGE"—Thomas R. Harkin, a staff member of a House of Representatives study team just back from Southeast Asia, says this picture shows political prisoners peering up from a "tiger cage" cell on Con Son Island, a South Vietnamese prison.

July 9

I peered up through the bars at them. I did not want to speak, to define our experience. I was aware of the outside of the bars. It was simple enough really. I did not want to experience the inside of the cage, nor give them a refuge in words. I myself would have liked to break out of the words. I know who you are, I thought to myself, your insubstantiality. We exist here. I know every word I use. I don't want to use up the language at my disposal. What does it mean to say that the cages were fetid, or to speak of the urine and filth? It is amazing, I thought, as they looked at me, how empty experience is. They want to fill it out, to circumscribe it. I turned to one of my companions: don't you see, I said to him, we are what they see. I looked back up through the bars; I felt that my eyes made a link. July 9, I thought to myself, with the layers of language, we are here now. It is this transparency with our presence that I want to say. Can't they see that we are here, that 'we exist? However much I say, it will not be any clearer to them. I know that I and my companions, and the hundreds of others, are here in terms of language, that we will be taken by them as language. To describe these conditions, our physical and emotional context, would only give them more language material. We live in frames of language, they must be stripped to a minimum, words detract from our being, our presence.

Maj. Gen. George W. Casey, missing in Vietnam.

AP.

July 10

Maj. Gen. George W. Casey was killed in this language. The wreckage of Gen. Casey's helicopter was found on a mountainside etc., there was no sign of survivors, United Press International reported. Gen. Casey knew he was included in this framework, in the sense that he had recognized the frames in which he was set on June 30. He knew the language contained his death. He was not able to review this language, but his death was certainly not unexpected. He knew that he was frozen in these words, just as they all were. He would have liked to return home. The blood; ever since he had that intuition about the language, he knew that this would be the case. He was no freer than its grammar. Of course he could have chosen otherwise, but these were his words. He did not foresee in any way his death of course, but he realized it would occur in this general context. At that time, ten days ago, when he directed etc., he knew that the words he spoke, the words that governed his every action, the atmosphere charged with language were all a part of this context. And his death was no freer. He thought: I would like to say something else. But he knew it was impossible. How could he move outside his own language? Maj. Gen. George W. Casey, missing in Vietnam. Was it not possible to be more flexible with the language, to manipulate it in some way? It had a rigidity that was inhuman, that did not belong to flesh and blood. But it was their language.

At the same time, the Army disclosed that Maj. Gen. George W. Casey, who directed the withdrawal of the last American ground troops from Cambodia on June 29, has been missing in the field since Tuesday.

[The wreckage of Gen. Casey's helicopter was found on a mountainside today by an aerial search party. There was no sign of survivors, United Press International reported.]

Associated Press.

BIVOUAC—A desolate bomb-scarred hilltop about 20 miles from Da Nang serves as bivouac area for the South Vietnamese 51st Regiment after a period of combat.

July 11–12

A desolate bomb-scarred hilltop; I walked through this landscape with a feeling of recognition. I reflected on the words as I
walked across the bomb-scarred hilltop. My friends were walking
around, smelling the air. I sat down against a tree-trunk, looking
at the scene. It was ironic, I thought, realizing that there could
be no refuge in the language of sense impressions, of the sensuous. This, I felt, could be compared to an interior landscape. I
put my hand onto the ground and looked at it a moment. My
mind was still reverberating from the combat. I looked about me.
At first it was difficult to recognize the various features of the
landscape, aside from the remains of the trees. I watched my
friends walking around. I thought: it becomes clearer, in this
situation, to what extent we are dependent on our immediate
context. Of course you could say that these surroundings are as
sensuous as any. But it has been reduced as far as possible, you
feel that a kind of language has been applied which leaves no
room for the senses to flee to. I stood up, and walked a short way
over the bomb-scarred ground. It was curious how we used each
other for reference. I asked one of my friends, what do you think
of this, I mean the desolate landscape etc.? He looked at me a
moment. Listen, he said, by now we know this is where we are.
What else is there for us? It is a suitable bivouac area for us after
a period of combat. I smiled, appreciating his use of these words.
This is nothing, really, I said, squatting and picking up a stone.
We are learning to live in our language. · A desolate bomb-
scarred hilltop; don't you see how appropriate the words are for
us? We are living here on our terms. It is proper after a period of
combat. We looked off towards the remains of trees. The language was consistent, I felt, reproducing, repeating itself. This
was necessary in view of the poverty of the language available.
There was very little it was possible to say. I felt satisfied by the
bareness of the surroundings. I reflected on the paucity of what
I was moving through; of the stripping down of the words. I
thought back a few moments. A desolate bomb-scarred hilltop, I
repeated to my friend. Now as I look at these surroundings, I recognize them clearly. I recognize them in the language itself.
There is nothing more than these few words! He looked at me:
this is ours to inhabit, to act in, he said. What else do we have?
We looked off to the remains of the trees again.

July 13

I was intensely conscious of the vegetation as we explored the
still-smoking jungle hills yesterday. I looked at a body split open

on the green background, counting. This murder and torture, I thought, horrifies us, but it is part of the poetry, it fits in with this language.

> Exploring the still-smoking jungle hills yesterday, South Vietnamese troops found 143 bodies and a large amount of weapons and equipment strewn in the area of the raid. Today at least 65 more bodies were reported to have been found.

I smelled the air, still smoking. I realized that I was a part of the same poem, the streams of blood, the green. I was particularly curious about the raid. Whose vocabulary, I wondered, did this belong to? We found 143 bodies yesterday. It was always surprising to find one, however conscious one was in the language, suddenly a body would appear in the middle of this literary context, and I would look at it as a man. I wondered about the relation of the bodies and the raid, I mean the words did not conjugate well. When I looked at a body, I recognized it. I mean there was something in the twist of the limbs, or in the eyes, that I recognized. But the raid was different, it belonged to another vocabulary. The flesh, the vegetation; there was a sensuousness in the words. But the raid was too distant, too playful, it did not fit. I knew after all that I had considerable freedom in this context. I knelt beside one of the bodies, to look at it closely. There was no face, it was turned away into the green, invaded by greenness. I touched it on the shoulder, and kept my hand there for several moments; it was a bond. I realized that the sensuousness, the depth of language did not detract from the context, did not make a pocket of silence in the middle of the words. I wanted to look clearly at everything, not to invent words and escape from the facts, the observable. I smiled to myself, as I arose, and looked about me, thinking of that last phrase. What truth could be in the observable, if already nothing could be said about these jungle hills. I looked about me and continued on my way. I looked back at the body a moment. I knew we were exchangeable, I mean that I could claim nothing for myself which it did not have. I looked out across the hilltops trying to sort out these words in my head. There was a homogeneity in them which made it difficult to experience anything. I walked for some time, counting the bodies. The bodies and the walk through the jungle hills were implicit in the factual description. I looked down for a moment at my hand, and smiled. I remembered the feeling of the body, the movement of the flesh. This word, for example, held some substance. Even if it were lifeless, it came closer to life than anything else in this framework. And today, at least 65 more bodies were reported to have been found. I could see where the relation between the words, ourselves, and the bodies was. The flesh was the central matter here, it gave us coherence. It was necessary not to confuse the words, the report, with the flesh.

Associated Press.

BACK IN THE FIELD—Gen. William C. Westmoreland, U.S. Army chief of staff and former Vietnam commander, inspects an honor guard of People's Self-Defense Force at a training center in Vinh Long province. Gen. Westmoreland is checking on progress in Vietnamization on a week-long visit to South Vietnam's war zones.

July 14

Gen. William C. Westmoreland looks at the men. One of them, conscious of his looks, stands rigidly at attention, the muscles of his arm tense. He is aware of the ground under his feet. Consciousness is collected about his flesh, the flesh of his arm muscles, the softness of his body. Gen. Westmoreland is checking on progress in Vietnamization. The sky is empty, it seems to partake of the nature of language. The soldier is aware of the scrutiny, he is conscious of his body, he feels clearly the confines of his flesh, he is reduced to his flesh. It is as if he could not see, his eyes darkened. Gen. Westmoreland looks through the soldiers. He knows better than they do their transparency. They are shadows, barely visible here, merging. He also understands that there is

hardly room for life in this language; that is, inspecting an honor
guard of People's Self-Defense Force at a training center etc. He
thinks: there is little enough left of myself. Their flesh is vibrant.
He looks through them. He knows the chain of words. There is
an impersonality in his inspection. Each one of them is fixed, defined in his flesh, in his own mind. They are at a training center
in Vinh Long province. Their context is clear. Gen. Westmoreland reads them, as he is checking etc. One of the soldiers thinks:
I am aware of the ambiguity of our presence, I mean the fluctua-
tion of this set of words. Gen. Westmoreland is checking etc. and
we are involved in that. Then I feel the urgency of my flesh. I
know of course this is part of the same context, that the language
is the same. What is my consciousness of my flesh in the context
of Vietnamization, etc. What place does it have in this kind of
language? He is right of course, Gen. Westmoreland is dealing
with the correct language, he inspects an honor guard of People's
Self-Defense Force at a training center etc. These words belong
to Gen. Westmoreland's vocabulary. The rest is in the shadow.
There is in fact little room for life; their self-consciousness reduced to their bodies is negligible. Gen. Westmoreland deals with
the plain language. Only a shell of consciousness is left with him.

July 15

I walked along the pretty jungle road, I knew there was irony in
this language, but it was all that was available. I walked along
the road, thinking about the picturesque spa, and looking at the
bodies. Eyewitness reports said etc., I knew I was in the context.
Sometimes I wondered if I had become too self-conscious about
the language, but there were images which imposed themselves,
such as the jungle and the dead, and it was necessary to realize
this was a part of the facts, included in the language used. I
looked at the bodies carefully as I walked by. I thought about
these words   again. I realized of course   Eyewitness reports from the pic-   that I was in
d a n g e r   o f turesque spa. 58 miles southwest   b e i n g l o s t
                    of here, said the pretty jungle road
among these   leading out of the town was lit-   words. It was
not possible to   tered with the bodies of govern-   see and feel
                    ment troops.
much of the   t i m e .   T h e
pretty jungle road was littered etc. These are the facts, the language is there. I could not or would not make out their faces,
what were they except bodies? Of course it is true that I was
particularly attracted by the picturesque spa and the pretty
jungle road. Eyewitness reports etc., I felt myself the object of a
huge eye. The pretty jungle road led out of the town; after glanc-

ing at the picturesque spa, I walked down the road, watching for the bodies. The road was littered with bodies. I recognized the banality of the language, death was a shallow thing, it floated up to the surface of language also. Was there any more weight to those bodies, than to the picturesque spa? I would have liked to reach out to one of those bodies, and embraced it, but I realized this was impossible in the present context. I did look about at the pretty jungle setting. I knew well what I was involved in. Eyewitness reports etc. I also was perfectly aware of my own language, of the repetitions and variations. But here, how else was it possible to move, except on the surface?

July 16

I was taken by the heavily wooded Kiri Rom plateau. I wandered through these woods with my companions. We set up blocking forces etc. but at the time this seemed irrelevant. In effect, the most amazing thing was to breathe for a while, to take advantage of this plateau. I film of trees, pools of light of branches whatever else plied in those heavily wooded watched the leaves, the in the midst and leaves, and could be im- words, heavily

Regular Cambodian troops reportedly set up blocking forces east and west of the heavily wooded Kiri Rom plateau, and American-trained Cambodian mercenaries, once known as the Mike Force, were trying to drive into the town from the north.

wooded, with nostalgia. I knew it was an accident of factual language, but I was unable to resist a few moments of pleasure and memory. I spoke of it to my companion. He said: I'm afraid this language is not credible. You forget that it is a part of our context—regular Cambodian forces reportedly set up blocking forces etc. Yes, I said. I knew of course that it was difficult to extend the language, but was our context so closely defined? You said that regular Cambodian troops reportedly etc. There's an emptiness, a breathing space in the framework. Yet as I spoke I realized it was naive to hold on to this language. It was the vocabulary of another time. One can no more mix lexicons than times. Besides, I knew that this same time, American-trained mercenaries were trying to drive etc. I thought about the words an instant, but could not find them credible either. I walked about in the woods, but there were evidently less and less contents to the heavily wooded Kiri Rom plateau. I was aware of the usual trees and plants, but this language was incompatible with our framework. For example, I said, regardless of whether we realize the drive of the American-trained Cambodian mercenaries, it's in keeping with countless other phrases. But, I thought, we are excluded from the life processes by these frames of language—we set up blocking forces, and the heavily wooded plateau is just a parenthesis; the American-trained Cambodian mercenaries were trying to drive etc. and their deaths are out of context. The experience of death is as removed as life. I looked at my companion. I was no longer affected by the woods, they were a setting. But, I said, in spite of the reduction of our experience here, we have a freedom which was unforeseeable. I mean, the regular Cambodian troops reportedly etc. There is an oscillation in the language which always constitutes our freedom. I am not afraid of using our little freedom, however uncertain or even inexistent the zone may be. I think that is the way they are dying in this context; the mercenaries at this time for example. Let's continue our walk through the woods; they are dying, there is a smell of wild flowers. I saw him smile, and knew of course that the language was unstable, unfounded in fact, but I felt this was the beginning of freedom.

GOD CARES, BUT WAITS

James B. Hall

I. Behind Our Lines

First the prisoner and his interrogation. Of my final mission into their territory, more later.

Beyond our village the highway crosses a narrow bridge of concrete, and then in a gorge of stone goes north. At four o'clock the subject came pedaling beneath the row of palm trees; I stepped from behind the abutment and grabbed his handle bars. When asked did he "want a drink of our water," the prisoner's face turned white: I had taken another courier headed north.

Our procedures of Search and Interrogation are prescribed: with the subject facing a wall, legs apart, we search first for the knives or other weapons of offense. Only then may we place our hands first on the crown of their heads, rumpling well the hair, then on the seams of clothing where the saw blades are, then down to the shoes—in his case, rope sandals. Inspection of the body cavities, especially females who wear pads or tampons, takes place at my private office in the abandoned schoolhouse. Only after complete inspection may interrogation begin.

Subject courier carried no weapons of offense, but when I placed my hands on the crown of his head I noted a soft innocent odor, a coconut oil pomade. His trousers had neither seams nor fly. When I removed the cycling clips from his ankles, the trousers came apart and exposed completely the lower part of his legs. His "trousers" were only a single piece of cloth, gathered at the waist; the legs were formed very cleverly by use of steel clips. Not until my second interrogation, however, did I see the absolute symmetry of his whole body.

Looking back on that instant of capture, I now wish the prisoner had tried to run. As a C.I. Captain, long in the field, I do not miss; as it was, the subject prisoner pushed his bicycle toward my detachment headquarters. The other natives smiled at me pleasantly—a kind of salute; they knew this was planned at Babe Ruth, and besides, my previous two hundred and seventeen captures are a matter of informal record in the village. That night the prisoner's interrogation began.

But first a word about my methods. In addition to obtaining military secrets and/or agent-contacts in the Territories, I also take unofficial information for my private files: if subject is married, then admitted infidelities; if single, then deviant sexual practice, relations with Self, and all "chance" encounters. These personal notes I send into the village for "secret" typing and reproduction. In this way I am an indirect moral force in the community.

"You are by profession a *Siziar*"—one who professionally washes the dead.

Subject prisoner declined reply.

I then methodically disclosed other items of his file form Babe Ruth. Our files from Corps Headquarters are very complete and contain, chronologically, all instances of unconscious confession as well as the implications from household wastes; at Babe Ruth our specialists analyze evidence from the field for patterns of conduct and consistent routes of travel.

"Your profession and one living relative—your grandmother— are your excuse to go north. Sixty-eight percent of the time you go via the bridge—at four o'clock."

Subject prisoner declined reply. I then came back to a phrase he had heard before because I had carefully planted it in his subconscious: "How would you like to drink our water?"

Concerning our water this much should be clearly understood. Although the *Rossiter* or the "Lawyer" may be delegated for morale purposes to the enlisted men, including my detachment barber, I alone—in private—administer all water. One half gallon in each nostril is often enough. The head fills, rationality departs, and by delicate adjustments the subject is suspended for some hours in a twilight state of full confession. When the technique is professionally administered, fatalities are almost unheard of. At that moment the prisoner remained suspiciously calm and so I put my question once again ". . . the water?"

As though to reply, as though to begin his interrogation of *me*—a Captain six years in rank—my subject reached down and took a cycling clip from his right ankle. The cloth fell away from his leg, and the light turned his thigh to silver.

Without hesitation, I did the only responsible thing. I kneeled before him, and I forcibly *replaced* the cycle clip around his ankle. Then I rang for my orderly. Instead of suggesting the prisoner might wish to "Talk with a Lawyer," I ordered this subject held under special guards, in a stone cell in our stone outbuildings. I now felt this particular prisoner might be a rewarding exercise, after all.

The next morning, I sent my entire C.I. Detachment, including the barber, into the field for ten days. I wished to complete this interrogation under Ideal Conditions. When I asked him again if he wanted a drink of our water, the prisoner looked directly into my eyes, but everywhere in his face I saw genetic weakness. At that time I disclosed, completely, the secondary information in his file: he had washed the young girl overly long. Why? Consider those unhealthy relations with Self. Why? The light behind my desk shone full into his eyes.

My prisoner did not either reply or change expression. Instead, he bent gracefully and removed both cycle clips from his ankles. It was the flesh of his thigh that glistened and winked and moved like liquid metal in the folds of cloth. For the first time I saw the symmetry of his whole body.

As a matter of command decision, I opened my interrogation drawer. On my desk, I placed a bamboo rod, one end flayed. To my surprise the prisoner neither asked for mercy nor made assertions contrary to our cross-filed data from Babe Ruth. Instead, he took the rod from my desk and somewhat awkwardly—like a girl trying to throw a baseball—flayed the sunlight.

"No. Like this," I said, and brought the "C.I. Lawyer" down across my own leg. The prisoner's face was ecstatic. Once he saw our correct methods, he went around and around my private office, striking desk and chairs and the plaster walls.

Only after I removed my own shirt and placed myself on the interrogation bench did he see the obligations of continuity. He himself cried out as he brought the bamboo "Lawyer" across my flesh. As I had known he would, the prisoner broke down and began to weep. So ended my second interrogation.

Such was the pattern of our next four days: early each morning I suggested our water; in response, the subject removed his cycle clips. Each day I placed a new mode of investigation on the desk; avidly, he learned our methods. In order, I submitted myself to the knout, the *Rossiter*, the Penis Key, and the Fire Stubbs. Toward the end I even dreamed of the prisoner, head down beside our carboys, a nostril hose swinging in the sunlight like a vine. Still, I held back, and so it was, at night, our bodies exhausted, that we began to talk.

"You have told me of your past," he said. "You came from an

outlying Province, and because your father was a Tax-Fraud In-
vestigator, your parents often moved. Only your mother is now
alive."

On those nights I disclosed even the secondary information
about my childhood: all our white cottages behind picket fences
in a hundred villages; helping mother pack china in the barrel of
straw for still another move; the ways I kept my teachers morally
strong by the little notes addressed to the superintendents of all
my old school districts. . . .

As though it were his voice speaking, I heard about my interesting past: recruit days, my medals for services in the Territories as
Chief of Patrol; my sought-for commission, and my satisfactory
advance to Captain, Counter Insurgency. Sometimes his hand lay
on my breast and in the darkness of my room we were prisoner
and interrogator, almost intimate, almost One. Very much I
wanted to administer our water, but this he denied me in the
following way.

"Captain," he said on the final night, taking care to speak with
appropriate respect, "I will now do the thing within my power."
He raised me by the hand, and I followed to a room where already he had laid out the ritualistic towels of a *Siziar*.

His insistent hands bathed and bathed me until at three
o'clock the telephone beside my bed—my direct line to Babe
Ruth—began to ring.

The voice on the wire was Tiger, at Babe Ruth. In code, our
Operations Major gave me the coordinates of a new transmitter—
deep in the Territories to the north. At once I volunteered for
this mission. Tiger denied my request. I remonstrated. At last he
sensed the urgency in my voice and he agreed I should draw
grenades at Dump Two. In less than thirty minutes, crepe-soled
scouting sandals on my feet, my body covered by a native burnoose, I began my last patrol.

Subject prisoner wept without restraint at my departure. Only
once did I look back: from the door of the abandoned schoolhouse, his back to the light, he was watching me go. When I
returned he would be gone, for as a token I had given him my
private key to his outbuilding cell. Under formal orders once
more, I walked steadily across the valley. At dawn I drew grenades from a watchman at Dump Two, and then crossed easily
into their Territories to the north.

On the second day, high in the mountains, I crawled beneath
bushes and came to the barbed wire surrounding their transmitter. This place was of hard, swept clay, the red and white tower

clean and erect in the open space beyond the fence. Beside the tower I saw a house of cinder blocks, with a low, square, green door. Pacing the strict limits of his post, a very large man—a guard—sometimes shouted cadence to himself as he walked. With grenades and the machine pistol held close to my belly, I covered myself with my leaf-colored burnoose and waited for dusk.

Shortly past noon I saw the relief guard arrive on the back seat of a motorcycle. To be far behind the lines and to see them talking in their green uniforms and arm bands is always sinister. This new guard was slender, and obviously less military. At once the new guard went into the transmitter house and in the quiet of the afternoon I heard the noise of a toilet flushing.

Finally the new guard returned to the post—with a folded beach chair. The guard leaned the rifle beside the door and unfolded the chair. With the motorcycle now far away, the guard removed first hat, and then blouse. After an almost knowing look around the perimeter fence, the guard took off her brassiere. She reclined in her chair, her face to the sun, her red hair winking in the light. This new guard—a woman—apparently drifted off into sun-bathed sleep.

All afternoon, through a little opening in the briers, I watched the woman "guard" their transmitter. Clearly she was my enemy and yet from time to time she roused herself and peered very innocently, yet very intently, into the hand mirror in her purse. Aways before on my patrols I had used explosives, guile, disguise, appeals to pride, or bribery where possible. Now, for reasons I did not understand, I felt beyond Tiger and even Corps; in fact, although I still say our war is Just, I felt beyond the entire chain of our command, both tactically and politically. I began to tremble in my burnoose, and yet with grenades and automatic pistol warm near my belly, I forced myself to wait.

What happens next is perhaps strange: some will say I wanted to die, but the fact of my victory proves otherwise. Boldly at dusk, I stood up. I went directly to the main gate: she did not challenge. Therefore I went to the place where she lay. At close range she was much younger than I had imagined. Provocatively —innocently—in the half light from the transmitter tubes, I saw her teeth and her half-parted lips. For one moment, pistol at full automatic, I stood above her.

Suddenly her eyes opened. Without trying to rise she spoke to me in my mother tongue and she said, "You have come."

In fury I remembered Corps and Tiger. I armed and then I

threw my first grenade. I threw it with great force inside the transmitter. Only then did she cry out. Too late, she saw my face bent very close above her lips.

She cried out again, but I threw my last grenades into the now flaming house. Suddenly, I heard laughter. This was my own voice. As I ran across the clearing and leaped the fence and ran down a ravine of stones, I heard the transmitter tower crash down into the clearing somewhere behind me.

I repeat: although the woman guard awoke and positively identified my face, I did not shoot.

On the trails through low jungle to the south, I sometimes wept. Too late I saw that my prisoner—now escaped—and the woman guard were in league: what the prisoner began, the woman finished. And it was a fact: I had spared them both.

Therefore imagine my intense joy when I arrived back at the village and crossed the narrow concrete bridge. I found the schoolhouse still abandoned—except for my prisoner. He had remained faithful. He had even prepared for my return, for food was already on the table. At once I slipped out of my burnoose and my sandals and together we ate.

From gratitude and from some apparently deeper understanding, I very willingly taught my prisoner—at last—to administer the water. His confession was lyrical, complete.

Awkwardly at first, then with greater control, he administered the same to me. One half gallon in each nostril is often enough.

Painfully at first, then in a visionary way, all consciousness left—and then returned. In the end, my body outraged by water, I sank again into the isolated darkness of the abandoned school-house. Toward dawn, I very clearly heard the prisoner going through the drawers of my interrogation desk, taking one of each thing I had taught him—correctly—to use.

Unable to arise, impotent, my Detachment still in the field, I heard the back door slam. The prisoner, after all, was going north. Somewhere this side of the mounain he would meet the woman guard. They would cross-file their notes and together they would view all of the things he had taken from my interro-gation desk; together they would go to some house I would never see and there, late at night, they would make their full report. As for myself, I knew well enough what both my sergeant and the barber would report to Tiger and also to Babe Ruth.

Not far .up the gorge of stone I heard men counting cadence lustily as they came. I heard my own Detachment march across the narrow concrete bridge and then up the path toward this abandoned schoolhouse.

II. Outside the Cave

The buildings of the city and of the prison itself were fire under the sky, and the land beyond the city's edge with no rain in the past two years was cracked as an old woman's hand: cattle with legs apart in the fence corners, mouths slobbering foam, eyes glazed by the memory of water. In that heat he passed walls of stucco where the noise of buckets swinging empty above empty cisterns echoed among the small shops that lay beside the railroad tracks going north across the valley until the rails became a sliver of steel between two hills and then went on into the Territories beyond. To himself he said, "No. Not yet."

"Going on?" the barber asked, and with a white paper bib in place the barber began with the clippers. "*Very* far?"

The man said nothing for truly he had no plans. Although he had waited years for his release, and although his papers were correct, he now accepted something for the first time: in a coastal city where they had interrogated and arraigned and had tried him, indeed in the whole world, there was no one waiting for him. Years ago his only sister had stood by him for a while, but now even the judges were dead.

"Shorter than that," he ordered the barber, and because he was now free, with good papers, his voice was contemptuous.

"Yes indeed, sir," and the barber went on: so this year not one land owner planted a crop. And to be honest about it, in the whole town only one garden remained green. That one, by rail, twice weekly, got barrels of water marked Salt Cod—it was said. Also: young girls roamed the streets after dark, the government did nothing, and so who was to blame?

The man in the barber chair said nothing, but he heard well enough that girls ran alone in the streets after dark. In the sky overhead he felt some grotesque fowl—all fire—beat its wings.

"Good luck," the barber finally said, and with false enthusiasm whipped off the paper bib. Released prisoners often ducked into his shop like this for they wanted to pay someone to do a personal service, perhaps for the first time in years. The barber resolved to say no more for this one was very pale and very hard and very possibly a murderer—or worse. When the ex-convict looked at him coldly the barber added nervously, "Ahhh, good luck. Ahhh out *there?*"

As the prisoner walked along the railroad tracks going north, he happened to look up and see the cave. Because he was going nowhere at all, he climbed the high bank to see about it. This cave was in a ledge of rock and not much larger than his old cell. Inside the cave there was nothing at all; outside the cave's entrance was a large, smooth square of clay.

Because he was fatigued, the convict sat for a while on the square of earth to rest. Toward the town at dusk he saw the lights of the prison workshops suddenly blaze in the heat; along the tracks to the north he saw only the landscape and the rampant heat of the valley flow across the hills like a river.

With no possessions except for the suit of blue serge and the small amount of money they had paid him for work at the stamping machines in the prison, with no very real hope of a future, the convict saw no reason to move on. The money left over from the barbershop was not enough for either bribery or a train ticket; therefore he threw all his coins over the bank toward the railroad tracks. He took off the prison-made suit coat and the shoes and placed them behind a rock in the cave. In the old way, exactly at nine o'clock, he slept.

At daylight the convict sat again in the mouth of his cave. For the first time in his life, without rancor, he observed the sun's first rays come up and then spread across the curve of the earth. On the train tracks below, the first peasant walked toward the white buildings of the town; past noon a released prisoner in a blue serge suit walked north, eyes on the gravel. No one looked up at the cave in the limestone ledge so the ex-convict who had committed so many crimes against both women and animals did not call down. He watched his morning shadow disappear at noon; he watched his afternoon shadow grow longer and disappear at night when the sun went down.

On the third day the ex-convict slept upright, and awoke to find a youth standing on the square of clay before him.

"Are your lips black because of no water?" was what the boy said, for he was an unemployed drover who had found several coins on the clay bank. One after another these coins had led him upward to this cave. Because the convict had been so long in a cell, he had somewhat lost the habit of speech and so he made no reply at all. As a little joke he even pretended not to see the money that the young drover showed him.

From guilt and also from the joy of having found coins that a man in a cave did not claim as his own, the drover boy went at once into the town. At cafés, a little at each place, he spent the money and he recounted also his adventure with a black-lipped hermit. Old women begging at tavern doorways heard this story and each one knew in her heart that if one coin were found there was always another.

At dawn the convict awoke to see a half circle of towns-people staring into his blackened, sun-warped face. A beggar-woman had found the last of his coins on the clay bank above the tracks; in a respectful voice, she gave thanks. The drover boy stepped forward to ask all of their questions: In fact, had The Hermit been without food *or* water for seven months? Did or did not one melon roll down from the bank above the cave each night and thus sustain him? In what manner were certain of the clay-bank coins changed overnight, in merchant's tills, into gold?

The former convict felt laughter deep in his belly. Once he had been a stonemason but much drink and a vicious temper had caused him to kill a fellow workman. The body had floated many days down a canal, and his first crime was not discovered; after that his violence became more open, and there were others. Finally, almost by chance, he was questioned about a woman's body and the child's body dead beside her. At the trial other things were established. To hear their deferential questions made him feel superior, much in the way his crimes had made him feel beyond the judgment of all men. In addition, he saw one of these "pilgrims" was a young girl with black, serious hair down around her shoulders. The old echoes of desire clanged and clanged in his mind but because he had worked as a mason he thought, "Let's first see how this little job goes. . . ."

With all of the guile and dissimulation he had learned in prison, the convict solemnly raised his right hand, palm outward toward their faces. Well enough he saw the young woman was frightened: this was good for he knew from experience that gen-uine fright may easily become passion.

As protection against the dust, one man had cloth over his face and so the convict did not at once recognize the barber. As though on official business, the barber walked slowly around the convict: very closely the barber inspected the half-moons of scalp above the ears, the slope of the forehead, the gray-tipped hair growing wildly from each nostril.

"Of course I would know the prisoner by his neck and his hair. Besides, I never forget a customer who tips generously. This man is not the man who came into my shop. I give you my word, this hair was not recently trimmed by a fine barber such as myself."

The first delegation from the town walked back along the railroad tracks and the beggarwomen followed, making little pods of dust with their sticks, looking for more coins.

The convict watched them go and then rolled backward into his cave and laughed until tears came into his eyes. He felt these people were even bigger fools than either wardens or prison guards, themselves always prisoners but because of the pay never admitting it. Nevertheless, to keep up appearances, the prisoner sat again outside his cave and was surprised to see that one visitor—beyond any doubt the barber—had donated a few coins. This new money the convict also threw over the bank: others would find it when the sun rose the following day.

Then it began. Beggars and the small shop owners who sold cloth and crushed maize walked out along the railroad tracks. They left melons, gourds of water, or coins; each night the convict threw these coins wildly across the landscape for the people who found the money also spread his fame most swiftly to the larger cities where now all canals were dry.

Because trainloads of people came early and a great many stayed to imitate the convict's peculiar cross-legged posture or to imitate the way he stared at the landscape, the prisoner found he could not easily retreat into his cave either to laugh or to take a long, secret drink of gourd water. He saw new respect in their faces, and this he had not known as either a prisoner or an honest but violent stonemason; he felt he deserved this attention for none of his trials had been covered well enough by the Press.

Unfortunately, their gifts and coins were in such profusion around his crossed legs that he could scarcely move. This effect of opulence distracted his pilgrims from closely inspecting his almost black body and neck and face. In the past week the barber had closed his shop and was now living at the foot of the clay bank beside the tracks. In his loud warden's voice the barber lectured each day's crowds and told them what to expect when they climbed the bank, and also of the miracles: Copper into Gold, and the Profusion of Melons.

Partly to offset these distractions, on the ninety-sixth day the convict, who now really did look much like a hermit, motioned for the young girl to remain beside him for the night. Each day, without fail, she had walked to his cave and he understood she wanted to experience his body for herself.

"Do . . ." and he was surprised at his own voice for he had imagined his first words to her as sounding not coarse, "This, do . . ." and he picked up one coin from the heap and managed to toss it almost to the railroad tracks.

The young girl did likewise. He saw she liked very much to throw the gifts and the melons down upon the barber who suddenly found himself kneeling under a shower of coins.

Desire was what the convict felt, desire clanging in his blood. His hands ached as he thought of the white throat of the girl and of twisting fiercely her black hair around her throat until at the same instant he both defiled her and broke the neck with his remembering, stonemason hands.

"Place me inside our cave," he said. "Pour all water gourds over my unclothed body."

This the girl did, and then without having to be asked she threw herself on his breast and sobbed, "Yes . . . Yes."

Ironically, the convict now knew his lust was only in his mind. His gulps of water late at night when the barber slept, his fast, the sun all day and the dust, all those things had wasted his body to . . . oh, to these crossed sticks that were his legs, to these bones that were his thighs, to a protruding, black forehead, to flesh that now seemed almost stone.

She wanted to revive his flesh, but she could only weep in the cave. In his pretension he could only say to her, "Believe, believe." Then he, himself, was taken by her innocent, smooth-handed desire. To her, yes; but to himself nothing happened.

"But we could," the girl told him softly as she carried him once more to his customary place at the entrance of his cave. "If you will only permit rain to fall. In the valley."

Partly to please her, partly to fulfill the role he had drifted into over the months, partly to perpetuate this joke on the herd-minded bourgeois that he so much despised, but most of all for revenge, the convict said it solemnly, one eye on her white throat:

"Rain," he said to the dry moonlight. It was the kind of joke another convict might understand. "Rain. *Comes.*"

After the girl called those words down over the railroad bank, the convict saw the barber running along the tracks toward the town, already making manifest this promised miracle.

Yet in the days that followed, the heat overhead beat the entrance of the cave with wings of fire. Now he wore no clothes at all; bleached by the sun, his hair waved across his rutted breast. In his mind he saw what he had become: a thing of influence, his words recorded by the friends of the barber. To men who left much gold where he could see it, the convict passed on a convict's evasive, worldly wisdom; these men of substance used his words to justify business schemes that were both devious and cruel. For this service they left water he could not now drink in gourds of gold.

For two weeks, with longing, he watched the smoke plumes and fire of the railroad trains going across the valley toward the lighted cities on the coast. He thought upon it seriously: he would take only the coins of gold and he would bribe the drover boy to sit in his place for one night. Secretly he would leave this cave and board the train and disappear forever. Yet at summer's down; behind and high above on the mountain where once they had camped, they heard the noise of woodchoppers at work in the fir trees. The man raised his head. Beneath the guardrails, as always, he saw the road curving away, to reappear at last near a fountain in a green park and go on then into the town below.

The woman turned on her side of their blankets. By raising her head she could also view the place where they sometimes felt they wanted very much to go—at least after long discussions they had agreed once on that point. Now it seemed mostly a matter of time, and the time was not yet.

"Fires," and she tried to take exactly her share of their blankets. Because she was domestic and responsible and hungry she said, "Other women—down there—are at breakfast."

The man took it as a criticism, but did not reply. He was more philosophical and he often thought back to see how it had all begun—so to speak. For a few minutes he looked at the gorge where tiers of young fir trees rose above them, sparkling with moisture in these first minutes of another day. Higher up on the mountain the woodchoppers worked steadily in the larger trees.

He threw back his side of the blanket: the vine was still there. He had known it would not go away during the night, but its new growth each day was always shocking. Nevertheless, he was always anxious to see how much it really had grown during the night while they slept.

Yes. This morning really a great deal—as he pointed out to her. Whether this growth was caused by these longer, late-summer days, or by the night's humidity, he could not say. At first he had thought the vine's growth was in relationship to phases of the moon; now he was equally convinced that new growth was related to the water level in the trout stream in the bottom of the gorge. Water, from somewhere, must surely give the vine both food and useful minerals in solution; otherwise, how would the green convoluting vine with its leaves like hammered green metal, tendrils soft as his wife's flesh, continue to grow?

Actually, they had come here in late spring. They had walked down a trail from the melting end of the mountain glacier. When lights of the town seemed very close they had camped in this spot below the guardrails for the night.

The vine, so tiny then, had been there when they awoke. She had intended to throw back their blanket, but he was already sitting upright, examining very intently this small green thing, the first leaf emergent and tender and silly there between his great toe and his second toe. He had said, "Fungus," but as they both watched, a new tendril curled up and out, and by nine o'clock this first new, green leaf was a little bit larger.

"What about stockings?" she had asked, for it was still a few miles to the town, or at least to the green park where the fountain was.

He might have said, "No," or he might have argued that this, too, was a living thing, but he did not; instead, he accepted it without either fear or discussion. He saw it was without roots and loved the sun and that seemed enough; therefore, they stopped all activity and all future plans in order to contemplate this new, tiny thing that was even then growing larger from between his toes.

Some days he lay with his head on the rucksack, and she lay beside him, and both of them watched his foot and the vine growing. At noon she went to the trout stream and brought back small cups of water to pour over his foot—and also to inspect more closely this new thing that was now really much larger and much more beautiful. Then past noon, when the woodcutters stopped chopping, they slept.

Toward nightfall they awoke and she took a little of their food from the rucksack and they ate together. Even after they went to sleep again beneath the stars they felt the vine's newest tendril rustle a little around his ankle and—later—around the calf of his leg. Even in the nights of late summer they did not dream and at dawn they contemplated his new green leg, made green by the vine growing.

At the end of their second month, she realized the vine itself had become his life. This she accepted. His single-minded attention, his hard-minded exclusion of everything else, in fact his adoration of the vine, instead of either her, or their own relationship, made her feel lonely. Once she cried in the night, but he did not awaken. The bad, blue feeling came and she, herself, wished for the green vine to grow inside her belly. But no, and that mood also passed.

Nevertheless, during that night, she recalled a great deal about their old life before this vine came to them: at a place, a town it was in the Territories to the north. They had met when young. What it was like before they met, she did not now care to remember. At first they had gone out at night with other young people in groups; later, alone, they had experimented with drugs and went for long, harmless trips of the "mind"—singly, of course—but still much closer than ever before.

Finally when they were truly together, they had gone into the mountains toward the foot of the glacier. For several days they had camped near beds of wild flowers in bloom—of that much she was certain. Now each day the vine grew a little bit—like a habit—and now it held them both. She did not cry about this anymore and when the tendrils of the vine took his thigh, when she could no longer see all of his body in the old way, she accepted it.

Acceptance, however, was not enough. At times he urged her to leave him, to go on alone into the town. She felt this was neither ultimate affection, nor even mercy on his part for now the roots of the vine had pierced through the blankets and went deeply into the rocks and the soil. If he urged her to leave, it was his way of being a hero; besides, he would have the vine alone and unadulterated for himself. That he could tell her to go on alone made her sad. After all, she had carried all of the water from the trout stream. She had accommodated the vine in their bed from the first day it appeared—innocent and tender—between his toes.

In September, before the rains, the thing finally happened. Deeply, she had wanted it to happen: she awoke but could not get up to serve either him or his vine. During the night, because she had always placed her legs close to his in sleep, the tendrils of the vine had taken her ankles. As they watched, the tendrils ravished her flesh and took her strength as though the vine needed this new thing on which to grow.

When the first rains of fall came down the gorge they did not move for they were both with this vine and—at last—a part of it.

At noon she felt him tremble beside her. What she saw was the first spume of snow, blowing down from the glacier and across the upper rim of the gorge. His breath at noon emerged from his part of the leaves, and she saw his breath turn white against the vine. Worse, the vine itself was now, ever so little, turning to brown.

In fear, in panic, with their rusted camp knife, he began to hack at the vine. When the vine drew back, she saw his neck and his breast. When she saw him again, for the first time in many months, she too began to pull and to cut each tendril frantically. Then each of them got a knife and the vine seemed to pull back and away—but not one tendril withered.

Still, she urged him on. Together they worked at each tendril in order; beginning at the top they pried tendrils from flesh, and did not stop when blood came from each place where the vine had to let go. That night, very late, the first flakes of snow fell in their camp and the vine was almost gone from their bodies.

"Tomorrow," he told her, and she too felt they were free to go. "Tomorrow we will go down into the town."

To her it seemed only an act of the Will, and so she put everything she could reach into small piles. Very early in the old way they would get up and pack and go on down the road which they had seen each day all summer. Oh, she knew they were exhausted but she knew they were also together in the old way, in the time before they watched this thing which they had nurtured and had finally accepted and which had, in the end, almost overwhelmed them both. "Good."

And then she added, "I still do." And he answered her and said, "Yes. I still do. I love you."

And then it was morning.

During the night the vine had surrounded them, had grown back tighter than ever before. Now they could not see each other.

Because snow was coming down the side of the mountain very fast, the woodcutters—two of them—doubled-bitted axes over their shoulders, also came down the trails to the road.

That morning the two woodcutters saw this strange thing not far from the guardrails: a vine growing, with great roots going down into the soil. Furthermore, the vine had grown in upon itself—had not climbed either the guardrail or a tree, nor had it run across the rocks of the gorge toward the water, as might be thought natural. More strange than its shape was this: the coiling, triumphant vine seemed to breathe in and out. When the woodchoppers placed their woolly ears close to the leaves they heard voices—or something—crying out from the core.

Therefore the woodcutters chopped this very large vine off at its roots. They also chopped away the stray tendrils. With left-over vines they made the whole thing into a long, mummylike bundle. They also cut down a small fir tree and stripped off the branches to make a carrying pole. With the bundle of vine tied to the pole, they placed the pole on their shoulders. With axes and pole and all they went down the road and around the curves. Whistling as they walked along, the woodcutters soon entered an astonished village.

In that way, riding on a pole, intimate in vines, concealed from the people who watched with much interest as they passed, the man and the woman came to the place which they had looked at from afar for a very long time.

In the town square all of the following week the children and beggarwomen and men going home from barbershops or factories on the hill and home from prison or from some army post not far from the frontiers, all of them walked past, and some of them paused for a little while to look. More than one said, "Yes. Something is singing all right, somewhere inside those wrapped-up vines."

And then they walked on.

DATE DUE